Confronting Crime

Confronting Crime

edited by
**Roger Matthews and
Jock Young**

SAGE Publications · London · Beverly Hills · New Delhi

SAGE Publications Ltd
28 Banner Street
London EC1Y 8QE

 SAGE Publications Inc
275 South Beverly Drive
Beverly Hills, California 90212

SAGE Publications India Pvt Ltd
C-236 Defence Colony
New Delhi 110 024

British Library Cataloguing in Publication Data

Confronting Crime.
1. Crime and criminals—Great Britain
I. Matthews, Roger   II. Young, Jock
364'.941   HV6947

ISBN 0-8039-9731-0
ISBN 0-8039-9732-9 Pbk

Library of Congress Catalog Card Number 85-062748

Printed in Great Britain by
J. W. Arrowsmith Ltd, Bristol

Contents

Acknowledgements

The preparation of this book was helped greatly by discussion with colleagues at the Centre of Criminology, Middlesex Polytechnic. Many of the papers were given at the annual Clacton Conferences of the MA Deviancy and Social Policy. Thanks go, as always, to the staff and students on the MA.

R.M. J.Y.

Notes on contributors

John Auld teaches sociology of deviancy and social policy at Middlesex Polytechnic. He is the author of *Marijuana Use and Social Control* (Academic Press, 1981), and has also written on the sociology of health. He studied at Leicester University and at the London School of Economics where he obtained his PhD.

Steven Box is a Senior Lecturer in Sociology at the University of Kent at Canterbury. He specializes in teaching criminology and the sociology of deviance. His current research programme (with Chris Hale) is centred around an empirically based critique of the present British Government's 'Law and Order' campaign. His recent publications include *Power, Crime and Mystification* and *Deviance, Reality and Society* (2nd ed.), and he is just completing a new work entitled *Recession, Crime and Punishment*.

Jill Box-Grainger is currently a Lecturer in Further and Adult Education and a Community Arts Adviser at Brixton Recreation Centre. For some years she has worked with campaigns against criminalization and the abuses of prison, and practical women's organizations. She is a member of the editorial group of *The Abolitionist*, the magazine of Radical Alternatives to Prison.

Nicholas Dorn is Assistant Director (Research) at the Institute for the Study of Drug Dependence, London. He is the author of *Alcohol, Youth and the State* (Croom Helm, 1983) and *Helping Drug Users* (Gower, 1985, with Nigel South). He studied psychology at London University, the sociology of deviance and social policy at Middlesex Polytechnic and gained his PhD from the University of Kent. He maintains a broad interest in the relations between international and sexual divisions and social policy.

Jeanne Gregory is a Senior Lecturer at Middlesex Polytechnic. She has recently completed a PhD thesis on the employment provisions of the Sex Discrimination Act and has published a number of articles on this subject. Her main areas of interest are feminist criminology and the impact of the law, in all its aspects, on women and racial minorities. She is currently writing a book which assesses the potential and actual achievements of civil rights legislation.

Chris Hale is a Lecturer in Quantitative Social Science and Management Science. He has published papers in econometric theory in various journals including the *Journal of the American Statistical Association* and the *International Economic Review*. He has co-authored (with Steven Box) work on women's liberation and crime (*British Journal of Criminology* (1983), *Criminology* (1984)), and recession and imprisonment (*Crime and Social Justice* (1982) and *Contemporary Crises* (1985)). His current research interests include misspecification in econometric models and improved estimation techniques.

John Lea teaches Social Policy at Middlesex Polytechnic. His areas of interest include race relations and criminology. He has published articles on race relations legislation, urban violence and political marginality, and co-authored (with Jock Young) *What is to be Done about Law and Order?* (Penguin, 1984). He has also worked on the development of local criminal victimization surveys for Merseyside County Council and Islington Council.

vii

Roger Matthews is a Senior Lecturer in Sociology at Middlesex Polytechnic. He received his doctorate in 1984 from Essex University for his thesis on 'Prostitution and Social Structure'. He is currently working on a book on the history of prostitution and engaged in research into penal policy.

Alan Phipps is Lecturer in Social Sciences at Stockport College where he specializes in courses for workers with offenders and the mentally handicapped. He also teaches criminology for The Open University. He has published articles on victims of crime and sociological approaches to mental handicap. He is involved in the management of a support scheme for crime victims and is conducting research for a book on autobiographical accounts of prison life.

John Pitts is a Senior Lecturer in Social Work at the West London Institute of Higher Education, which he joined in 1977. After teacher-training he became a youth-worker in the Elephant and Castle area of London and in the early 1970s was Intermediate Treatment Organizer for the Borough of Lewisham, also in London, developing community-based services for young people in trouble with the law. Between 1981 and 1982 he chaired the London Intermediate Treatment Association and is a member of the National Intermediate Treatment Federation Working Party on Racism and Juvenile Justice. He has published articles on youth and crime and contributed to books on juvenile justice and social work with black clients.

Nigel South is a Research Sociologist, Institute for the Study of Drug Dependence, London. He studied at the University of Essex and as a Research Associate at the Centre for Occupational and Community Research where he gained his PhD. He has taught criminology in London and New York, published on private justice, the informal economy and drugs issues and is co-author (with Nicholas Dorn) of *Helping Drug Users* (1985) and *Message in a Bottle* (1983).

Jock Young is Reader in Sociology at Middlesex Polytechnic and was educated at the London School of Economics where he received his PhD in 1972. He has also written *The Drugtakers* and is co-author of *The New Criminology*, amongst others. He is co-editor of several books including *Critical Criminology* and *Policing the Riots*. His most recent books are *Losing the Fight Against Crime* (with R. Kinsey and J. Lea, Blackwell, 1985) and *Realist Criminology* (Gower, 1986). His present principal area of research is criminal victimization and he has worked on the Merseyside and Islington Crime Surveys.

Editors' introduction: confronting crime

The tide is turning for radical criminology. For over two decades it has neglected the effect of the crime upon the victim and concentrated on the impact of the state — through the process of labelling — on the criminal. There was nothing wrong with this per se. It was a necessary antidote to orthodox criminology which was neither concerned with the impact of the state on the criminal, *nor* the criminal on the victim. It focused almost exclusively on the offender who operated, it seemed, in a vacuum, while both the state and the victim were held in parentheses. Against this background the focus on the state was progress indeed. There is no doubt that the exposé of expert partiality, of prison conditions, of police prejudice and brutality, of courtroom bias and legal posturing was needed. It is *still* needed — as is the necessity of pointing to the theoretical bankruptcy of what purports to be 'scientific' criminology. But radical analysis also lost touch with the most obvious focus of criminology — crime itself. It became an advocate for the indefensible: the criminal became the victim, the state the solitary focus of attention, while the real victim remained off-stage.

Thus the basic triangle of relations which is the proper subject matter of criminology – the offender, the state and the victim – has yet to be fully developed. It is to this task that the new radical criminology addresses itself. Indeed the articles in this book seek to trace out and relate the causes of crime, the impact on the victim and the appropriate role of the state. In doing so the various contributions to this book aim to fulfil the promise of radical criminology to link critical theory to radical practice. Thus each of the articles in this book is concerned not only with the failures of the present policies, but also with the construction of more progressive alternatives. Gone is the 'impossiblism' of the sixties which claims that nothing works or that intervention only makes matters worse. In its place is being developed a form of radical criminology which is able to compete with its more orthodox rival. That is, the two paradigms begin to compete rather than co-exist in a scientific universe where little that either could say to the other was sufficiently commensurable to allow proper evaluation. And this more abrasive relationship occurs at a time when, as Jock Young points out in his introductory article, there is a considerable crisis in orthodox criminology. At a time when criminology is becoming increasingly atheoretical and unreflexive it is all the more necessary for radical voices to be heard.

There is then a pressing social and political need to take the question of crime seriously and to break with the romantic and idealist conceptions

1

which have been conveyed by radical criminology. For in withdrawing from the theoretical debate about the question of crime and its regulation, it has left the arena wide open to conservative and liberal theorists.

The limits of the romantic conception of crime and the criminal were brought home most forcibly by the growing feminist concern during the 1970s with the problem of rape. Discussions around this issue served to reintroduce into radical criminology discourse neglected issues of aetiology, motivation and punishment. Central to the development of these concerns, Jill Box-Grainger argues, is the formulation of a coherent and effective sentencing policy for rapists. The impact of feminist criminology also forced a fundamental rethink of criminology theory itself, and particularly the ways in which sexist assumptions can affect our general approach to crime. Jeanne Gregory discusses the deficiencies of traditional androcentric criminology and sets out some conditions for the construction of a non-sexist criminology.

An enduring theoretical problem which both feminist and radical criminology have continually confronted is that of crude determinism. In their article on 'unemployment, crime and imprisonment', Steven Box and Chris Hale question the conventional wisdom which posits a deterministic causal relationship between these phenomena and suggests that the relationship is more complex. They argue that the problem of prison overcrowding would not necessarily be overcome by reducing the level of either unemployment or crime. For conscious social and political decisions counterpoise themselves within the previously imagined mechanistic model of cause and effect.

Part of the problem of analysing the relation between crime, unemployment and imprisonment rates is the problematic nature of the central concept of crime and particularly of assessing the so-called 'dark figure' of crime. Alan Phipps suggests that victimization studies can be useful in overcoming some of the deficiencies of official offender-based statistics. He argues that victimization studies can be a valuable and illuminating resource, not only for radical criminologists but for radical politicians as well. Thus, if the women's movement has indicated the way forward in terms of the creation of a radical victimology, it is time now to extend its theoretical and political potential.

If it is vital to introduce the social category female into the meta-discourse of criminology, it is also vital to include ethnicity. There has recently in Britain been a growing interest and debate around the relationship between race and crime. John Pitts suggests that this debate has often proceeded with little regard for the available empirical evidence. He poses the question of whether black juveniles are treated differently than their white counterparts by the police and the judiciary, and whether they are engaged in a higher or different level of criminal activity. Taking another element of the debate around race and crime John Lea focuses specifically on the question of police racism. In opposition to the 'rotten apple' or 'occupational culture' theses, or the view of 'institutionalized racism' propounded by some radical criminologists, he argues that police racism is best understood as a product of the necessary generalizations and stereotypes which the police adapt from the dominant culture and reproduce through their own particular occupational structure. This alternative conception carries important implications for the way in which police racism might be confronted.

Alongside the growing interest in the organization of the police in Britain in recent years has been the mounting concern with drug abuse and with heroin in particular. Just as it became impossible for radical criminology to continue to dismiss the problem of working class crime, it became necessary for them to confront the growing problem of heroin abuse occurring in working class areas. John Auld, Nicholas Dorn and Nigel South identify the expansion of heroin use with the growth of the informal economy which is neither organized around the familiar rules of work and the home, nor the usual modes of consumption. Any policy initiative, they argue, must take into account the central role of the informal economy in which the distinction between users and pushers is often blurred and in which heroin use itself is bound up with sexual divisions and conceptions of 'masculinity'. Thus they attempt to situate heroin use at both micro and macro levels of analysis informed by a socialist perspective on the operation of the informal economy, and by feminist discussions of gender.

Formulating a coherent policy initiative around heroin abuse has proved extremely difficult. Similarly with prostitution. As Roger Matthews argues in the final article, the current movement by a number of radical groups towards a policy of decriminalization, as a response to the growing problems in the operation of the existing legislation, is neither as progressive or as radical as it might appear and there is a need to develop an alternative response.

We have brought together these articles in this reader to illustrate the changing direction and focus in British radical criminology in the present period. In doing so we hope to stimulate further theoretical debate in the discipline and to suggest some ways in which progressive policy initiatives might be constructed.

Roger Matthews
Jock Young

1

The failure of criminology:
the need for a radical realism

Jock Young

> Why should it be that a century of theorizing and research should have made
> little or no apparent impact either upon the trends of crime in our society or
> upon our ability to modify criminal tendencies in individuals? (Radzinowicz
> and King, 1977: 93).

There has been much talk of a crisis in radical criminology; the truth
is that the crisis is in the mainstream of the discipline. Ironically, it was
this deepening crisis that brought radical criminology into being and its
solution which was high on the agenda of the new criminology.

If there has been a measure of lack of success on the part of radical
criminology it has been its failure to rescue mainstream criminology from
the conceptual mess in which it has increasingly found itself. It is my
contention that the core of this problem revolves around the causes of
crime and that this aetiological crisis emerged most blatantly in the 1960s,
engendering a period of intense creative development within the discipline
including the emergence of radical criminology. However, by the eighties
the Thermidor set in and a silent counter-revolution occurred within the
mainstream with the emergence of what I will term the new administrative
criminology involving a retreat from any discussion of causality. For we
have now a criminology which has well nigh abandoned its historical
mission of the search for the causes of crime.

The aetiological crisis and the failure of positivism

Let us examine the dominant tendency in mainstream criminology in
Britain and the United States in the sixties — the period which experienced
most traumatically the aetiological crisis and heralded the emergence of
the new deviancy theory and hence radical criminology. Mainstream
British criminology, as Stan Cohen (1981) detailed in his short history,
was characterized by pragmatism, an eclectic multidisciplinary approach,
correctionalism and positivism. Such a positivism was profoundly atheoretical, a product of British intellectual culture in general (see Anderson,
1968) and it was formed in a social democratic mould which set itself
up intransigently against the classicist sphere of the legal profession. Thus
Baroness Wootton, a prominent Fabian, wrote:

Traditional conceptions of criminal responsibility. . .have already been modified to a point where they can no longer be logically defended. . .they have, in fact, been effectively undermined by the advance of medicine into what used to be the sphere of morality. They may, it is true, linger for a long while yet there are plenty of precedents for the survival of illogical practices and institutions. And she continues: The struggle between the rival empires of medicine and morality seems to have become the contemporary equivalent of the nineteenth century battle between scientific and religious explanations of cosmic events or of terrestrial evolution. True, the modern battle is much more decorously conducted. . .But the issues are akin and the victory seems likely to go the same way (Wootton, 1959: 338–9).

She seemed remarkably unaware that such arguments had occurred, without resolution, half a century previously. The important exceptions to British atheoreticism in criminology were the German emigré Hans Eysenck (1964) — a biological determinist — and a few scattered writers such as Terence Morris (1957) and David Downes (1966) at the London School of Economics who had bravely championed and transposed American sociological ideas to the British context.

It would be difficult to exaggerate the crisis of criminology at this time. Above all it had lost any explanatory grip on the phenomenon that it was supposedly studying. For example, Wootton in 1959 surveyed twelve of the most likely criminological hypotheses, ranging from broken homes to low social status, as causes of delinquency, and came to the conclusion: 'all in all. . .this collection of studies, although chosen for its comparative methodological merit, produces only the most meagre, and dubiously supported, generalizations' (Wootton, 1959: 134). It is, indeed, surprising how her adamant faith in positivism was reconcilable with its obvious intellectual bankruptcy.

Ten years later, one of the largest and most expensive pieces of criminological research in Britain came up with the conclusion that there was a link between poverty and delinquency although it was not at all sure why. D. J. West concluded the report on this longitudinal study of 400 boys with the forlorn: 'These preliminary observations raise many questions. It is our pious hope that with the passage of time. . .at least some answers will emerge' (West, 1969: 149).

But there were worse problems than this: for if the crime rate had remained static at least some semblance of stumbling scientificity might have been preserved. But in the post 1945 period, official crime rates continued to rise remorselessly, year by year, even accelerating as we entered the affluent sixties. Real incomes became the highest in history, slums were demolished one by one, educational attainment rose, social services expanded in order to provide extensive welfare provisions and safety nets, and yet the crime rate continued to doggedly rise! All of the factors which should have led to a drop in delinquency if main-stream criminology were even half-correct, were being ameliorated and yet precisely the opposite effect was occurring. Such an aetiological crisis was an empirical anomaly which, if it did not immediately shake the somnolent mainstream paradigm, certainly encouraged the emergence of others.

In the United States the aetiological crisis was even more anomalous and threatening to positivism. For not only was crime rising in pace with affluence — it was much more of an actual threat than in any other part of the Western World. Street crime became a number one fear of the American public and there seemed little advice that establishment criminology could give that would effectively stem the tide.

In addition, the American muckraking tradition and the pioneering work of E. H. Sutherland were revived at this time by the twin feed-ins from self-report studies — which showed that there was a considerable dark figure of *middle class* delinquency – and the journalistic exposés of crime in the high echelons of political and corporate power. These constantly threatened the positivist conventional wisdom which associated crime with poverty and lower class socialization patterns etc.

In the United States, as in Britain, there was a parallel reformist tradition, positivism in its outlook and interventionist in its policy. This was dominant, not only in criminology, but also to a remarkable extent in the rehabilitative ideals of the 'new penology' which held the centre ground in prison reform from the thirties onwards. As Simon Dinitz put it:

> Intellectually, the reformist impulse was made respectable by the victory of positivism over classicism, by empiricism over speculative philosophy, by the clinical over the legal perspective. . . and by elevating the actor over his act. On the policy level, this liberal-reformist impulse focused, to the exclusion of nearly all else, on humanizing the prisons and jails and on rehabilitating the inmates (Dinitz, 1979: 105).

But just as orthodox criminology failed to explain the extent, distribution and change in the official crime rate, establishment penology plainly failed to control crime or rehabilitate. For crime increased at the same time as did recidivism rates from the prisons.

But the Americans were more theoretically capable of tackling the aetiological crisis than were the British. True the same current of eclectic positivism dominated criminology in both countries — witness the Gluecks and the McCords in the United States. But it was not hegemonic for there was also a sophisticated tradition of sociological criminology involving the Chicago school, symbolic interactionism and structural functionalism. It was these theoretical strands which were mobilized to attempt to explain the aetiological anomaly. Out of these theoretical bases three separate and politically different schools of criminology emerged. Thus labelling theory, with its roots in symbolic interactionism, attempted to explain the problem in terms of the differential and unjust administration of justice. Unfair labelling explained the fact that middle class deviancy was hidden, increased policing and moral panic gave rise to the crime-wave and stigmatization caused recidivism. Subcultural theory, derived from Mertonian structural functionalism, utilized the concept of *relative* deprivation to explain the rise in crime despite the decrease in *absolute* poverty. It pointed to the way in which subcultures are solutions to such deprivation and that the pains of imprisonment gave rise to an inmate subculture which increased commitment to criminality and recidivism. It even got around to acknowledging that relative deprivation need not be solely a working class phenomenon. Lastly, deriving from the Chicago school of the thirties, social disorganization theory talked of community disintegration. Thus breakdown of informal controls engendered crime amongst the poor and throughout the stucture of society, *and* provided no community to which the ex-prisoner could be returned.

Their political attachments: libertarian, social democratic and conservative kept them apart, as did their emphasis on what were usually seen as alternative aetiologies and levels of analysis. What was often forgotten was that these three perspectives on deviance: that which emphasizes social reaction, that which stresses the cause of deviant action and that which focuses on the organizational context of action are not per se mutually exclusive. They were fragmented because of politics, not because of reality. A few American sociologists in the creative debates at that time sensed this — for example Albert Cohen (1965), Cloward and Ohlin (1960) and David Matza (1969). It was this American tradition which formed the basis of the development of the new deviancy theory in the United States, which was subsequently imported wholesale to Britain.

The rockbed influence on the new deviancy theory was labelling theory but there were substantial, and sometimes forgotten, influences of subcultural theory and of the Chicago School. Certain pieces of theory were incorporated, others rejected in this bricollage and reorientation. For example, from the Chicago School new deviancy theory inherited a healthy scepticism and cynicism about the basis of order and the honesty of the powerful. But perhaps more significantly it explicitly rejected any notions of social disorganization as a cause of deviancy. Organization and counter-organization, culture and contra-culture, differential socialization and pluralism became the order of the day.

All theory can be illuminated by understanding its chief sparring partners. For new deviancy theory, this was mainstream positivism. The debate between the new deviancy theory and positivism continued the tradition of critique by inversion with a vengeance. In place of the grinding determinism of positivism was replaced a capricious voluntarism. Instead of condemnation of the deviant, there was advocated an 'appreciation' of deviant realities from the perspective of the controlled not the controllers. Whereas positivism denuded deviant action of meaning, new deviancy theory granted meaning and full blown rationalism. Consensus was replaced by radical pluralism, pathology ousted by differential definitions of normality and correctionalism by a condemnation of the expert. On every dimension of understanding crime and deviancy positivism was inverted (see Young, 1975).

New deviancy theory was the seedbed of radical criminology: the first attempt, in this period, to create systematically an alternative paradigm to positivism without reverting to an updated version of classicism.

The tasks of the radical paradigm

By far the most helpful circumstance for the rapid propagation of a new and revolutionary theory is the existence of an established orthodoxy which is clearly inconsistent with the most salient facts of reality, and yet is sufficiently confident of its intellectual power to attempt to explain these facts, and in its efforts to do so exposes its incompetences in a ludicrous fashion (Johnson, 1971).

The retreat from theory is over, and the politicization of crime and criminology is imminent (Taylor, Walton and Young, 1973: 281).

A senescent positivism facing with woeful inadequacy the aetiological crisis was ripe for paradigm change. This is indeed what happened but the changes both in conventional and radical criminology which emerge out of the skirmish were largely unforeseen.

What effect did the revolt of these Young Turks have on the Sultanate of mainstream criminology? Its major forum in Britain was the National Deviancy Conference, formed in 1968, which had a remarkable, almost spectacular, growth in the first few years of its existence. But as Stan Cohen noted, the impact of radical criminology was much less devastating than was believed in the more heady days of the early seventies.

There are more corners and cavities than ten years ago, but for the most part the institutional foundations of British criminology remain intact and unaltered, for the Establishment saw the new theories as simply a fashion which would eventually pass over or as a few interesting ideas which could be swallowed up without changing the existing paradigm of all (Cohen, 1981: 236).

What radical criminology did not do to any significant degree was to challenge the criminological establishment. For the policy centres in British society were, and remain, remarkably unaffected both in the Home Office itself and the university institutions which it helps to finance.

Both in Great Britain and the United States the size and power of the criminological establishment has actually grown over the last ten years. Thus a weak and unsuccessful positivism was not dislodged from its position by the emergence of radical criminology. It was displaced, however, but ironically the challenge to positivism emerged quietly from within its own ranks. As we shall see this was due to the rapid growth both in Britain and the United States of what I have termed administrative criminology. Thus, the qualitative transformation of establishment criminology, the decline of positivism, occurred autonomously from the rise of radical criminology as a competing paradigm.

Administrative criminology: the silent revolution

The liberal reformist impulse in criminology and corrections institutionalized a century ago...[are] now utterly spent (Dinitz, 1979: 105).

If we have little effect in making people more honest and loving we can at least make stealing more difficult and increase the risk of getting caught and punished...Wilson is the eloquent spokesman for more than a few of us (Marvin Wolfgang in his Review of *Thinking About Crime*, 1975).

A silent revolution has occurred in conventional criminology in the United States and in Great Britain. The demise of positivism and social democratic ways of reforming crime has been rapid. A few perceptive commentators have noted the sea-change in the orthodox centre of criminology but the extent of the paradigm shift has been scarcely analysed, or its likely impact understood.

The first sighting of realignment in Western criminology was in a perceptive article written in 1977 by Tony Platt and Paul Takagi entitled 'Intellectuals for Law and Order' (Platt and Takagi, 1981). They grouped together writers such as Ernest van den Haag, James Q. Wilson and Norval Morris and noted how they represented the demise of 'liberal', social democratic ways of understanding crime and prisons in the United States. 'Intellectuals for law and order are not a criminological fad', they write, but 'a decisive influence in criminology' (Platt and Takagi, 1981:54). Developing this line of argument Donald Cressey writes:

The tragedy is in the tendency of modern criminologists to drop the search for causes and to join the politicians rather than develop better ideas about why crime flourishes, for example, these criminologists Wilson, and van den Haag, Ehrlich, Fogel, Morris and Hawkins — and hundreds of others — seem satisfied with a technological criminology whose main concern is for showing policy-makers how to repress criminals and criminal justice work more efficiently, [and he adds:] If more and more criminologists respond — and they seem to be doing so — criminology will eventually have only 'handcuffs 1a' orientation (Cressey, 1978).

There is an unfortunate tendency to conflate these various thinkers together as if they were politically similar. But van den Haag is very much a traditional conservative whereas Morris is a 'J. S. Mill' type of liberal and Wilson differs explicitly from both of them. Such a confusion makes it difficult to understand the particular purchase which writers such as

James Q. Wilson in the United States and Ron Clarke in Britain have had on the new administrative criminology and their ability to mobilize writers of various positions in support for a broad policy. The basis of this is what all these writers have in common, namely: (1) an antagonism to the notion of crime being determined by social circumstances — 'the smothering of sociological criminology' as Cressey puts it; (2) a lack of interest in aetiology. As Platt and Takagi note: '[they] are basically uninterested in the causes of crime. For them, it's a side issue, a distraction and a waste of their valuable time' (Platt and Takagi, 1981: 45). The historic research programme of criminology into causes and the possibilities of rehabilitation is thus abandoned; (3) a belief in human choice in the criminal act; (4) an advocacy of deterrence.

The key figure in this shift is James Q. Wilson in his role as a theoretician, as author of the bestselling book *Thinking About Crime* and as an adviser to the Reagan administration. His central problem and starting point is the aetiological crisis of social democratic positivist theory and practice:

> If in 1960 one had been asked what steps society might take to prevent a sharp increase in the crime rate, one might well have answered that crime could best be curtailed by reducing poverty, increasing educational attainment, eliminating dilapidated housing, encouraging community organization, and providing troubled or delinquent youth with counseling services...
>
> Early in the decade of the 1960s, this country began the longest sustained period of prosperity since World War II, much of it fueled, as we later realized by a semi-war economy. A great array of programs aimed at the young, the poor, and the deprived were mounted. Though these efforts were not made primarily out of a desire to reduce crime, they were wholly consistent with — indeed, in their aggregate money levels, wildly exceeded — the policy prescription that a thoughtful citizen worried about crime would have offered at the beginning of the decade.
>
> Crime soared. It did not just increase a little; it rose at a faster rate and to higher levels than at any time since the 1930s and, in some categories, to higher levels than any experienced in this century.
>
> It all began in about 1963. That was the year, to over-dramatize a bit, that a decade began to fall apart (Wilson, 1975: 3–4).

What then can be done about crime? Wilson does not rule out that crime may be caused by psychological factors or by the breakdown of family structure. But he argues that there is little that public policy can do in this region. He adamantly rules out the option of reducing crime by improving social conditions. In terms of his interpretation of the aetiological crises — the amelioration of social conditions has resulted in an exponential rise in crime rather than its decline. Thus reform on any level is discarded and with it the notion that the reduction of crime can be achieved by an increase in social justice. But there are other factors that policy can manipulate and it is to these that Wilson turns his attention.

Although the poor commit crime more than the rich, he notes that only a small minority of the poor ever commit crimes. People obviously, then, have a choice in the matter; furthermore, these moral choices can be affected by the circumstances decreed by governments. And here he focuses in on the jugular of liberal thinking about crime and punishment:

If objective conditions are used to explain crime, spokesmen who use poverty as an explanation of crime should, by the force of their own logic, be prepared to consider the capacity of society to deter crime by raising the risks of crime. But they rarely do. Indeed, those who use poverty as an explanation are largely among the ranks of those who vehemently deny that crime can be deterred (Wilson, 1975: xiv. See also van den Haag, 1975: 84–90).

The goal of social policy must be to build up effective deterrents to crime. The problem is not to be solved, he argues, by the conservative measures of draconian punishments but rather by an increase of police effectiveness, the certainty of punishment, not its severity, is his key to government action. Thus Wilson differentiates his view from both conservatives and 'liberal'/social democrats. He advocates punishment but punishment which is appropriate and effective. He sees the informal controls of community as eventually more important than the formal, but that in areas where community has broken down and there is a high incidence of crime, formal control through policing can regenerate the natural regulative functions of the community (the influential Wilson-Kelling hypothesis, see Wilson and Kelling, 1982).

This intellectual current is immensely influential on policy making in the United States. Thus, the working party set up in the United States in the early years of the Reagan administration under the chairmanship of Wilson gave a low priority, amongst other things, to 'the aetiology of delinquency and a high rating to work in the area of the effects of community cohesiveness and policing for controlling crime' (see Wilson, 1982; Trasler, 1984).

A similar 'social control' theory of crime has been dominant in Britain at the Home Office Research Unit in the recent period particularly influenced by their major theoretician Ron Clarke (see Clarke, 1980). Here, as with Wilson, causal theories of crime came under caution as unproven or impractical (Clarke calls them disposition theories). Situational factors, however, are eminently manipulable. The focus should, therefore, be on making the opportunities for crime more difficult through target hardening, reducing the opportunities for crime and increasing the risks of being caught. This represents a major shift in emphasis against the dispositional bias in almost all previous criminologies.

This move to administrative criminology (or varieties of 'control theory' as Downes and Rock, 1982, would have it) represents the re-emergence of neo-classicist theory on a grand scale. The classicist theory of Beccaria and Bentham had many defects, among them a uniform notion of the impact of the various deterrent devices legislated to control crime (see Rutter and Giller, 1983: 261–2). By introducing concepts of differential risk and opportunity as variables which can be varied by policy makers and police on a territorial basis, they add a considerable refinement to this model of control.

The story so far

The nature of the crisis in criminology should by now be a little clearer: positivist criminology of the social democratic mould, the major paradigm in Anglo-American criminology for the last fifty years, has suffered a precipitate decline. True there are, of course, positivists around but they have simply failed to hear the last bugle call. In its place a new administrative criminology has quietly and quickly gone ahead with the business of research and policy recommendations. Its empiricist approach often disguises the fact that is has abandoned the search for causal generalizations and instead adopted a neo-classicist problematic centring around the principles of effective control. Social democratic criminology with its search for the aetiology of crime within the realms of social injustice has been replaced by an administrative criminology interested in technology and control. A rump of biological reductionists — some of the most naïve variety — remain to carry the torch of aetiology for conventional criminology. Ironically, it was radical criminology which was left with the task of carrying on the tradition of sociological criminology and which was formulated as a project intent on solving the recurrent problems of the discipline.

In the next section I will turn to how this first flush of radicalism lapsed into left idealism and end this article with the emergence of left realism in the most recent period.

Left idealism: the loss of a criminology

I have detailed elsewhere the fundamental characteristics of left idealism (Young, 1979; Lea and Young, 1984). Suffice it to say that the tenets of left idealism are simple and familiar to all of us. Crime is seen to occur amongst working-class people as an inevitable result of their poverty, the criminal sees through the inequitable nature of present day society and crime itself is an attempt — however clumsily and ill-thought out — to redress this balance. There is little need to have complex explanations for working-class crime. Its causes are obvious and to blame the poor for their criminality is to blame the victim, to point moral accusations at those whose very actions are a result of their being social casualties. In contrast, the real crime on which we should focus is that of the ruling class: the police, the corporations and the state agencies. This causes real problems for the mass of people, unlike working-class crime which is seen as minor, involving petty theft and occasional violence, of little impact to the working-class community. If the causes of working-class crime are obviously poverty, the causes of upper class crime are equally obvious: the natural cupidity and power-seeking of the powerful as they enact out the dictates of capital. Criminal law in this context is a direct expression of the ruling class; it is concerned with the protection of their property and the consolidation of their political power. The 'real' function of policing is political rather than the control of crime per se; it is social order rather than crime control which is the raison d'être of the police.

I want to trace how the various tasks of radical criminology were abandoned by left idealism, how the building blocks for a new criminology, although available, were discarded. Part of this process is explicable internally in terms of the ideas inherited from labelling theory and the New Left, and others, in terms of the changes externally in terms of crime and politics: the rise of the New Right in Britain and the United States.

Koshering: the loss of the past

> We need to develop something more than a 'new criminology' that takes most of its form and method from the 'old'. . . . We need, in short, to forget 'criminology' as we have known it altogether (Currie, 1974: 113).

> 'The New Criminology' which seemed to open up new perspectives in the criminological debate is only part of the historical development of bourgeois science designed to secure the position of the ruling class (Werkentin et al., 1974: 28).

Left idealism claimed a paradigm change of such a degree that most of the findings of the old criminology were discarded as not sufficiently kosher to fit the new Marxist credentials. If a theory did not have the correct conception of human nature in social order it would not be possible to learn from its findings. So the critical work of such innovative theorists as Goffman, Becker, Matza and Albert Cohen, became pariah. Paradoxically, they unconsciously took on board the more limited concepts of the old criminology whilst consciously discounting much that was of worth from the extremely productive period of the late sixties and early seventies.

The process of excavation — the re-discovery of the past of criminology was thus put to a halt. Koshering is of particular significance as there was, in fact, little Marxist criminology to fall back on. Within classical Marxist theory there is precious little written about crime. Apart from some extremely positivistic articles by Marx in the *New York Daily Tribune*, which there are grave doubts that Marx – or Engels for that matter – actually wrote, there remain a few disparaging remarks by him on the lumpen-proletariat and a cynical joke about the function of the criminal to the police, hangmen, locksmiths etc. And Engels, despite an interesting discussion of crime in *The Condition of the Working Class in England in 1844*, manages to be both totally positivistic and extremely idealistic about crime in different parts of the same book. What passed as a Marxist input into radical criminology was, as Tony Platt has noted, various New Left commentaries, often of a Fanonist complexion, extremely voluntaristic in their notion of criminal behaviour and having more anarchist than Marxist sensibilities (see also Kettle, 1984). From socialist historians, particularly of the Warwick school, came extremely interesting analyses of the nature of law but remarkably economistic conceptions of criminal action. Sophisticated legal theory was matched with a very undeveloped notion of criminality (see for example, Hay, 1975). All in all, their input into radical criminology was an extremely developed sociology of law but an absence of a criminology.

Koshering had several consequences, one, the loss of middle and ground level of analyses of crime which structural functionalist and interactionist sources could have provided; two, a regression in terms of many of the debates of the sixties; three, a loss of ethnographic and qualitative methods of research, and four, because of the hiatus in terms of discussion of the aetiology of crime, an easy acceptance of very economistic New Left ideas on the subject.

Such a process of Koshering can be seen in some of the very best works of this period. Thus subcultural theory occurred in two waves: a structural functionalist current in American sociology of the early 1960s and a Marxist version, particularly in Britain, in the late 1970s. The American work was pioneered by writers such as Albert Cohen, Richard Cloward and Lloyd Ohlin. The British work was — and still is — epitomized by the writings stemming from the Centre for Contemporary Cultural Studies at the University of Birmingham. There are considerable convergences between the two waves. As Stan Cohen put it:

> It is worth noting, though, that for all its obvious novelty and achievement . . . the new theory shares a great deal more with the old than it cared to admit. Both work with the same 'problematic' . . . growing up in a class society; both identify the same vulnerable group: the urban male working-class late adolescent; both see delinquency as a collective solution to a structurally imposed problem (Cohen, 1980: iv).

Structural functionalist, subcultural theory was a high point in criminological theory. The use of relative deprivation was developed in order to cope with the aetiological crisis; there was an attempt to unite macro and micro-levels of analysis; the distinction between individual and collective deviance was made and the basis of a programme to deal with delinquency by wholescale social intervention developed (e.g. Cloward and Ohlin, 1960). A whole series of problems in theory were executed and attempts at solution made, for example, the problem of reconciling cultural diversity and disorder (e.g. Valentine, 1968); the recognition of the different position of women in subcultural theory (e.g. Ward and Kassebaum, 1966) and the problem of the degree of adherence to deviant values (e.g. Matza, 1964; Downes, 1966). Yet despite the remarkable similarities both in theoretical structure and in the problems which the theorists faced, it is rare for the second Marxist wave to refer to the first. For example, it is extraordinary that Paul Willis' book on delinquency and the school (1977) does not refer back to Albert Cohen's *Delinquent Boys* (1955) given the parallels between them.

The development of Marxist subcultural theory with regards to explanations of youth culture and deviance simply did not learn from the past. In fact, it re-encountered many of the problems which had confronted structural functionalism and in some instances, made real advances whereas in others it remained relatively undeveloped when compared to past theory.

And to conclude this section let me stress that this was a high point of theory within the radical tradition — for the majority of mainstream left idealist criminology there was a dramatic break with the past and a wholesale embracing of the most simplistic notions of crime and criminality.

Keep on going round in circles: the loss of disorganization
I have noted how the history of criminology involves a series of inversions: voluntarism and determinism, romanticism and pathology. These alternatives become inverted in the process of critique. Thus radical criminology — with its roots in the voluntarism of labelling theory and the New Left, and in its commitment to anti-correctionalism — ended up by inverting positivism. As John Ainlay put it: 'the strategy has been to invert it: if correctionalism presupposes pathology, then anti-correctionalism must presuppose anti-pathology. Consequently, the essential features of radical criminology's alternative conception of deviance are defined *antithetically* by the inverse of each of the correctionalist terms, i.e. by free choice, authenticity and rationality' (Ainlay, 1975: 222). Yet as a putative Marxist theory, left idealism cannot reject determinism – rather it is cast as a distant determining force whilst immediate action is the sphere of freedom, of commitment and decision. Thus pathology is discarded yet determinism exists all the same, people are very definitely under the propulsion of class forces but their choice in the last instance is mediated by ideas and is extraordinarily voluntaristic. Determinism, in Stan Cohen's pertinent phrase, has become a 'taken-for-granted backdrop against which the whole play [is] enacted' (Cohen 1979: 33). Thus in terms of class-consciousness, the material forces which make socialism obviously necessary impinge on the lives of working-class people. It is

only false ideas emanating from the mass media and the State which hold the population in thrall. Correspondingly, it only needs the correct ideas and people will realize their destiny and freely *choose* the radical path. The Left-wing intellectuals will click their fingers and the working-class dreamers will awake! (see Young, 1981; Greenberg, 1983).

Conversely, the deviant, the criminal, and the various members of counter-cultures are portrayed as having seen through the inequalities of everyday life. This results in the problem of granting an over-rationality to the criminal actor, of overemphasizing the level of organization of deviant groups and ignoring their disorganization of bestowing the 'primitive rebels' too much coherence and rebelliousness when their actual opinions are often incoherent and conventional, and of picturing them as acting with free will when they are, to a great part, propelled by immediate circumstances.

In short, to reject the concept of pathology with its medical and reductionist connotations should not result in a denial of disorganization, determinism and unreflectiveness in deviant actors and activities.

The centrality of disorder: the loss of crime

> During the seventies the challenge to property relations and the smooth repro-
> duction of capitalist social relations increasingly came from working class youth
> in general. The decade began with a fairly narrow set of youth singled out
> for attention — skinheads, hippies, student militants and blacks. There followed
> constant rumblings about vandalism, hooliganism and truancy and from 1976
> onwards both media and state were glancing anxiously at the militancy and
> self-organization of Asian youth. By the end of the decade politicians, media
> and the state functionaries were talking of youth as a whole as being a 'problem'.
> The number of crimes recorded as committed by young people rose throughout
> the period. . .(Friend and Metcalf, 1981: 156, 161–2).

This is the authentic voice of contemporary left idealism: the community adapts to its material predicament, it pulls itself up by its own bootstraps in order to cushion and overcome deprivation. Above all it *sees through* the misconceptions of 'middle-class values' and the false consciousness of the conformist 'respectable' poor. All of this is true *in part*; it is the positive creative moment in the histories of oppressed people but what is omitted is the dark side of the dialectic: the ritual conformity and social disorganization which is also a result of oppression (see Young, 1975). Thus the positive fightback of leisure culture and militant youth is mixed up with the negative demoralization of theft, vandalism and truancy. Left idealism cannot countenance contradictions, it ignores the fact that most working class crime is directed at working class people and that the 'challenge to property relations' is more often the appropriation of working-class property than any threat to capitalism.

But at least Friend and Metcalf acknowledge that crime exists even though they blunt its antisocial edge and turn it into a form of fightback. More frequently, left idealism simply ignores crime as a problem of any significance. Disorder remains central to the study of society — left idealism has, at least, achieved that aim of radical criminology. But it is disorder purged of crime.

Top-down explanations: functionalism, instrumentalism and the loss of political economy

From the outset a sizeable section of radical criminologists followed Paul Hirst's (1975) lead and declared that radical criminology was incompatible with Marxism. As Bankowski, Mungham and Young trenchantly put it: 'criminology and crime [were] not areas or resources worthy of study for a radical analysis of present (capitalistic) social arrangements. . . As social scientists became concerned with the objects (mode of production etc.) that [would] allow a radical analysis, then crime and criminology became peripheral and marginal' (Bankowski, Mungham and Young, 1977: 37–8). Many of these radicals moved to the sociology of law where their object of study became the relationship between law (its form and content) and capital. A whole discipline grew up where one could find a sociology of law without a sociology of infraction, a sociology of rules and rulemaking without any focus on rulebreakers, and socio-legal studies independent of criminology. Some of this, of course, reflected departmental splits which, as David Matza pointed out, had managed for so long to help separate crime from politics and it is this thoroughly conventional split which many radicals merely endorsed.

But for those remaining in the field of criminology a parallel process occurred. We have seen how crime disappeared from being the subject matter of radical criminology. What replaced it was a focus upwards to the state and its agencies, coupled with an analysis downwards of their impact upon both offenders and non-offenders. And, of course, to the extent that crime was seen as a non-event of little impact, the latter distinction became increasingly difficult to make.

Left idealist criminology thus centres around the nature of the state and its impact upon its citizens. It does not concentrate on why people become criminals but how the state criminalizes people. Thus the impact of the administration of justice becomes paramount in a top-down fashion whereas the structural determinants of crime — so to speak from the bottom up — are ignored or relegated to the obvious.

What is striking about left idealist theorization about the state is its almost unwitting functionalist mode of explanation coupled with a strong, instrumentalist notion that the operation of every agency or action of powerful individuals is linked in some one-to-one fashion to the needs of the ruling class and capital and that all of the state agencies gear frictionlessly together to promote capitalism — there is no contradiction between them. Furthermore, the process of criminalization itself is a key element in this: serving to create scapegoats which divert public attention from the real problems of a capitalist society.

Such a position, is of course, riddled with problems. Functionalism is a teleological form of explanation which does not supply the sufficient and necessary conditions which would give rise to an institution. Alternatives tend, therefore, to be ignored and in left functionalism this means that the possibility of progressive reforms to existing institutions is ruled out of court. The instrumentalist notion of the state does not incorporate the idea of progressive reforms which have occurred because of popular struggle and contradictions within the state agencies. At its most ludicrous, for example, left idealism in radical social work texts tends to portray the totality of the welfare state as being an agency of social control. Capitalism, is it argued, needs to take care of its members so that they can have fit workers with a basic modicum of housing, health care etc. Furthermore, welfare measures placate popular revolt particularly amongst the unemployed. QED the welfare state is an agency of social control. And, the argument continues, when one enters into the areas of the welfare state which are concerned with delinquency — probation, intermediate treatment, social work with children in trouble, youth work etc. — one is dealing *despite the rhetoric of care* with the extension of the net of a coercive state.

Left idealism is not only non-dialectical in the way it rules out the possibility of progressive measures investigated by the state ignoring contradictions within and between different institutions, it is non-dialectical about the actions which are overtly in the interests of capital. Central to a Marxist perspective is that capitalism creates the conditions and possibilities for its own demise: that is that functional equilibrium is *not* achieved (see Frank, 1966). It is the assumption that the values and institutions of capitalism obviously aid its equilibrium which is a key weakness in left functionalism. Even sophisticated bourgeois functionalists, like Robert Merton, indicate how the ideology that merit finds its reward (e.g. 'The American Dream'), which serves to legitimate capitalism, contradicts with the class-based opportunity structure to create a massive basis for discontent (see Young, 1981). And further than this they claim that the whole basis of mass democracy constantly poses a threat to an inegalitarian social order. As Piven and Cloward write in a powerful auto-critique of their previous left functionalist approach:

> There has been an accumulated history of democratic victories institutionalized with government. Left analysts have tended to view these victories as co-operative, as new systems of social control. They are systems of social control, to be sure. But that is not all they are. Social control is never complete, and never enduring. The very mechanisms that effect such a control at one

historical moment generate the possibilities for political mobilization at another. If that were not true, the history of insurgency from below would have ended long ago (Piven and Cloward, 1982: 143).

The loss of aetiology

As we have seen, David Matza described the débacle of positivism as arising from the attempt to study crime without analysing the state. Well, no one can fault left idealism for its inattentiveness to the state. Political economy, theories of the state, are analysed in detail, if sometimes simplistically, in every book and article. But what is missing, this time round, is a sociology of crime. Left idealism has managed to construct a theory of crime without a criminology! For if one looks at the underlying — and invariably unstated — theory of the motivation for crime behind most left idealist criminology one finds the most naïve postulates.

Thus Dario Melossi, in an extremely apposite critique, writes:

> On the issue — which is crucial for critical criminology — of the relation of economy to crime and punishment, there has traditionally been an unspoken alliance of the most primitive Marxism and traditional economics in portraying 'the criminal' as a utilitarian puppet who, by means of simple cost-benefit analysis, reverts to property crime when out of work and desperate but who can be deterred by punishment if the costs that he might have to pay for his crime are raised high enough. By the same token, unemployment, crime and punishment are seen as 'naturally' destined to move together in the same direction. It has been noted that the 'economic man' of the textbooks in economics is not even a good ideal type for the community of business persons after which s/he is supposed to have been remodelled. Is there any special reason why this ideal type should work better with these people who happen somehow to break the criminal law? Conversely, while unemployment and imprisonment rates move together with great synchrony, nobody has explained why they do so. What passes for explanation is some magic structuralist formula about 'the needs of capital' or the need for social control! (Melossi, 1983: 17–18).

And this puts it in a nutshell. On the level of criminology left idealism has taken up precisely the same monetarist notion of human nature as has the new administrative criminology. Furthermore, almost exactly the same thing has happened in the area where they are supposed to be more sophisticated, the area of social reaction. If you read the pages of the journal *Race and Class*, for example, you would be led to believe that every action of the police in Britain from Swamp 81 to the constitution of Neighbourhood Watch Schemes is a wilful act pursued by the agents of capital — as are the activities of other agencies like teachers or social workers (see for example, Bunyan, 1982; Bridges, 1983; Gutzmore, 1983).

It is a strange world, bourgeois economists may argue about the logic of capital — as do Marxist economists — but seemingly a local police chief has no problem in understanding what capital requires of him nor does the lone school teacher facing a disruptive class.

The aetiological crisis is a non-event for the left idealist. First of all, if crime is not much of a problem then there is little point in explaining it. Secondly, any increase in crime is seen as simply a consequence of an increase in policing rather than a real increase in crime. So the problem becomes why has there been an increase in criminalization, not why is there an increase in crime? And the answer comes back: the crisis in capitalism. Thirdly, without having to posit an increase, the answer to why crime occurs is seen as obvious. Unemployment causes crimes — isn't it obvious? Poverty leads to delinquency — is it necessary to spell it out? A decline in living standards gives rise automatically to riots — doesn't everyone know this? The truth is that none of these laws has a universal validity and the shame is that it has taken arch-conservatives like Ernest van den Haag (1975) to point it out.

So the crisis of aetiology was neatly sidestepped by left idealism. And this was underscored by the real rise in unemployment, poverty — all the *obvious* causes. The rise in crime during the affluent sixties which had caused such a strain in the 'more crime is due to more police' thesis had faded into the past. The crisis had passed over and was forgotten.

The convergence between left idealism and administrative criminology

I have noted that the anomaly which traditional positivist criminology confronted was what I have termed the aetiological crisis; that is, a rapidly rising crime rate despite the increase in all the circumstances which were supposed to decrease crime. This was coupled by a crisis in rehabilitation — the palpable failure of the prison system despite decades of penal 'reform'. With the passing of the sixties the new administrative criminology concluded that, given that affluence itself had led to crime, it was social control which was the only variable worth focusing upon. On the other hand, left idealism forgot about the affluent period altogether and found the correlation between crime and the recession too obvious to merit a discussion of aetiology. If administrative criminology side-stepped the aetiological crisis, left idealism conveniently forgot about it. Both, from their own political perspective, saw social control as the major focus of the study, both were remarkably unsophisticated in their analysis of control within the wider society — and anyway were attempting the impossible, to explain the crime control whilst ignoring the causes of crime itself — the other half of the equation.

In a way, such a convergence suggests a stasis in criminological theory. And, of course, this is precisely what has occurred over the last ten years. But, as I have tried to indicate, theory is very much influenced by changes in empirical data and in social and political developments. And it is in this direction, particularly in the phenomenal rise of criminal victimization studies, that we must look for the motor forces which begin to force criminology back to theory.

The empirical anomalies arising from both radical and conventional victimology were a major spur to the formation of realist criminology. Paradoxically, findings which nestled so easily with administrative criminology caused conceptual abrasions with left idealism. Thus, as the crisis of aetiology waned, the problem of the victim became predominant.

The nature of left realism

The basic defect of pathology and of its romantic opposite is that both yield concepts that are untrue to the phenomenon and which thus fail to illuminate it. Pathology reckons without the patent tenability and durability of deviant enterprise, and without the subjective capacity of man to create novelty and manage diversity. Romance, as always, obscures the seamier and more mundane aspects of the world. It obscures the stress that may underlie resilience (Matza, 1969: 44).

The central tenet of left realism is to reflect the reality of crime, that is in its origins, its nature and its impact. This involves a rejection of tendencies to romanticize crime or to pathologize it, to analyse solely from the point of view of the administration of crime or the criminal actor, to underestimate crime or to exaggerate it. And our understanding of methodology, our interpretation of the statistics, our notions of aetiology follow from this. Most importantly, it is realism which informs our notion of practice: in answering what can be done about the problems of crime and social control.

It is with this in mind that I have mapped out the fundamental principles of left realism.

Crime really is a problem

It is unrealistic to suggest that the problem of crime like mugging is merely the problem of mis-categorization and concomitant moral panics. If we choose to embrace this liberal position, we leave the political arena open to conservative campaigns for law and order — for, however exaggerated and distorted the arguments conservatives may marshal, the reality of crime in the streets *can be* the reality of human suffering and personal disaster (Young, 1975: 89).

To be realistic about crime as a problem is not an easy task. We are caught between two currents, one which would grotesquely exaggerate the problems of crime, another covering a wide swathe of political opinion that may seriously underestimate the extent of the problem. Crime is a staple of news in the Western mass media and police fiction a major genre of television drama. We have detailed elsewhere the structured distortion of images of crime, victimization and policing which occur in the mass media (see Cohen and Young, 1981). It is a commonplace of criminological research that most violence is between acquaintances and is intra-class and intra-racial. Yet the media abound with images of the dangerous stranger. On television we see folk monsters who are psychopathic killers or serial murderers yet offenders who even remotely fit these caricatures are extremely rare. The police are portrayed as engaged in an extremely scientific investigative policy with high clear-up rates and exciting denouements although the criminologist knows that this is far from the humdrum nature of reality. Furthermore, it grossly conceals the true relationship between police and public in the process of detection, namely that there is an extremely high degree of dependence of the police on public reporting and witnessing of crime.

The nature of crime, of victimization and of policing is thus systematically distorted in the mass media. And it is undoubtedly true that such a barrage of misinformation has its effect — although perhaps scarcely in such a one-to-one way that is sometimes suggested. For example, a typical category of violence in Britain is a man battering his wife. But this is rarely represented in the mass media — instead we have numerous examples of professional criminals engaged in violent crime — a quantitatively minor problem when compared to domestic violence. So presumably the husband can watch criminal violence on television and not see himself there. His offence does not exist as a category of media censure. People watching depictions of burglary presumably get an impression of threats of violence, sophisticated adult criminals and scenes of desecrated homes. But this is of course not at all the normal burglary — which is typically amateurish and carried out by an adolescent boy. When people come home to find their house broken into there is no one there and their fantasies about the dangerous intruder are left to run riot. Sometimes the consequences of such fantastic images of criminals are tragic. For example, people buy large guard dogs to protect themselves. Yet the one most likely to commit violence is the man of the house against his wife, and there are many more relatives — usually children — killed and injured by dogs than by burglars!

In the recent period there has been an alliance between liberals (often involved in the new administrative criminology) and left idealists which evokes the very mirror image of the mass media. The chances of being criminally injured, however slightly, the British Crime Survey tells us, is once in a hundred years (Hough and Mayhew, 1983) and such a Home Office view is readily echoed by left idealists who inform us that crime is, by and large, a minor problem and indeed the fear of crime is more of a problem than crime itself. Thus, they would argue, undue fear of crime provides popular support for conservative law and order campaigns and allows the build up of further police powers whose repressive aim is political dissent rather than crime. For radicals to enter into the discourse of law and order is to further legitimize it. Furthermore, such a stance maintains that fear of crime has not only ideological consequences, it has material effects on the community itself. For to give credence to the fear of crime is to divide the community — to encourage racism, fester splits between the 'respectable' and 'non-respectable' working class and between youths and adults. More subtly, by emptying the streets particularly at night, it actually breaks down the system of informal controls which usually discourage crime.

Realism must navigate between these two poles, it must neither succumb to hysteria nor relapse into a critical denial of the severity of crime as a problem. It must be fiercely sceptical of official statistics and control institutions without taking the posture of a blanket rejection of all figures or, indeed, the very possibility of reform.

Realism necessitates an accurate victimology. It must counterpoise this against those liberal and idealist criminologies, on the one side, which play down victimization or even bluntly state that the 'real' victim is the offender and, on the other, those conservatives who celebrate moral panic and see violence and robbery as ubiquitous on our streets.

To do this involves mapping out who is at risk and what precise effect crime has on their lives. This moves beyond the invocation of the global risk rates of the average citizen. All too often this serves to conceal the actual severity of crime amongst significant sections of the population whilst providing a fake statistical backdrop for the discussion of 'irrational' fears.

A radical victimology notes two key elements of criminal victimization. Firstly, that crime is focused both geographically and socially on the most vulnerable sections of the community. Secondly, that the impact of victimization is a product of risk rate and vulnerability. Average risk rates across a city ignore such a focusing and imply that equal crimes impact equally. As it is, the most vulnerable are not only more affected by crime, they also have the highest risk rates.

Realism must also trace accurately the relationship between victim and offender. Crime is not an activity of latter day Robin Hoods — the vast majority of working class crime is directed within the working class. It is intra-class *not* inter-class in its nature. Similarly, despite the mass media predilection for focusing on inter-racial crime it is overwhelmingly intra-racial. Crimes of violence, for example, are by and large one poor person hitting another poor person — and in almost half of these instances it is a man hitting his wife or lover.

This is not to deny the impact of crimes of the powerful or indeed of the social problems created by capitalism which are perfectly legal. Rather, left realism notes that the working class is a victim of crime from all directions. It notes that the more vulnerable a person is economically and socially the more likely it is that *both* working class and white-collar crime will occur against them; that one sort of crime tends to compound another, as does one social problem another. Furthermore, it notes that crime is a potent symbol of the antisocial nature of capitalism and is the most immediate way in which people experience other problems, such as unemployment or competitive individualism.

Realism starts from problems as people experience them. It takes seriously the complaints of women with regards the dangers of being in public places at night, it takes note of the fears of the elderly with regard to burglary, it acknowledges the widespread occurrence of domestic violence and racist attacks. It does not ignore the fears of the vulnerable nor recontextualize them out of existance by putting them into a perspective which abounds with abstractions such as the 'average citizen' bereft of class or gender. It is only too aware of the systematic concealment and ignorance of crimes against the least powerful. Yet it does not take these fears at face value — it pinpoints their rational kernel but it is also aware of the forces towards irrationality.

Realism is not empiricism. Crime and deviance are prime sites of moral anxiety and tension in a society which is fraught with real inequalities and injustices. Criminals can quite easily become folk devils onto which are projected such feelings of unfairness. But there is a rational core to the fear of crime just as there is a rational core to the anxieties which distort it. Realism argues with popular consciousness in its attempts to separate out reality from fantasy. But it does not deny that crime is a problem. Indeed, if there were no rational core the media would have no power of leverage to the public consciousness. Crime becomes a metaphor but it is a metaphor rooted in reality.

When one examines anxiety about crime, one often finds a great deal more rationality than is commonly accorded to the public. Thus, frequently a glaring discrepancy has been claimed between the high fear of crime of women and their low risk rates. Recent research, particularly by feminist victimologists, has shown that this is often a mere artefact of a low reporting of sexual attacks to interviewers — a position reversed when sympathetic women are used in the survey team (see Russell, 1982; Hanmer and Saunders, 1984; Hall, 1985). Similarly, it is often suggested that fear of crime is somehow a petit bourgeois or upper middle-class phenomenon despite the lower risk rates of the more wealthy. Yet the Merseyside Crime Survey, for example, showed a close correspondence between risk rate and the prioritization of crime as a problem, with the working class having far higher risk rates *and* estimation of the importance of crime as a problem. Indeed, they saw crime as the second problem after unemployment whereas in the middle class suburbs only 13 percent of people rated crime as a major problem (see Kinsey et al., 1986). Similarly, Richard Sparks and his colleagues found that working class people and blacks rated property crimes more seriously than middle-class people and whites (Sparks et al., 1977). Those affected by crime and those most vulnerable are the most concerned about crime.

Of course, there is a fantastic element in the conception of crime. The images of the identity of the criminal and his mode of operation are, as we have seen, highly distorted. And undoubtedly *fear displacement* occurs, where real anxieties about one type of crime are projected on another, as does *tunnel vision*, where only certain sorts of crime are feared, but the evidence for a substantial infrastructure of rationality is considerable.

The emergence of a left realist position in crime has occurred in the last five years. This has involved criminologists in Britain, Canada, the United States and Australia. In particular, the Crime and Justice Collective in California have devoted a large amount of space in their journal for a far-ranging discussion on the need for a left-wing programme on crime control (see e.g. *Crimes and Social Justice*, Summer, 1981). There have been also violent denunciations, as the English journalist Martin Kettle put it:

> For their pains the [realists] have been denounced with extraordinary ferocity from the left, sometimes in an almost paranoid manner. To take crime seriously, to take fear of crime seriously and, worst of all, to take police reform seriously, is seen by the fundamentalists as the ultimate betrayal and deviation (Kettle, 1984: 367).

This, apart, the basis of a widespread support for a realist portion has already been made. What remains now is the task of creating a realist *criminology*. For although the left idealist denial of crime is increasingly being rejected, the tasks of radical criminology still remain. That is, to create an adequate explanation of crime, victimization and the reaction of the state. And this is all the more important given that the new administrative criminology has abdicated all such responsibility and indeed shares some convergence with left idealism.

Conclusion

I have traced the extent of the crisis which has occurred within criminology in the last twenty years, attempting to place it in its empirical, social and political context. Central to this has been the demise of social democratic positivism, the major paradigm, within British and American criminology over the period. This has been primarily a response to what I have termed the aetiological crisis — the continued rise in the crime rate all the way through the affluence of the sixties wherein all the familiar 'causes' of crime were systematically diminished and ameliorated. And this was supplemented on a slightly different time scale by a collapse in positivist beliefs in rehabilitation within the prisons.

The most immediate response to this crisis was a remarkable creative ferment within the discipline. From different perspectives labelling theory, strain theory and to a lesser extent theories of social disorganization attempted to tackle the anomaly. It was out of these roots that the new deviancy theory and radical criminology emerged. What happened at that time was — despite widespread disagreements — the widening out of the subject. The need for placing crime in the context of the wider society, of relating macro- to micro-levels of analysis, of studying action and reaction, and of placing the discipline within the context of wider social theory had become paramount. For a period the often hidden philosophical and sociological underpinnings of the various currents in criminological thought were uncovered and there was a time of re-examination of the classic texts in terms of what light they would shed on the debate. Marx, Durkheim, Mead, Merton and the schools of symbolic interactionism, phenomenology and Chicago were all invoked and critically examined. It is no accident that criminology and the sociology of deviance during the 1960s and 1970s became a major focus of many of the debates within methodology and sociology.

The potentiality for a sophisticated radical criminology was, for a time, enormous. And indeed it expanded rapidly in influence within the expansion of higher education and the dissemination of New Left ideas. But there were substantial flaws both in its roots and in the social and political context which it developed. The old story of critique by inversion, which has dogged criminological thinking since the 1900s returned with a vengeance. The new deviancy theory gravitated towards an inverted positivism: its actors rendered too rational, and criminal action either minimized or romanticized, whilst social disorganization as a notion disappeared from its vocabulary. The dictates of 'really' radical thought inflicted a cauterization of the past. It became no longer fashionable to learn from structural functionalism or labelling theory — the process of Koshering had begun. Ironically, as Mertonian structural functionalism was shown to the door, Althusserian functionalism entered in the back way. Many thought that radical criminology was itself a conceptual impossibility and moved to the sociology of law, others that crime itself was a minor problem not worthy of consideration — the majority that the real concern must be with the state. All in all this created a one-sided, top-down type of theory, functionalist to its core, whose concern was not the causes of crime but the relation of state reaction to the political and economic needs of capitalism. And in such a functioning totality reform, whether it was in the streets or in the prisons became an impossibility. Thus left idealism emerged, its dominance within socialist criminology confirmed by the recession. For as unemployment and poverty soared there no longer remained a problem of why the crime rate increased — the answer was obvious and unworthy of reflection. The aetiological crisis for the radicals had *temporarily* disappeared.

Meanwhile a silent palace revolution occurred within orthodox criminology with the emergence and rapid expansion of the new administrative criminology, whose dogged empiricism made it appear like positivism, yet nothing could be further from the case. For the historic search for causation had been abandoned and a neo-classicism had taken its place. No longer was there a notion of solving crime through increasing social justice; rather the emphasis became surveillance, policing and control.

A convergence between left idealism and the new administrative criminology unwittingly emerged. Both thought that investigation of causality was fruitless, both agreed that rehabilitation was impossible, both thought that crime control through the implementation of programmes of economic and social justice would not succeed, both focused on the reactions of the state, both were uninterested in past theory, both attempted to explain the effectiveness of crime control without explaining crime and both believed it was possible to generalize in a way which profoundly ignored the specificity of circumstances.

Thus a nadir has occurred within criminology. However, the discipline develops in a way which relates to changes in its empirical and social context. If the aetiological crisis was the empirical motor of the sixties, criminal victimization studies are the motor of the eighties. And whilst for radical criminology victimology is a veritable creator of anomalies, for the new administrative criminology it creates few surprises. There is little in the paradigm which is particularly jolted by asking the question who is the victim? Indeed by providing maps of the targets of crime it fits unabrasively into control theory. But the evidence for the high criminal victimization of the working class and its intra-class nature sets up real problems in left idealist theory — not the least that it inevitably highlights problems of community disorganization. And the pioneering work of feminist criminologists both in the field of women as victim and as offenders has been of prime importance in forcing radicals to re-examine their positions on punishment and the causes of crime. This has been underscored by a widespread concern over the problem of racist attacks within working class communities and the spread of heroin use to the working class of many European cities. Politically, this has combined with the need for socialist councils in the inner cities to develop a policy which tackles these problems and which cannot, with rising unemployment, depend on the traditional focus within the workplace. Thus all the prerequisites for the emergence of left realist criminology are now present.

This article has argued for the need for a systematic programme within radical criminology which should have theoretical, research and policy components. We must develop a realist theory which adequately encompasses the scope of the criminal act. That is, it must deal with both macro- and micro-levels with the causes of criminal action and social reaction, and with the triangular inter-relationship between offender, victim and the state. It must learn from past theory, take up again the debates between the three strands of criminological theory and attempt to bring them together within a radical rubric. It must stand for theory in a time when criminology has all but abandoned theory. It must rescue the action of causality whilst stressing both the specificity of generalization and the existence of human choice and value in any equation of criminality.

On a research level we must develop theoretically grounded empirical work against the current of atheoretical empiricism. The expansion of radical victimology in the area of victimization surveys is paramount but concern should also be made with regard to developments in qualitative research and ethnography (see West, 1984). The development of sophisticated statistical analysis (see for example Box and Hale in this volume; Greenberg, 1984; Melossi, 1985) should not be anathema to the radical criminologist nor should quantitative and qualitative work be seen as alternatives from which the radical must obviously choose. Both methods, as long as they are based in theory, complement and enrich each other.

In terms of practical policy we must combat impossibilism: whether it is the impossibility of reform, the ineluctable nature of a rising crime rate or the inevitable failure of rehabilitation. It is time for us to *compete* in policy terms, to get out of the ghetto of impossibilism. Orthodox criminology with its inability to question the political and its abandonment of aetiology is hopelessly unable to generate workable policies. All commentators are united about the inevitability of a rising crime rate. Left idealists think it cannot be halted because without a profound social transformation nothing can be done; the new administrative criminologists have given up the ghost of doing anything but the most superficial containment job. Let us state quite categorically that the major task of radical criminology is to seek a solution to the problem of crime and that of a socialist policy is to substantially reduce the crime rate. And the same is true of rehabilitation. Left idealists think that it is at best a con-trick, indeed argue that unapologetic punishment would at least be less mystifying to the offender. The new administrative criminologists seek to construct a system of punishment and surveillance which discards rehabilitation and replaces it with a social behaviourism worthy of the management of white rats in laboratory cages. They both deny the moral nature of crime, that choice is always made in varying determining circumstances and that the denial of responsibility fundamentally misunderstands the reality of the criminal act. As socialists it is important to stress that most working class crime is intra-class, that mugging, wife battering, burglary and child abuse are actions which cannot be morally absolved in the flux of determinacy. The offender should be ashamed, he/she should feel morally responsible within the limits of circumstance and rehabilitation is truly *impossible* without this moral dimension.

Crime is of importance politically because unchecked it divides the working class community and is materially and morally the basis of disorganization: the loss of political control. It is also a potential unifier — a realistic issue, *amongst others*, for recreating community.

Bertram Gross, in a perceptive article, originally published in the American magazine *The Nation*, wrote: 'on crime, more than on most matters, the left seems bereft of ideas' (Gross 1982: 51). He is completely correct, of course, in terms of there being a lack of any developed strategy amongst socialists for dealing with crime. I have tried to show however, that it was the prevalence — though often implicit and frequently ill-thought — of left idealist ideas which, in fact, directly resulted in the neglect of crime. There is now a growing consensus amongst radical criminologists that crime really is a problem for the working class, women, ethnic minorities: for all the most vulnerable members of capitalist societies and that something must be done about it. But to recognize the reality of crime as a problem is only the first stage of the business. A fully blown theory of crime must relate to the contradictory reality of the phenomenon as must any strategy for combatting it. And it must analyse how working class attitudes to crime are not merely the result of false ideas derived from the mass media and such like but have a rational basis in one moment of a contradictory and wrongly contextualized reality.

In a recent diatribe against radical criminology Carl Klockars remarked: 'Imagination is one thing, criminology another' (Klockars, 1980: 93). It is true that recent criminology has been characterized by a chronic lack of imagination — although I scarcely think that this was what Klockars lamented by his disparaging remark. Many of us were attracted to the discipline because of its theoretical verve, because of the centrality of the study of disorder to understanding society, because of the flair of its practitioners and the tremendous human interest of the subject. Indeed many of the major debates in the social sciences in the sixties and seventies focused quite naturally around deviance and social control. And this is as it should be — as it has been throughout history both in social science and in literature — both in mass media and the arts. What is needed now is an intellectual and political imagination which can comprehend the way in which we learn about order through the investigation of disorder. The paradox of the textbook in orthodox criminology is that it takes that which is of great human interest and transmits it into the dullest of 'facts'. I challenge anyone to read one of the conventional journals from cover to cover without having a desperate wish to fall asleep. Research grants come and research grants go and people are gainfully employed but crime remains, indeed it grows and nothing they do seems able to do anything about it. But is it so surprising that such a grotesquely eviscerated discipline should be so ineffective? For the one-dimensional discourse that constitutes orthodox criminology does not even know its own name. It is often unaware of the sociological and philosophical assumptions behind it. James Q. Wilson, for example, has become one of the most influential and significant of the new administrative criminologists. Yet his work and its proposals have scarcely been examined outside of the most perfunctory empiricist discussions. The discipline is redolent with a scientism which does not realize that its relationship with its object of study is more metaphysical than realistic, an apolitical recital of facts, more facts and even more facts then does not want to acknowledge that it is profoundly political, a paradigm that sees its salvation in the latest statistical innovation rather than in any ability to engage with the actual reality of the world. It is ironic that it is precisely in orthodox criminology, where practitioners and researchers are extremely politically constrained, that they write as if crime and criminology were little to do with politics. Radical criminology, by stressing the political nature of crime and social censure, and the philosophical and social underpinnings of the various criminologies is able to immediately take such problems aboard. The key virtue of realist criminology is the central weakness of its administrative opponent.

We are privileged to work in one of the most central, exciting and enigmatic fields of study. It is the very staple of the mass media, a major focus of much day to day public gossip, speculation and debate. And this is as it should be. But during the past decade the subject has been eviscerated, talk of theory, causality and justice has all but disappeared and what is central to human concern has been relegated to the margins. It is time for us to go back to the drawing boards, time to regain our acquaintanceship with theory, to dispel amnesia about the past and adequately comprehend the present. This is the central task of left realist criminology: we will need more than a modicum of imagination and scientific ability to achieve it.

2

Sentencing rapists

Jill Box-Grainger

Since January 1982 there has been much media and public comment on the appropriate sentences for convicted rapists.[1] However, such comment has almost exclusively concentrated upon the appropriate length of prison sentence a rapist should receive; with very little attention being paid to which principles of justice underlie such sentences and what effect upon rapists or the incidence of rape such sentences seek to achieve. Significantly, it has been left to feminist women to raise, time and time again, the issues of the extent to which legal sanctions against rapists do or can offer *all* women some genuine protection from rape (see Medea and Thompson 1974; Clark and Lewis 1977; London Rape Crisis Centre 1984; Edwards 1981).

In this article I shall examine demands made by some feminists from rape sentencing policy. However, I stress at the outset that change in sentencing policy for rape is only one, and not necessarily the most important, area of concern for women campaigning for the protection of all women from rape. Feminists have campaigned, and continue to assiduously campaign, for changes against:

— *the degradation of rape victims* by police questioning and (medical) examination
— *the frequent police disbelief of the rape allegations of some women*; especially from women who have been raped by someone they know, allegations of rape from black women and white women from ethnic minorities, and allegations of rape from prostitute women
— women victims of rape, 'put on trial' by the court procedure
— a law of rape that currently does not recognize the existence of rape in marriage.

It is therefore obvious that womens' war against rape needs to be, and is, comprehensive, making an attack on all aspects of the criminal justice 'management of rape' which directly and indirectly degrades women and reproduces the social conditions and acceptance of rape. Demands for changes in rape sentencing policy are just one tactic in a unified strategy against rape, and for the genuine protection of *all* women from male violence.

Introduction

It is not possible to even begin an evaluation of the principles and effects of current or proposed rape sentencing policy without prior recognition of the facts of rape (see M. Amir 1971; Walmsley and White 1979; Wilson 1978; Hall 1985). From a number of research sources, it is clear that if rape laws and the criminal justice 'management' of rape are to protect all women from rape they must take the following factors into account:

1. That rape in marriage must be legally recognized as existing, with consequent available legal sanctions.

2. That rape is committed far more often than official statistics suggest. To encourage the reportage of all rape attacks and the successful prosecution of those who rape, the police, the public prosecutors, legal advisers, etc., must reconsider their interpretations of 'founded' and 'unfounded' rape allegations, must employ tact and understanding in their treatment of rape victims, and must eradicate racist assumptions and practices from their investigation of rape allegations.

3. That although the conventional profile of the rapist is that of an average young man of lower economic status, the evidence shows that rapists are from all social backgrounds and of all ages.

4. That rapists attack at least as frequently indoors as out, and are often victims' relatives, friends, acquaintances, and men in positions of authority over them.

5. That rarely are rapists mentally ill.

6. That rape is frequently a planned event, sometimes involving more than one offender — and is not merely the expression of explosive, individual pathology.

7. That rape may involve racial attack and abuse on the woman victim, and may be motivated by racial-sexual violence.

8. As an offender, the convicted rapist's criminal record is often for non-sexual as well as sexual offences; in this sense the rapist does not belong to a clearly defined class of offender.

9. That because by definition rape is sexual intercourse against a woman's will, women do not want, or ask to be raped.

10. That *all* women are entitled to be protected from rape and whatever a woman's behaviour, *there is no justification for rape*.

These factors implicitly or explicitly inform my assessment and critique in later discussion of current and proposed rape sentencing policy and practice.

Current practice

Penalties

The maximum penalty for attempted rape is seven years imprisonment, and for full rape is life imprisonment. In 1980, of 420 rapists sentenced in that year 391 received a custodial sentence and only 29 non-custodial. Of those receiving custodial sentences 339 were sent to prison, 26 to borstals, 7 to detention centres, 6 to special hospitals and 13 young men were detained at Her Majesty's Pleasure. Of those receiving non-custodial sentences 18 were placed under a suspended prison sentence, 5 on probation orders, 3 on community service orders, 1 on a juvenile supervision order, 1 under a care order and 1 was conditionally discharged (Durisch, 1982). Of 1,114 men convicted of rape in England and Wales over the past three years, only one received a fine for the offence (Zander, 1982). In Scotland, the latest figures (1979) show that all 34 rapists convicted in that year were detained in custody. However, since 1973 there has been a 12 percent decrease in the custodial rate for convicted rapists (see Walmsley and White, 1979; and Cross, 1981).

The lengths of sentence given to rapists convicted in England and Wales vary widely. In 1976 (the year that the Sexual Offences (Amendment) Act was passed) of 238 convicted rapists who received a prison sentence 16.4 percent received a sentence of under two years, 47.9 percent a sentence of two to four years, 30.25 percent of between four and seven years and 5.7 percent of seven years or more, including life imprisonment. This range of sentence lengths has generally remained stable over the past few years. For the 80 percent of rapists who were detained in 1980, 16 percent received a sentence of under two years, 57 percent a sentence of two to four years, 1 percent a sentence of between four and seven years and 6 percent a sentence of seven years or more, including life imprisonment (Cross, 1981).

Two things can be seen from the above figures. The first is that, like sentencing for other offences, sentences given for rape typically fall well short of the maximum — and where they do approach the maximum the indeterminate life sentence appears to be preferred to a determinate sentence of over ten years. Secondly, during the period 1976–1980 there was a noticeable decline in the numbers of rapists receiving the middle range of prison sentences (between four and seven years) and an increase in those receiving sentences at the lower end of the range (between two and four years). Unfortunately there is no available evidence to explain the reason for this shift — i.e. whether it reflects the difference in severity of rape presently coming before the courts or whether more recently courts are tending to penalize rapists less.

However, it is this apparently increasing leniency by the courts towards rapists which concerns many feminists. Later in this paper I shall look at particular tough sentencing proposals made by feminists but it is first necessary to investigate the principles that presently govern sentencing and the practical consequences of their application.

Principles of sentencing

David Thomas's *Principles of Sentencing* is a seminal documentation of the principles that govern current sentencing practice in England and Wales. In his opening paragraph Thomas notes that during the past fifty years sentencing policy has undergone an important change. He says that as late as 1932 the Departmental Committee on Persistent Offenders could describe sentencing behaviour almost entirely in terms of a tariff system — based primarily on the concepts of retribution and general deterrence. But by 1961 the report of the Streatfield Committee was aware of a shift:

> the courts had increasingly come to consider the offender as an individual, whose needs, rather than whose guilt, would form the basis of the sentence passed (not always, of course, to his immediate advantage in terms of the extent of deprivation of liberty) (Thomas, 1970: 3).

However, individualization of sentences has not meant that tariff sentencing has disappeared. What we now have instead is a dual system of sentencing.

What this means in practice is that the *primary decision* of the sentencer is whether the choice of sentence should be governed principally by the 'needs' or the 'guilt' of the offender. Once the primary decision of tariff or individualized measures has been made, the *secondary decision* of what type or length of sentence tends to be relatively straightforward. However, the primary decision is the key one, and is one which Thomas says often presents difficulty. A typical example is where a serious and prevalent offence has been committed, suggesting a deterrent (tariff) sentence and yet it appears that this particular offender is less likely to reoffend if placed on, say, probation (an individualized sentence). How this conflict is resolved is a matter of policy — i.e. whether the court feels that against such offences or offenders the need to adhere to a particular type of policy is paramount. In the case of rape, Thomas argues that the primary decision is nearly always to follow the tariff, and to this extent it can be presumed that rape sentencing policy follows the principles of deterrence and retribution.

Thomas notes that although in practice the distinction between deterrence and retribution is a fine one, the primary decision to use the tariff is following a policy of deterrence and the secondary decision as to sentence length is a retributive consideration. The calculation of the latter must not be out of proportion to the gravity of the offence and places the sentence at an appropriate point within the tariff range, with regard to the gravity of that particular offence as an example of its species and to any mitigating circumstances.

Lord Chief Justice Lane was recently quoted (Lane, 1982) as giving eleven aggravating circumstances in rape cases which will affect the length of sentence — i.e. circumstances which make greater punishment appropriate. These include the use of a weapon, excessive violence, causing serious injury, the age of the victim, and whether the rapist was in a position of trust with the victim. Thomas generally agrees with the significance of these factors and shows that these types of rape will attract sentences at the upper end of the tariff (seven to ten years).

However, Thomas goes on to note that for the lower range of sentences to be used (approximately three years) the court has probably taken account of some elements of invitation or what might be called 'contributory negligence' on the part of the victim. Examples of this category of rape event are a woman raped whilst hitch-hiking, or a woman who goes with a man to a flat after a party. Furthermore, this consideration holds good even when a woman is raped by a group of men. [2] What is noticeable here is that it is the victim's behaviour that is under scrutiny — and if that behaviour is labelled as deviant in some way, punishment of the rapist (retribution) is seen as less appropriate.

Rape events of the type cited by Thomas as having elements of invitation appear to be those where the relationship between the victim and offender would be categorized as one of 'general acquaintance'. It is interesting to note Walmsley and White's study where the length of sentence is related to the type of relationship between victim and offender. They found that 66.5 percent of their rapists who were strangers to their victims received a four year prison sentence or under; 76 percent of rapists who were well known to their victims received sentences of similar length whilst 81.5 percent of rapists who were 'casually acquainted' with their victims received sentences of four years or under. We can not only here quite possibly see how the rape of some women is considered less reprehensible but also why Clarke and Lewis are unhappy about the practical consequences of interpreting brief meetings between strangers as casual acquaintanceships (Clarke and Lewis, 1977: 72–3).

One other factor influencing the secondary decision in rape sentencing is that of the offender's criminal record. [3] Walmsley and White found that where a rapist did have a previous conviction for a sex offence it affected the length of his subsequent sentence for rape. These authors state that those offenders in their study whose sentence exceeded four years for rape or two years for attempted rape, more often had previous convictions for sexual offences that those who received shorter, or non-custodial sentences. Yet given that many convicted rapists may well have no previous convictions for sex offences, the principles that are probably most likely to affect sentences for rape are those given by Lord Lane and Thomas.

Overall then, despite the apparent emphasis rape sentencing policy places upon deterrence, the actual length of sentence given is the exaction of retribution proportional to the gravity of rape compared with other offences, and the gravity of this particular rape amongst all rapes. It can be seen from the above that what appears quite starkly when these principles are applied is that not only is the crime of rape treated as no more grave than many property offences (for the sentences given are frequently equivalent) but that the gravity of one rape amongst many is decided by what sort of woman was raped. This entirely unsatisfactory state of affairs is discussed again when I look at feminist proposals for sentencing, and is challenged by the recommendations at the end of this paper.

The effects of current sentencing practice

It is impossible to measure the effects of sentencing policy accurately since the incidence of crime is affected by many variables outside the control of sentencing. Nevertheless, despite this caution I feel it is important to look at the claims made by current rape sentencing policy and attempt to make some measure of their success.

As noted earlier, rape sentencing policy is based on concepts of deterrence and retribution, the latter almost automatically involving custody as the appropriate sentence for rape. Hence, it could be said that current policy aims to deter rape through the exaction of what is to be considered harsh punishment.

The effects of deterrence are assumed to be general, individual or both. The former is typically claimed to affect the law-abiding, where it serves to maintain the distinction between the already law-abiding and the already lawless. However, such an effect is obviously impossible to measure. On the other hand, individual deterrence can theoretically be measured according to the recidivism rates of individual offenders although there is unfortunately a paucity of information about recidivism amongst rapists. Nevertheless, I shall make the best of available information.

The Cambridge Department of Criminal Science made a study of all sex offenders convicted in 1947 (CDCS, 1957). In their four-year follow-up of the sample they found that the overall recidivism rate during the period was 15 percent. But of those previously known as sexual recidivists, 50 percent committed at least one other sexual offence in the following four years. Christian et al., carrying out a survey in Denmark in 1965, found that only 10 percent of sex offenders later reconvicted in the courts were actually convicted of a sex crime and that the likelihood of recidivism to the same type of sexual crime was greatest in the case of the more deviating forms of sexual criminality (indecency towards boys and girls and exhibitionism) (Christian et al., 1965: 84).

The risk period for sexual reconviction after release seems long for sexual offenders. Christian et al., (1965) found that 22 percent of those reconvicted of another sexual offence did not reappear until ten years after their original conviction under study. A somewhat similar finding was made by Soothill and Gibbens (1978: 269) which noted with respect to a reconviction follow-up of rape cases over a twenty-two year period that over a quarter or so of the reconvicted (twelve out of forty two) did not reappear until ten years had elapsed. In contrast to these two studies, Frisbie and Dondis' (1965) study of sexual psychopaths discharged from Atascadero State Hospital between 1954 and 1961 found that of reoffending sexual aggressors, including rapists (41.5 percent of total sample), the key times for reoffending were the first and second years after release (15 and 14 percent). This difference in finding may be accounted for by the type of offender ('psychopath') studied by Frisbie and Dondis and the comparatively shorter follow-up period (six years).

One of the overall conclusions reached by Frisbie and Dondis regarding sexual offender recidivism was that the more dangerous the sex offence the less recidivistic was the offender and vice versa. Other studies dispute this conclusion but, nevertheless, one could still presumably argue here that the more dangerous the sex offence the less tolerable the reoffence is, despite the lesser likelihood of it happening. From their study of sexual offenders (including rapists) convicted between 1951 and 1961 and their reconviction patterns, Soothill and Gibbens (1978) found that by the end of the five-year follow-up period there was no evidence of a decline in the seriousness of the type of offences committed. This conflict of evidence may be accounted for by Soothill and Gibbens' finding, supported by that of Christian et al. (1965) 'that a past career of crime is a decisive factor of recidivism'; a factor not taken fully into account by Frisbie and Dondis.

Returning to the CDCS study their analysis of the relationship between rates of reconviction and types of penal disposal is interesting, given that the principles governing current rape sentencing place great emphasis on the deterrent and retributive value of imprisonment. CDCS found that when the fine was used for the first time sexual offenders only 12 percent were reconvicted; and only 26 percent of sexual recidivists who were fined were reconvicted. Overall, CDCS found that the rate of reconviction from penal institutions was 22 percent, from probation 19 percent (although they note that no rapists were placed on probation), 13 percent from discharges and 12 percent from fines (see Wright, 1982: ch. 8).

The conclusions that can be drawn from the above evidence are limited, given that only one of the studies mentioned expressly looks at the reconviction rates of rapists and that many of them were undertaken in different countries during different time periods (presumably with different sentencing systems operating). However, it does not seem too rash to suggest that although recidivism is lower among sex offenders than, say, property offenders, those who do reoffend are likely to be long-term risks whose seriousness of crime does not necessarily diminish over time. In the light of the above it may be that the retributive nature of rape sentencing is of greater importance than the deterrent value. If this is so, the effects of retribution are probably ideological rather than practical, and thus unassailable in terms of a demand for tangible results from sentencing. Yet despite this, or perhaps because of this, demands for an effective rape sentencing policy have recently increased and I shall now look at these new proposals and the principles that guide them.

Feminist proposals for a new rape sentencing policy: rape as a special case

Background
Since the mid-seventies feminists have demanded that the criminal justice process take a tougher line against rape. A recent decision made by Judge Bernard Richards to fine a rapist £2,000 because he considered the victim guilty of contributory negligence has received much publicity and brought many of the long-standing criticisms of rape sentencing to the fore.

To my mind there are two key issues that have arisen out of (although they did not originate in) the recent 'rape debate' — and I mean key issues for feminist analyses and proposals for rape sentencing. The first is the explicit or implicit argument that rape and violence against women should be treated as a special case by the criminal justice process; and the second is that all rapes should be treated as equally serious, that the degree of seriousness should not be decided according to the status of the victim.

The idea that violence against women should be treated as a special case is one which arises out of radical feminist analysis of the position of women in society. Up until the mid-sixties the penal reform movements tended to be dominated by traditional Marxist thought. Attention tended to focus on property crimes and the relationship between capital and the proletariat, state oppression and working-class crime. However, with the rise of the Women's Movement in the late sixties and early seventies feminists began to challenge traditional Marxian ideas of class, i.e. white and male, and showed how under capital women were oppressed in a particular way — in fact to such an extent that it was possible to talk of women's oppression as crossing class boundaries. This analysis led some feminists to argue that because of this deep-rooted oppression (which was also present in other guises before the emergence of capital) violence against women could not be explained as simply the result of working-class oppression, because it was in fact an act committed by the dominant class of men against an oppressed class of women.

One consequence of this analysis is that some feminists who would otherwise probably view most working-class crime as a response of the oppressed to capital, and thus should be treated with leniency, view violence against women as crimes committed by the oppressor (men) — and thus a special case to be treated harshly. The dilemma that then presents itself for this group of feminists is how sentencing and the use of custody — which when used for 'ordinary' crime supports oppression by capital — can serve a useful purpose in curbing the oppression of women.

The second issue of importance here is whether, and if so how, degrees of gravity of rape are to be established. As was shown in the section of this paper 'Principles of sentencing', it is the idea of contributory negligence (rearing its ugly head again in the Ipswich judgement) which presently determines the degree of severity of rape and which in practice denies some women the right of equal protection against rape. Feminists are vehemently against this type of principle being used to establish the seriousness of particular rapes – and in fact many feminists swing entirely the other way suggesting that all rapes are equally serious and once guilt has been established all rapists should be treated equally harshly, for reasons given in the special case analysis.

This equality of treatment argument stems directly from the feminist critique of legal support for the idea of 'appropriate' and 'inappropriate' rape (see Reynolds 1974: 63–4). On the one hand feminists demand that all women must be equally protected from rape since no rape should be justified or 'normalized'. However, on the other hand some feminists would claim that the very fact that some rapes can be said to be normalized shows that the rape of certain women is considered normal in male/female relations. And if this is the case, some feminists are arguing that not only should the law offer equal protection from rape to all women but that feminist sentencing policies should also attempt to attack these 'normal' male/female relations. How or whether this can be done is obviously extremely contentious.

However, it must be understood that the following feminist proposals for sentencing are suggested as short-term tactics in the war against rape.[4] This is important because although some of the proposals may appear drastic in their severity, some feminists would defend them by saying that in the short term there is no alternative but to 'hammer' convicted rapists. What I shall be concerned with in the following section is not so much the question of whether rapists deserve a hammering but whether the type of hammering some feminists are proposing is actually a useful and effective *short-term* tactic in an overall strategy against rape.

Denunciatory sentencing
Many feminists believe that harsher sentences for rape would have a denunciatory effect.[5] The principle of denunciation through harsh sentences is not new and, as Walker (1971) points out, has found many proponents including Beccaria, Fitzjames Stephen, Durkheim, Lord Denning and at least one Home Secretary (Lloyd-George). But there are two aspects of denunciatory sentences which are problematic; the first is what it is that is

to be denounced, and the second is what the denunciation is supposed to achieve and by what that means (see King, 1978).

In the case of rape, some feminists would argue that harsh sentences for all cases of rape would publicly denounce violence against women and show that because all rapes will be treated the same no one type of rape can be considered justified. However, what first must be asked here is whether denunciation through harsh sentences is a necessary medium for denunciation or whether it is one that seems appropriate for feminists in the particular case of rape. Walker argues that harsh sentences are not a prerequisite of denunciation and that to consider them so is a confusion of principle.

> The question which should disclose a denunciator's underlying philosophy would ask whether the criminal must actually suffer, or whether it is sufficient merely to indicate society's abhorrence of his crime — for instance, by a suspended sentence. If he says that the criminal must suffer, he must answer the question why? If he says 'to reduce crime', he is really just a desperate reductivist. If he says to 'satisfy our feelings', he is asking us to treat the criminal sacrificially, as a mere instrument of ritual. But if he says, as he probably will, 'because he ought to suffer', he is just a retributist in fancy dress (Walker, 1971: 19–20).

I believe that feminists are right in attributing some form of denunciatory quality to sentencing. However, it seems to me that such an effect is actually achieved more through the severity of a sentence in relation to others rather than through the actual severity of a sentence in itself. Although I am only guessing here, I believe that feminists who advocate denunciatory sentences for rape are looking for sentences which are both relatively harsh and harsh in some absolute way. And if this is the case for reasons more than simply vengeance, there is the problem of how denunciation works and whether retribution in any form is one of its necessary ingredients:

> Does it simply deter those who fear society's condemnation, or does it set up some subtler psychological process which leads to conformity? In either case, is the effect one which would not be achieved by the mere fact of public conviction? Certainly, those who simply fear society's condemnation should be deterred by the mere stigma of public conviction (Walker, 1971: 19–20).

It seems to me that feminist demands for harsh and denunciatory sentences for rape are problematic on three counts. Firstly, despite the fact that many feminists deliberately avoid discussions of degrees of severity of rape for ideological reasons, the practical consequences of this are that if courts are likely to introduce harsh sentences to denounce rape they will apply these against offences which they consider grave and which have no mitigating circumstances — in other words the distinction between 'appropriate' and 'inappropriate' rape will be retained and perhaps even increased. To me, the real problem here is that instead of rejecting the present distinction made between degrees of severity in rape — and proposing severity according to different criteria — they have ditched any idea of degree altogether. I cannot think of any criminal offence in which sanctions are *not* graded according to the degree of severity of the crime species. It seems highly unlikely that the courts will make rape a special case in this sense, even if it is treated as a special case according to the severity of the penalty given.

Secondly, I believe that feminists are looking for an effect from denunciatory sentencing. As mentioned earlier, apart from the problems of by what means an effect is achieved, there seems to be a strong element of retribution contained in the feminist argument for denunciatory sentencing, and possibly even suggestions of deterrence (see Zimring and Hawkins, 1973). If this is so, then the principles guiding denunciatory sentencing in this instance are no different than the principles already in operation for rape sentencing. This is not necessarily a problem as long as these feminists are willing to recognize that they are therefore not suggesting anything but a modification of the old 'rules' of the criminal justice system.

Finally, returning once again to the question of what is to be denounced, there is a suggestion that since the rape of all women must be denounced equally — and because the law fails to do this in current practice because some rapes are considered a normal extension of male/female relations — some feminists are in fact arguing that rape sentencing should be a direct critique of normal male/female relations. However much one would like sentencing to have the power to achieve such an end, I feel that any attempt to attribute to it such an effect must surely fail. For rape sentencing policy to have an effect it is as much a question of demanding it be used to its full potential as recognizing that sentencing in itself has severe limitations.

Exemplary sentencing

I have heard some feminists argue that, if denunciatory sentences for rape have their shortcomings, sentences for rape should instead be exemplary. But immediately this proposal raises a question — are these two types of sentencing substantially different, and if so, how?

Exemplary sentencing is currently, in some circumstances, an accepted practice, for instance, exemplary sentences were passed on people convicted during the Notting Hill riots and those convicted on football hooliganism — particularly in the mid-seventies. The actual concept of exemplary sentencing relies heavily on the idea of deterrence. Walker (1971) notes that in current practice exemplary considerations guide sentencing in two situations; (a) when a judge believes that more severe sentences will influence potential offenders but is unsure whether colleagues will adopt his policy. Here, exemplary sentences are markedly more severe than the norm, and the judge acts almost as an individual campaigner; and (b) when there is a local outbreak of a particular type of crime. In this situation the judge passes a severe sentence in the hope that making an example of an individual will deter others. [6]

However, there are general problems for exemplary sentencing, the major one being that claims for its success or otherwise are largely anecdotal, says Walker. Furthermore, since the concept is imbued with ideas of deterrence there is the necessity for certainty and the similarity of punishment if it is to have the desired effect. If exemplary sentencing aims to have more than just local effect (and even that possibility is questionable), then it faces the problem of the use of judicial discretion in other courts — and thus the risks involved for the offender are tempered to some extent.

It can be seen from the above that there is a distinct similarity between denunciatory and exemplary sentencing — that is that they both seek to have some kind of effect on public consciousness. But in their pure forms there is a difference between them. Denunciatory sentencing aims primarily at some kind of ideological effect, an effect which need not necessarily rely on harsh penalties. In contrast, exemplary sentencing appears to aim at achieving some kind of concrete effect on a potential body of offenders, and practically involves harsh sentences according to retributive deterrent principles.

However, there are two problems for feminist proposals for exemplary sentencing. The first, quite simply, is that because feminist proposals for denunciatory sentencing are 'impure' (involving ideas of deterrence and retribution) they blur what small distinction there is between denunciatory and exemplary sentencing — and thus their proposal of the latter as an alternative to the former is somewhat misleading. Secondly, even if this confusion hadn't arisen, and all the general problems of exemplary sentencing were minimized — feminist proposals for exemplary sentencing for rape would have to confront the question of which offenders were to receive exemplary sentences.

For, by definition, exemplary sentences are exceptional sentences which make an example of selected individuals — exemplary sentences would not be such if they were applied to all offenders. But because when proposing exemplary sentences for rape, feminists neither state which offenders should be made an example of nor, in general, which types of offence are of greater severity, their demand for exemplary sentencing becomes logically untenable. And without this type of specification it is highly likely that if the judiciary were to apply exemplary sentences for rape they would select those cases which are already considered by the courts as heinous — i.e. most frequently stranger-rapes. This consequence would be totally against the spirit of feminist proposals for exemplary sentencing and would only be avoided if feminists offered some distinction between the degrees of severity of rape.

Protective sentencing and incapacitation

As noted in the background to this section, many feminists would consider imprisonment an inappropriate response to the non-violent property offender. However, in treating crimes of violence against women as a special case some feminists argue that prison can serve a purpose in dealing with men who offend in this way.

In my earlier discussions of denunciatory and exemplary sentencing it can be seen that feminists attempts to make a case in support of such sentencing by arguing that when used in an ideologically correct manner, and against the correct offenders, prison can serve a purpose other than that of shoring up an oppressive and bankrupt social system.

When proposing protective or incapacitation sentencing measures for rapists, feminists join with others on the left in an attempt to find solutions to the possibly perpetual problem of a comparative handful of serious offenders (a group which includes rapists). Again, there is the suggestion that, used sparingly, sentencing some offenders to terms of imprisonment can have to some extent a socially useful purpose. Brody and Tarling put the issues in the following way;

> As a means of dealing with crime, prisons face an uncertain future. On the one hand, recent advances in penological research and thinking have indicated that their rehabilitative value is negligible (Brody, 1976; Greenberg, 1977) and that their capacity to deter individuals is probably overestimated or at least misunderstood (Beyleveld, 1978; Brody, 1979) and that their use as a punishment is too often unjust and unconstructive (Von Hirsch, 1976; Advisory Committee on the Penal System, 1977). But these disadvantages have to be weighed against other considerations. It can by no means be ruled out that the threat of imprisonment exercises an important constraint on the readiness of a large part of the population to break the law. Prisons perform an essential function in containing under secure conditions a few people who would otherwise represent a genuine threat to public safety, and probably have a sort of symbolic significance in reassuring the public that its interests are being protected. It has also been suggested that by taking people out of circulation, prisons actually have a more general preventive function; that is, while they are locked up, prisoners are effectively prevented from carrying out those crimes they would otherwise be free to commit (Brody and Tarling, 1980).

Although feminist proposals for protective sentencing for rapists are comparatively new, the practical opportunity to apply protective sentencing principles has been available for some time. The concept of protective sentencing assumes that some offenders are a special case. The idea is that some offenders have shown a serious potential to behave dangerously and for this reason require a sentence to be passed which goes beyond that of normal proportionality, i.e. they serve a sentence whose length is calculated according to the future harm they may cause if at liberty, rather than according to harm caused in the past. The two actual protective sentences currently available to the courts are the indeterminate life sentence and the extended sentence.

The indeterminate life sentence is the maximum penalty available for rape, and some other non-homicidal offences. Two justifications for the life sentence are typically put forward: (a) that of the 'merciful life sentence' which, because of the indeterminacy of the sentence, allows a person to be released once their particular disorder or problem is successfully treated. It is believed that a determinate sentence in such a case would not allow for immediate release on successful rehabilitation; (b) that some offenders are a real danger to the public and must be locked up accordingly — and theoretically, the indeterminacy of the sentence allows for early release if the danger appears to have passed (see Floud and Young, 1981:70).

The gravity of the offence, the mental condition of the offender and the risk that he will commit a serious offence in the future are the criteria by which non-mandatory life sentences are given. However, the judiciary have always appeared to be reluctant to use the life sentence for rape. Between the period 1976 to 1978 only 17 out of 715 convicted rapists were given a life sentence (see Cross, 1981) and of the all of the non-homicidal life sentences passsed in 1976 (47) only five were for rape. It is difficult to know whether this reluctance stems from the apparently small number of really dangerous rapists appearing before the courts or whether, given the available evidence, the apparent normality of many rapists means that the merciful life sentence, presupposing the need for treatment and rehabilitation, is inapplicable in most cases.

The extended sentence is another protective sentence already available to the judiciary. According to the Powers of the Criminal Court Act 1973 (s. 28 5.5.3) an extended sentence may be passed on a persistent offender when: (a) his offence was committed within three years of a previous conviction or final release from custody; and (b) the offender has at least three previous convictions involving at least two sentences of immediate imprisonment since the age of twenty-one. However, the courts have made little use of this sentence. For in 1970 129 extended sentences were passed but by 1976 only fourteen were given. The length of extended sentences has also diminished, with two-thirds now of five years or less. Furthermore, Walker (1971:143) states that the extended sentence has failed to capture the real menaces at whom it was supposed to be aimed. Because the extended sentence does not, unlike the non-mandatory life sentence, specify the types of offence for which it can be used, it is typically passed upon property offenders. Overall then, it seems that the extended sentence is of little relevance for dealing with rapists.

Both the indeterminate life sentence and the extended sentence seem to be inapplicable as protective sentences for rape. I believe that feminist demands for protective sentences are for long mandatory sentences of a determinate nature to be available only against special case crimes. In this argument the lack of discretion is essential if feminist protective sentencing is to avoid the possibility of discretion being used against certain women; long sentences are considered essential so that if all else to do with prison fails at least this particular offender is out of women's way; and that such sentences are available only against special case crimes is important if feminists are to make a distinction between an appropriate use of long terms of imprisonment. However, if the already available protective sentences are unsuitable for dealing with rapists, the criteria upon which any other kind of protective sentencing can be established must be examined.

The chief problem with protective sentences, and Floud and Young, Cross and Walker all testify to this, is the near impossibility of establishing the probability of future harm, which is largely because each individual and the circumstances of his offence are different (see Gordon, 1982). However, even if future harm could be predicted with some degree of accuracy it is possible that protective measures could be applied which do not necessarily involve long terms of custody. But if we are to assume that custody will be essential as a protection against some offenders it seems that the best safeguard for passing protective sentences would be to pass them only against those offenders who have at least one previous conviction for an offence of a similar nature.

But the above considerations are perhaps not quite what feminists have in mind. For I interpret feminist demands for protective sentencing as presuming that any man convicted of rape is, by definition, dangerous and thus even a first offender should serve a long protective sentence. If this interpretation is correct, there is then no question of predicting the future harm that may be caused by individual offenders. Yet without taking into account prediction, the optimum length for a feminist protective sentence must either be arbitrarily decided or decided according to some kind of proportionality criteria. If the former is the case, feminists are demanding protective sentences whose length is determined according to non-rational criteria, and if the latter is the case feminist proposals for protective sentences are really no more than proposals for retributive sentences against rape. It appears, then, that as with denunciatory and exemplary sentencing proposals, the call for protective sentences against rape is a call for the return of a clearly retributive system of sentencing.

Incapacitation

The apparent failure of imprisonment to have useful effect on individual criminals or crime in general has forced some professionals and lay people to reassess the value of custody. The suggestion that, if nothing else, prison incapacitates those locked up, is one that derives as much from a serious investigation into how to deal with persistent and perhaps dangerous criminals as from the desperate attempt of some (usually statutory bodies) to insist that, despite the evidence, the widespread use of imprisonment does serve a purpose after all. I raise this issue here because I feel it is important to state quite clearly that feminists who are interested in the incapacitatory effect of imprisonment are concerned with its possible effect on rapists and rape (serious offences) and are not those who, as mentioned above, probably have a general vested interest in justifying the present system of law and order. However, because most of the research into the possible effects of incapacitation has been carried out by those with a non-feminist perspective I can only attempt to relate to the more general discussions of the specific case of serious offences, sexual offences and rape.

The chief difference between the ideas of protective imprisonment and incapacitation is that the former is concerned solely with the special case — the dangerous offender — whilst the latter is an effect on imprisonment regardless of the offender incarcerated. Brody and Tarling in their Home Office Study 'Taking Offenders Out of Circulation' (1980) concentrate exclusively on the issue of incapacitation and make an extensive survey of all the available research pertaining to the actual or possible effects of incapacitation.

Research studies cited by Brody and Tarling analyse the effects of incapacitation in three ways: (a) by estimating the incapacitatory effects of custodial sentences given under current sentencing systems; (b) by estimating the possible incapacitatory effects of modified sentencing systems; and (c) by estimating the effects of decarceration on the crime rate. However, none of the research findings are conclusive and there is quite a wide divergence in estimates of those effects.

From their examination of available research Brody and Tarling found that the possible effects of incapacitation upon crime could range from a 5 to 20 percent reduction — somewhat inconclusive evidence from which to attribute a significant effect to incapacitation (see also Clark, 1975; Shinnar and Shinnar, 1975). With regard to the incapacitatory effects of modified sentencing systems, the available research suggests that crimes could be reduced by anything from 6 to 8 percent, depending on the nature of the offence, whether or not the sentence is mandatory, and the length of increase of sentence (see Carr-Hill and Stern, 1979; Peterson et al., 1980; Pease and Wolfson, 1979). However, this type of projected effect study relies heavily on an enormous (and often dubious) range of predictions and this fact, coupled with the range of results produced by research in this field, leaves me in no doubt that any proposal to modify the sentencing system which is guided purely by incapacitatory claims is a proposal to build a house on sand.[7]

Finally, considering the possible effects of decarceration, as opposed to those of increased incarceration, Greenberg (1975) estimated that if prisons were entirely eliminated indictable crimes would increase between 1.2 percent and 8 percent. Although this evidence is too insubstantial for real comment, I have included it in order to put the discussion of the importance of imprisonment as incapacitation into some perspective. For it is far easier to become involved in investigating why we should use prisons rather than ask 'what would happen if we didn't use prisons?'

Furthermore, feminists who believe that the imprisonment of rapists will have an incapacitatory effect must be concerned that it is more likely to affect those individuals actually incarcerated than necessarily the incidence of rape in society. This serious limitation is noted by Brody and Tarling who, in conclusion to their own incapacitation study state:

> Imposing incapacitative prison sentences of eighteen months would not have prevented any one type of crime. Peter Silian and Greenwood and Van Dine et al. obtained similar results. From this evidence at least, there is little evidence that any one type of offence can be prevented by concentrating on those offenders convicted of it on any single occasion (Brody and Tarling, 1980:14).

However, it is theoretically possible to argue that some crimes are so serious that even if the imprisonment of the individual perpetrators has no effect on the incidence of these crimes in outside society, the fact that at least one serious offender is incapacitated for whatever period is of some significance. To my mind this is of significance but this is really an argument for protection from individuals through their incapacitation. Thus we are back once again to the question of protection and the related problem of how the length of an individual's sentence is to be determined. For, if it can no longer be determined according to the possible effect all such sentences may have on the incidence of the class of crime in question, it must be determined by criteria which relate only to the individual offender — i.e. the severity of the crime, the mental state of the offender, predictions of the possible harm to be caused by the offender, etc. Yet these are issues which properly belong within discussions of protective and retributive sentencing and they have been dealt with in previous sections of this paper. But there is one further point which must be raised that relates to the success or otherwise of individual incapacitation of rapists.

Brody and Tarling's study of the incapacitatory effects of eighteen month custodial sentences served for a variety of offences found that this incapacitatory technique did not affect the incidence of different classes of crime equally. They noted that, for instance, incapacitation prevented proportionally fewer sex offences than burglaries and robberies. They give no explanation for this discrepancy but I would suggest that it is most probably related to the type of criminal record of many sex offenders and their offence/reconviction patterns. For it is generally the case that sex offenders have mixed criminal records it follows that their pattern of sexual offending is often broken by non-sexual offending. This fact, coupled with the evidence that suggests sex offenders who commit further sexual offences may be most likely to do so after many years since their original conviction has elapsed, suggests that if an individual sex offender is incapacitated for, say, two years it may be the case that he is incapacitated during a period within which he would otherwise have offended but have committed non-sexual crimes; or not have offended at all.

The problem then for feminists who support the incapacitation of individual rapists is how to gauge the optimum period of imprisonment for affecting both their non-sexual and sexual offending. This seems quite a key issue to me since if, as I believe is the case, feminists who support incapacitatory/protective sentences are only interested in their use against and effect upon sexual offences and sexual offenders, it is essential that the success of such sentencing is offence-specific. If not, feminists will find themselves supporting incapacitatory measures which could be seen as one justification for generally oppressive and usually class-specific law and order policies.

Conclusion and recommendations

I believe that feminist proposals for rape sentencing are important not so much because in themselves they are effective proposals — but because they are underpinned (explicitly or implicitly) by a critique of the criminal justice process in general, and of the anti-feminist stance of particular law enforcement policies.

Through their critical exposé of the discriminatory application of the rape laws, feminists rebut the general assumption that the enforcement of law is the application of neutral justice — and in doing so necessarily imply that law enforcement is guided by ideological considerations. In the case of rape, feminists state that these considerations are anti-feminist — for they allow, and possibly encourage, the rape of women who are not stereotypical and in this way permit the material and ideological perpetuation of the oppression of women.

However, the issue is to what extent, and by what means, feminist rape sentencing proposals can affect the material and ideological oppression of women. In my opinion, a major drawback with the proposals discussed in this paper is that they overestimate the power of sentencing to effect change.

Many of the proposals attempt to incorporate an attack upon systematized and materially based oppression – i.e. 'normal' male/female relations — and in doing so fail to recognize the complex and often indirect relationship between expressions of power and sources of power. For although the imposition of legal sanctions is one expression of the authority and power of the state – and as such legitimates and perpetuates a system of oppression — it is not the only expression of that power and authority nor necessarily its source.

There is an extensive debate surrounding the relationship between ideological and material oppression and it is not within the scope of this paper to give it more than passing reference. But what I wish to stress is that because this relationship is complex it seems likely that in the short-term a feminist rape sentencing policy would only begin to erode one area of ideological legitimation of rape. However, the long-term effect of such a policy — when it operates in conjunction with other attacks against systematized oppression — may be to fundamentally alter the nature of male/female relations and end the oppression of women. But this could only be a long-term effect. What I am arguing about here is not the objective, i.e. to eradicate the oppression of women, but the fact that some feminists appear to demand long-term effects from expressly short-term sentencing policies. This inherent contradiction must mean that such policies will fail.

On a more practical level, because some feminists fail to recognize the limits of a short-term sentencing policy they propose principles for sentencing which would only have their desired effect if they operated within a framework different from that of the feminist proposals. For instance, the exemplary, denunciatory, deterrent and retributive effects of sentencing must be important considerations. But by constantly suggesting that such effects are achieved only through long-custodial sentences feminists ignore the possibility that such effects derive at least as much from the relative quality of the sentences as they do from their absolute quantity.

Furthermore, because some feminists refuse to acknowledge any degree of severity of rape their proposals not only circumvent the immediate problem of contributory negligence but are also a recommendation for a sentencing procedure for which there is no precedent whatsoever in this country. By failing to face up to what I consider to be one of the crucial short-term problems these proposals are neither a real challenge to current practice nor to an extremely oppressive ideology.

In the final part of his paper I shall make my own recommendations for a rape sentencing policy which attempts to reconcile a long-term feminist strategy with the need for realistic short-term tactics. As I go through the recommendations I shall try to explain the philosophy behind the chosen framework and principles rather than attempt a detailed description of their practical operation.

Recommendations

1. Rape should be treated as one of a set of special cases by the criminal justice system, in so far as, like other crimes such as premeditated murder, it is of an exceptionally serious nature and not merely the result of an oppressive economic system. In order that this set of special cases be recognized as exceptionally serious crimes judicial power must be curtailed, or at least rationalized, so that severe penal sanctions such as imprisonment would have an extremely restricted use.

2. Once imprisonment can only be imposed against those who commit

serious offences, it will be clear that these crimes will be unequivocally considered the most unacceptable.

3. The crime of rape should be distinguished by the degree of severity. For although there is never any justification for rape, some rapists use excessive force, threat or humiliation against their victims and they should be dealt with in the light of such aggression. I propose that the crime of rape be defined as sexual intercourse or any other kind of penetration, oral or anal, against the will of any woman; and that the crime of aggravated rape be the above where extreme force, brutality, humiliation or mutilation is present. The distinction between rape and aggravated rape is one of degree of force or threat and *not* according to the status of the victim.

4. Where allegations of rape and aggravated rape are corroborated, evidence of threat or force should automatically negate any presumption of consent and in this case a rape victim's sexual history would be categorically inadmissable evidence. However, where rape allegations have no corroborative evidence, evidence of a victim's sexual history would only be introduced when it referred directly to her sexual relationship with the defendant.

5. Short but mandatory custodial sentences should be imposed upon first-time rapists. Although short, these sentences would be viewed as a severe sanction in relation to all available sanctions and thus would denounce and exemplify rape as unacceptable. The sentences must be mandatory in order to exclude the possibility of judicial discretion and thereby the possibility of the penalties being graded according to present, unacceptable criteria; and also to ensure that there is a certainty and similarity of penalty in order to maximize any deterrent potential that the sentences may have. Although there is no logical necessity for custodial sentences to form part of the attempt to use sentencing to denounce rape and deter potential rapists, I recommend that they *should* be used for rape. This is not only because their use, in relation to other sanctions, has the effects mentioned in 1 and 2, but also because temporary custody offers women some protection from, and punishes, the individual rapist. I can see no reason why tempered punishment should not quite openly form part of a feminist rape sentencing policy. Mandatory custodial sentences should be given for both rape and aggravated rape although the latter will carry a relatively longer sentence.

6. In extreme cases where a first offender is found guilty of multiple rape or aggravated rape, or an offender is found guilty for a second, third, etc., time of rape or aggravated rape there should be a restricted availability of long, mandatory, fixed-term prison sentences where the length of sentence would be a protective measure as well as a punishment.

7. The mandatory sentences for rape and aggravated rape should be reviewed at frequent and fixed intervals. Reviews of these sentences should

be conducted by a publicly selected panel of representatives of women and men (*not* the present Parole Board) — and at the review the onus would be upon the custodial authority to prove the need for further custody. These reviews should also be conducted in the presence of the prisoner who should be entitled to a legal defence, etc.

8. Where someone convicted of the above offences is released from custody by review, he should serve the remainder of his custodial term under community licence of fixed duration — with the possibility of prison re-call to finish this sentence if his behaviour in the community warrants such a move.

9. Where someone convicted of rape or aggravated rape serves his full sentence he will automatically be released. If the custodial authorities still consider him a risk they just carry out a review as above to prove their case. If they succeed in doing so, the offender may be placed on a community licence perhaps with conditions attached. However, this licence must be of a fixed duration.

Notes

Many thanks to Radical Alternatives to Prison (RAP) for their kind permission to reproduce much of this article from their publication; Box-Grainger, J. (1982) *Sentencing Rapists*, London: RAP.

1. In January 1982 Judge Bernard Richards, presiding over a rape case in Ipswich, fined a convicted rapist £2,000 — a comparatively light sentence because the judge claimed that the victim was guilty of contributory negligence. She was a seventeen year old woman hitch-hiking.

2. See cases Turner and Arnfield, 12.5.64 — 407/64; and Morgan and Burrell 14.10.63 — 1234/63 — cited in Thomas (1970:3).

3. The other major factor influencing the sentencing of rapists is the offender's colour and racial background. For further discussion of this see Brownmiller (1975:215) and Pitts in this volume.

4. Some feminists propose that the specific legal crime of rape should be replaced with the more general legal category of 'sexual assault'. This proposal is, it is suggested, geared to both short-term goals (a greater number of rape convictions) and long-term goals (changing women's sexual consciousness. For further discussion see Clark and Lewis (1977); Brownmiller (1975: ch. 12) and Plaza (1980), and for a critique of SAL proposals see Box-Grainger (1982).

5. There is, however, another aspect of retribution which is frequently overlooked. It is that society, through the courts, must show its abhorrence of particular types of crime, and the only way the courts can show this is by the sentence that they pass, according to Lord Justice Lawton giving judgement in the Sargent case (1974) — cited in Cross (1981:143).

6. For example: 'The sooner it becomes recognized that people who indulge in this form of criminal activity will be faced with long and severe sentences, perhaps the sooner the streets and houses will be safer to live in' suggested Lord Wheatley, the Lord Chief Justice Clerk in the Court of Criminal Appeal in Edinburgh when passing judgement on a rape case. *Daily Telegraph* 22.1.82.

7. The problem of prediction in incapacitation studies includes:
(a) only crude estimates are made as to the real rates at which offences are committed

(b) the studies tend to assume that more unsolved crime, let alone unreported crime, has been or would be committed by those being incapacitated

(c) it is only possible to estimate the incapacitation effect for all offenders and not individuals.

3

Sex, class and crime:
towards a non-sexist criminology

Jeanne Gregory

Introduction

During the last ten years, the slow trickle of feminist contributions to the study of crime and deviance has grown into a steady stream, which it is increasingly difficult for those teaching courses in these areas to ignore. Unfortunately, the most frequent response is to add the topic 'female crime' to the list of areas to be studied while leaving the rest of the course untouched. By reducing the gender variable to a footnote in this way, a potentially valuable source of theoretical and empirical insights is thrown away and the field of criminology impoverished. Victoria Greenwood has pointed out that:

> The scientific study of criminality has focused on blacks and not whites, on the poor and not the rich, on men and not women, on the young and not the old (Greenwood, 1981: 76).

These were the concerns of traditional, correctionalist criminology, geared to helping governments solve the crime problem. When academics struggled free of this straitjacket, the theoretical and ideological focus of criminology was transformed. The assumption that crime could only be understood in terms of individual pathology was abandoned and the statistical pyramid of crime, in which the young, the poor and the black were consistently over-represented, was subjected to critical scrutiny. Drawing their inspiration initially from interactionism, the 'new' deviancy theorists focused on the ways in which the criminal justice system stigmatized certain social groups and so exacerbated the very problems it claimed to solve.

Even while the insights derived from this perspective were still being absorbed into the vocabulary of anti-correctionalist criminology, some of its exponents were beginning to ask questions that interactionism seemed less well equipped to answer. As they sought to understand the basis of social inequality and power relationships within capitalism, they turned increasingly towards Marxism; and so 'radical' or 'critical' criminology was born. It is proving to be an extremely fruitful perspective for exploring the class dimension of crime, thereby illuminating the ways in which the criminal law is selectively enforced against the powerless. Women however, cannot easily be accommodated within this account. Despite their subordinate economic and social position, they appear in the crime statistics much less frequently than men. In order to rectify this weakness in critical criminology and so complete the break with correctionalism, it is essential to consider the impact of gender, as well as class position, on criminality.

In the quotation given above, the sex dimension stands out like a sore thumb, an apparent exception to the association between crime and oppression. The temptation is to avoid the difficult theoretical questions which it raises and to justify this oversight in terms of the large numbers of males caught up in the criminal justice system, for whom interventionist strategies are urgently required. Such impatience is misguided: theoretical understanding will be enriched, not undermined, by investigating the relationship between women and the criminal law. Furthermore, political campaigns derived from this understanding will provide a sounder basis for genuine human liberation.

Female crime statistics

Students of criminology are usually advised to approach official crime figures with considerable caution. They learn of the existence of the hidden dimension of crime, the part of the iceberg that is not visible and has an unknown shape. This warning reduces the chances that they will be lured by government funds into research projects on the crime problem as officially defined, possibly spending several years in the elaboration of a theory based on a false premise. The crime statistics tell us a great deal about the ways in which law enforcement agencies operate, but to accept the statistics as given is to accept without question the priorities and assumptions of these agencies. The most serious challenge to the official picture of crime as a largely working class phenomenon comes from recent work on corporation crime. In terms of the vast sums of money involved and the social harm inflicted, the offences recorded in the crime statistics pale into insignificance when measured against the crimes of the powerful (see Pearce, 1976; Ermann and Lundman, 1978). Furthermore, if we consider only those categories of crime that feature prominently in the official records, the evidence from self-report studies suggests a considerable degree of middle class involvement in criminal activity (see Box, 1981).

When we turn to the question of female criminality, we find that the crime statistics of all countries, despite considerable legal and cultural variations, tell the same story: that women have a lower crime rate than men. Does this mean that women are consistently less criminal than men, or that they, like the middle and upper classes, are systematically under-represented in the statistics? It is best to respond to this question in two stages. Firstly, we can look again at the shortcomings that criminologists have identified in the statistics and consider whether these defects would tend to mask more female than male criminality. Secondly, we need to consider whether there are any additional factors which might be operating specifically to produce a gender bias.

On the first point, it has been argued that women tend to become involved in offences with a low reportability rate: crimes such as illegal abortion, infanticide and thefts by prostitutes are unlikely to be reported to the police because the victims are unwilling or unable to do so (Campbell, 1981: 10). However, for every 'female' crime with a low degree of visibility, there are several 'male' crimes for which the same points can be argued. For example, there is ample evidence that the victims of rape and domestic violence are most reluctant to inform the police that crimes have been committed against them (Clark and Lewis, 1977; Dobash and Dobash, 1979). Similarly, as women are the chief recipients of welfare benefits and tend to do the shopping, there are undoubtedly a number of women who have committed social security or shoplifting offences and escaped detection; at the other end of the financial scale, only a handful of women have had the opportunity to become involved in corporation crime, as the executive suite remains an almost exclusively male preserve. The argument that the crime statistics are systematically skewed in favour of one sex or the other, as a consequence of different reportability rates, cannot be sustained.

On the second point, it has been argued that the extent of female crime is comparable to that of males, but that women escape detection more frequently because of the private nature of their social position, combined with an inherent deceitfulness (Pollak, 1961). This thesis is largely speculative and cannot be substantiated; it fails to recognize that men as well as women operate in private spheres and are just as likely to develop strategies for avoiding detection. There is, however, an alternative version of the 'hidden female crime' argument which does have to be considered seriously. It suggests that law enforcement agencies are generally more reluctant to proceed against females than males, whatever the crime, so that women are treated more leniently than men at every stage of the criminal process (Adler, 1975; Reckless and Kay, 1967). When these assumptions are put to the test, the results indicate that the impact of gender is much more complex than this. There is some evidence of leniency towards women both in the different cautioning rates for male and female offenders and in the different incarceration rates of those found guilty. Although the number of males arrested but subsequently released with a caution is considerably larger than the number of females treated in this way, when these figures are expressed in percentage terms, they do point to the more favourable treatment of women. [1]

For those less fortunate women whose cases are not dropped, the picture becomes more complicated. An American study conducted in the

1960s found that female offenders were less likely to be remanded in custody or receive custodial sentences on conviction than male offenders (Silverstein in Nagel and Weitzman, 1972). In Britain however, although a smaller percentage of female than male offenders receive custodial sentences, a larger proportion of women are held in custody awaiting trial or sentence, often because a medical report is considered necessary. As most of these women are subsequently given a non-custodial sentence, remand serves as a form of punishment (see Dell, 1971; Greenwood, 1983). The same American study also concluded that women were less likely to receive a jury trial and more likely to receive an indeterminate sentence than their male counterparts (Nagel and Weitzman, 1972; see also Temin, 1973). Once imprisoned, women are likely to suffer greater deprivation than men; they are the forgotten minority, denied access to educational programmes and recreational facilities on the grounds of insufficient numbers and often situated in remote parts of the country so that relatives visit infrequently.[2]

At the time of writing there are some 48,000 men in British prisons and only 1,400 women. To explain this difference in terms of chivalrous attitudes towards women is to anticipate that those women who *are* incarcerated have committed extremely serious offences. This is however not the case; the vast majority of these women are in prison for stealing (and this does not refer to the serious crimes of robbery and burglary) or for non-payment of fines (Matthews, 1981). If the 'chivalry factor' is operating to keep some female criminals out of the official records, it apparently operates selectively. 'Paternalism' would seem to be a more appropriate term. It throws light on some otherwise puzzling and contra-dictory features of the official response to female crime, particularly in relation to juveniles. It can be used to explain why on the one hand a higher percentage of girls than boys who are suspected of crime are merely cautioned[3] and why on the other hand girls who do appear before the juvenile courts are often treated more severely than boys, with female first offenders five times more likely to receive an institutionalized sentence than male first offenders (Jay and Rose, 1977). The severity is invariably justified in terms of the girls' need for protection, with immorality and not criminality proving to be the major issue.

Separate studies in a number of countries have found that it is girls rather than boys who are charged with status offences — i.e. offences that are only regarded as crimes when committed by young people. The behaviour that gives such cause for alarm is variously described as running away, incorrigibility, truancy, beyond parental control and in moral danger.[4] If the status offence is combined with a minor crime such as petty theft, the court is more likely to deal with the boy on the basis of the petty theft and with the girl on the basis of the status offence. In terms of disposal, this usually means a longer period of supervision or incarceration for the girl. Girls are also more likely to be subjected to physical examination even if they are not being charged with a sexual offence. The juvenile court thus reflects the double standard of sexual morality that operates outside it and hence actively 'sexualizes' the mis-behaviour of girls (see Chesney-Lind, 1973 and 1977). These findings are confirmed by a number of self-report studies which suggest that with regard to non-serious offences, young females commit a similar range and type of offence as young males, although less frequently (see for example, Hindelang, 1971; Cernkovich and Giordano, 1979; and Smith and Visher, 1980).

It is in the official response to juveniles that the distortions of gender are most pronounced. There is however, no simple method of stripping away the gender bias in order to uncover the true picture. We have seen how notions of gender inform the decision-making processes within the criminal justice system. The same notions are also deeply embedded within the criminal law itself. The existence of sex specific offences such as prostitution is a clear case in point; this alone would ensure that the pattern of female crime was different from that of male crime. The activities of women are sexualized at the same moment that they are criminalized, so that the statistics produce the very differences that they are supposed to demonstrate. This is no more clearly seen than in the recent liberation thesis, which has given a new twist to the female crime debate and so further intensified the clouds of mystification which surround it.

Carol Smart, in launching her attack on criminology for neglecting women, recognized the danger that if the question of female crime became a visible instead of an invisible social problem, a moral panic might well ensue (Smart, 1976: xiv). If the media became sensitized to a new issue, an escalation of reports of female crime could well result in an increased diligence on the part of law enforcement agencies which would in turn appear in the statistics as a rise in the rate of female crime. Criminal activity is then equated with liberation and the women's movement is blamed for the growth in female crime, along with the increase in divorce rates and the incidence of female lung cancer. Freda Adler falls into precisely this trap when she writes of the phenomenon of female crimin-ality as 'but one wave in [the] rising tide of female assertiveness' and claims that crimes of violence are for women increasing at rates six or seven times as great as those for men (Adler, 1975). These staggering claims have prompted a response from various quarters, so that just about every statement on which the thesis is based has been discredited. To begin with, the assumption that liberation is an accomplished fact of women's lives is challenged by demonstrating the extent to which the male monopoly of social and economic power persists (Leonard, 1982; Crites, 1976). More specifically, the women who commit crimes can in no sense be regarded as liberated (Weis, 1976). It cannot be denied that female crime rates are rising, but as the initial figures are small, quite small numerical increases will seem large when expressed in percentage terms (Smart 1979; Mukherjee and Fitzgerald, 1982). Far from providing proof of liberation, these increases can be understood as a response to deteriorating economic conditions, as they occur mainly in non-occupational areas such as welfare fraud and minor property offences. Contrary to Adler's claims, women have not made a major entry into the masculine world of violent crime; the male rate in these areas continues to rise faster than the female rate (Steffensmeier, 1980; Mukherjee and Fitzgerald, 1982). As Steven Box argues, sex-role stereotyping still prevails in the world of organized crime, which could hardly be described as an equal opportunity employer! (Box, 1983: ch. 5). Women continue to play subordinate roles in the world of crime as much as in the legitimate world of business.

Having decisively rejected the liberation thesis, we can approach the question of the relationship between the women's movement and the female crime statistics from an entirely different perspective. Campaigns for the elimination of gender bias and hence for equality of treatment have not fallen entirely on stony ground. Their success will have both a negative and positive effect on the statistics. On the one hand, a reduction in leniency towards female offenders will produce an apparent rise in female crime. On the other hand, successful campaigns to liberalize the criminal law (in such areas as prostitution and abortion) and to establish 'justice for juveniles' will prevent the criminalization of many women and girls.[5] Such developments serve to remind us that the impact of gender varies over time and also makes cross-cultural comparisons difficult. However, although the precise effect of gender bias on a particular set of statistics is difficult to measure, no one has convincingly demonstrated the existence of a vast quantity of hidden female crime which would effectively wipe out the sex difference. There is no equivalent to the 'crimes of the powerful' studies, which exposed the working class bias of the crime statistics of all capitalist countries at one fell swoop. As we cannot satisfactorily explain away the low rate of female crime, we should instead accept it as an important variable for criminology.

Theories of crime and the sex variable

(i) Theories which ignore the sex variable
The importance of crime derives from its minority status and from its ability to call into question the existence of a value consensus. The very absence of crime amongst certain groups is no less important than its presence. Thus the apparent lack of criminal activity within certain groups is as pertinent to the explanation as the high concentration of

crime within other groups. The general tendency to ignore female crime leads to a double failure. On one hand it fails to analyse the specific conditions through which female conformity and non-conformity are achieved. On the other hand it fails to recognize the critical comparative role that the analysis of female criminality provides in illuminating the 'peculiar' nature of male criminality. Indeed, it is only through the full elaboration of female crime and control that a coherent and consistent 'criminology' itself becomes possible.

The consequences of allowing women to remain invisible in this way are superbly demonstrated by Eileen Leonard (1982), who exposes some serious errors in criminology; errors which become blindingly obvious as soon as one remembers the existence of women. For example, anomie theory as Merton formulates it is largely irrelevant to women. Merton has been criticized for assuming the existence of a common value system and for ignoring the existence of subcultural values, so that his categories of adaptation to anomie are too rigid and simplistic. If he had considered the very different goals, opportunities and strains experienced by women in American society, he might well have taken a different direction and explored a number of interesting avenues which, because of his blindness, were simply excluded from his theoretical map. Similarly, the labelling perspective provides only a partial understanding of criminality because it focuses almost exclusively on the societal reaction to deviance and is not concerned to explain variations in the rates of initial deviance. Eileen Leonard argues that this omission is particularly serious in relation to female deviance. Labelling theorists claim that it is the powerless who suffer the detrimental effects of labelling and yet they fail to explain why powerless women are less involved in crime than powerless men.

In order to anwer this question, the concept of power in labelling theory needs refining, so that it can be used to explore the ways in which the structures of power impinge on different groups (for example, on men and on women, on blacks and on whites). These two criticisms of the labelling perspective — that it neglects both the question of initial deviance and the structural dimension of power — are not new, but are brought sharply into focus the moment one attempts to apply the perspective to women.

It is clear then, that criminologists ignore the sex variable at their peril. Their blinkered perspective limits the way the subject matter is defined and the questions that the theory is designed to answer. The male bias is so ingrained that if women are then tacked on as an afterthought, the theory becomes absurd. Eileen Leonard gives as an example the idea that there is a direct relationship between poverty and crime. In order to accommodate women within this simplistic notion, one would be forced to deny either the lower female crime rates or the existence of female poverty.

(ii) Theories which conflate sex and gender

While the mainstream debates within criminology proceeded as though women did not exist, a small number of criminologists have chosen in the past to make a special study of female criminality. Without exception, they all started from the premise that women are fundamentally different from men, so that a totally different kind of explanation was required to account for their behaviour. Insights gained from the study of female crime could not therefore be used to enrich the main body of theory.

In practice, these studies drew heavily from existing theoretical ideas, adapting them to fit the 'facts' of female crime on the basis of commonly held assumptions about the nature of women. For example, Lombroso's theory of atavism, which held that criminals were throwbacks from an earlier stage of evolution, could not be applied directly to women because he believed that women were less evolved but also less criminal than men! He introduced a mediating factor: women were by nature more passive and conservative than men, due to the 'immobility of the ovule compared with the zoosperm' (Lombroso and Ferrero, 1895). Female criminals were therefore by definition biological abnormalities. Unfortunately, we cannot dismiss this 'masterpiece' as a quaint archaeological specimen, faintly amusing but without contemporary relevance. A particular study may suffer the same fate as Lombroso and become discredited on methodological or scientific grounds, but the search for the biological basis of criminal behaviour continues unabated. Female criminals are often seen as suffering from a double abnormality; their behaviour is both antisocial and unfeminine.

A study of delinquency in girls by Cowie, Cowie and Slater (1968) provides a clear example of this approach. Although they discover a high incidence of disruptive social factors in the backgrounds of their approved school sample, they dismiss these as unimportant. They claim that girls in general have a higher level of immunity than boys to environmental stress; only when 'constitutional predisposing factors' are present will the stress lead to crime. In their view it is the presence of masculine traits that is crucial: they refer to the uncouth appearance, aggressive manner and homosexual tendencies of delinquent girls, combined with the high incidence of psychiatric disorder. They insist that:

> It is more natural to suppose that the male-female difference, both in delinquency rates and in the forms that delinquency takes, would be closely connected with the masculine and feminine pattern of development of personality. This again would be related to biological and somatic differences, including differences in hormonal balance; and these would at the ultimate remove be derived from chromosomal differences between the sexes (Cowie, Cowie and Slater, 1968: 17).

Despite the lack of scientific evidence to substantiate biological re-ductionist arguments of this kind, they continue to enjoy considerable popularity both in academic circles and among those concerned with law enforcement. The arguments are appealing because they offer an explanation for the statistical differences in male and female criminality at the same time as confirming people's common sense understandings of those differences. They are nevertheless based on a fundamental error in that they fail to distinguish between socially constructed notions of gender and biologically grounded sex differences. Hence the prevailing sexual division of labour, together with the ideologies of feminity and masculinity that justify it, are regarded as natural and immutable: they are assumed to follow inevitably from the different roles that men and women play in biological reproduction.

(iii) Why the gender variable is so important
In the work of Lombroso, and Cowie, Cowie and Slater, the case for biological determinism is argued without equivocation. However, even criminologists who explicitly reject those arguments are still liable to make dubious assumptions about sexual difference. This is because the socially constructed categories of masculinity and femininity (i.e. gender) are so deeply embedded in the criminal law that they tend to be regarded as natural. Lemert's analysis of prostitution provides a vivid demonstration of this tendency. (Lemert, 1951). Although he investigates the socio-economic background of prostitutes, the significance of this information is lost because he does not question the accepted wisdom that prostitution is a form of sexual deviation (Heidensohn, 1968 and Leonard, 1982: 80). Because he ignores the impact of gender relationships, Lemert is unable to comment on them; consequently they are uncritically absorbed into the analysis. Matza makes precisely the same error. He actually chooses an example of female deviance in order to introduce his 'master' concepts of affinity, affiliation and signification (Matza, 1969). Superficially, such a choice would seem to strengthen the argument that the process of theory construction occurs at a level of abstraction which applies equally to men and women and assumes that: 'deviance is a form which is relatively autonomous, neither male nor female but androgynous' (Rock, 1977).

It is however, no accident that Matza, like Lemert, has chosen an example of sexual deviation: in Matza's case it is the process of becoming pregnant while unmarried. It is impossible to understand this process fully without considering the specific forms of social control that operate in relation to female reproduction. Such questions cannot be addressed within an androgynous framework because they would be regarded as irrelevant.

In the same way that value-free sociology failed to develop a critical perspective and became by default a justification for the status quo, so a sociology based on androgyny fails to provide a critical view of prevailing notions of gender and therefore simply absorbs them. Unfortunately, the development of one form of critique (attacking value-freedom) in no way implies the other (attacking androgyny). In criminology, critical contributions have concentrated either on exposing the ideology of correctionalism or exposing gender bias.

Critical criminology

A criminology rooted in Marxism is equipped with a sophisticated set of conceptual tools for analysing oppression and would therefore seem ideally suited to understanding the oppression of women. Yet although they broke with traditional theories on a number of fundamental issues, the exponents of the new, radical or critical criminology did nothing to remedy the neglect of women. Leonard points out that Taylor, Walton and Young's 'massive criticism of criminology does not contain *one word* about women' (Leonard, 1982: 176; emphasis in the original). The oversight was not a conscious one and yet the image of the criminal that emerges from The New Criminology is of a 'purposeful, rational human being [who] is, by implication, a male' (Greenwood, 1981). The deep sense of disappointment detectable in these comments echoes the growing dissatisfaction on the part of socialist-feminists with the political priorities of the left. It is no longer acceptable to argue that a consideration of women's issues must wait until the main revolutionary agenda has been accomplished, nor that the interests of women are automatically reflected in the general (i.e. male) programme. Such arguments are simply the political face of androgyny, which insists that the concerns of women and men are necessarily identical and in practice subsumes the former within the latter.

It is not difficult to see how the central concerns of Marxism have led to this sex-blindness. Marxists have arrived at a sophisticated understanding of the processes of commodity production and exchange as the central dynamic of capitalism; in doing so, they have reproduced the same fracture between the world of work and family life that capitalism itself created. It is men who relate directly to the means of production and participate in the processes of commodity exchange; for women such experiences are mediated through the sexual division of labour and a set of power relationships based on gender as well as class. Lacking the conceptual tools for exploring these mediations Marxist criminologists have focused on the criminality of men. In consequence, their work contains a number of serious errors and omissions. This is nowhere more vividly demonstrated than in some of the studies of youth culture in Britain (e.g. Young, 1971; Cohen, 1972; Hall and Jefferson, 1976).

The male bias in youth culture studies is manifested in two ways: firstly, there is very little consideration of the nature and extent of female youth culture; secondly, there is a tendency for the writers to identify with the 'oppositional' values of the culture. Consequently, they project a romantic image of youth culture as an embryonic form of political protest against the work ethic and family values of capitalism; at the same time they gloss over the more reactionary features of the culture, notably its pronounced sexism. Youth culture is seen to offer young males a temporary escape route from the oppressive features of working class life. The frequently oppressive implications of this escapism for women and girls are rarely explicated. As Angela McRobbie says:

> If we look for the structured absences of this youth literature, it is the sphere of family and domestic life that is missing. No commentary on the hippies dealt with the countercultural sexual division of labour, let alone the hypocrisies of 'free love'; few writers seemed interested in what happened when a mod went home after a weekend on speed. Only what happened out there on the streets mattered (McRobbie 1980: 39).

Not all students of youth culture remained totally insensitive to this problem. Some have apologized for the absence of females (Mungham and Pearson, 1976; Corrigan, 1979) or included a separate chapter on them (Brake, 1980: ch. 5). Paul Willis however, goes further than this and in so doing opens up a potentially rich field of insights. Although his study *Learning to Labour* (1977) perpetuates the traditional pattern in so far as it focuses exclusively on male youth culture, Willis breaks the mould both by acknowledging the reactionary aspects of the culture and by recognizing the crucial impact of gender. Despite their anti-authority attitudes, in the long run the boys collude in their own domination. They do this by placing a high valuation on manual labour and a low valuation on mental labour and so express no dissatisfaction with the low-status, low-paid work that is available to them. Willis argues that this inversion of the dominant ideology can only be understood by reference to the 'concrete articulation' of two structures within capitalism: the two structures are the distinction between manual and mental labour and the distinction between masculinity and femininity:

> Manual labour is associated with the social superiority of masculinity and mental labour with the social inferiority of femininity (Willis 1977: 148).

Manual work is highly regarded as an affirmation of masculinity, with the result that the alienating and exploitative aspects of the work are obscured. Two important lessons emerge from this analysis. Firstly, it is impossible to provide a meaningful account of youth culture without considering the impact of gender; its role is not peripheral but central. Secondly, the impact of gender is complex, contradictory and ultimately oppressive for working class males.

Because his main focus is working class 'lads', Willis does not explain how the construction of femininity, at the same time that it directs girls to the mental labour side of the occupational divide, simultaneously denies them the possibility of genuine upward mobility. Feminist accounts of this process are however available (e.g. Sharpe, 1976; Wolpe, 1976; Deem, 1978). The next step is to build on the framework that Willis has provided in order to bring together the insights from male and female youth culture research in order to ensure that the dimensions of class and gender are fully elaborated.[6] Marxist criminologists do not deny the existence of sexual oppression, but they tend to refer to it in passing, rather than allow it to shape their ideas in any fundamental way. Recently however, following the ascendancy of the political right in a number of Western democracies and the apparent fragmentation of working class movements, the need for a reassessment is increasingly acknowledged. In this context, the feminist critique assumes a new theoretical relevance and the women's movement becomes a potentially significant political force, For some feminists, this change of heart comes too late; they have walked away from the now open door and rejected a Marxist-feminist dialogue in favour of their own separate analysis. In making this choice, they can only replicate the shortcomings of Marxism.

Feminist criminology

A number of the feminist groups that mushroomed in the United States during the 1960s were a direct consequence of the rejection of women's issues by the male left. Jo Freeman (1973) recounts how Seattle's first group was formed following a political meeting at which one of the speakers described how white college youths developed rapport with poor whites by 'balling a chick together'. The Chicago group was also conceived in anger, following a political convention at which a women's resolution was considered too insignificant to merit discussion. The chairman patted one of the women on the head and told her: 'Cool down little girl. We have more important things to talk about than women's problems' (quoted in Freeman, 1973: 39). The 'little girl' did not cool down. Instead, she became a radical feminist and wrote *The Dialectic of Sex* (Firestone, 1971). You could not ask for a more vivid demonstration of the inter-relationship between the political and the theoretical than this!

Radical feminists who have severed their connections with Marxism in this way regard the break as permanent, despite their frequent indebtedness to the methods and concepts of Marxism (see especially Firestone, 1971; Delphy, 1977). They give theoretical priority to sexual divisions rather than to class divisions and argue that since the oppression of women predates capitalism, it is patriarchy (defined as the domination of women by men) and not capitalism that is responsible for this oppression (see also Millett, 1971). In contrast, socialist-feminists retain the long-term goal of 'dissolving the hyphen' (Petchesky, 1979) and so achieving theoretical and political integration between feminism and Marxism. For them, separatism is a tactic and not a strategy. Its purpose it to provide time and space for the development of a Marxist-feminist theory and practice which would make the subordination of feminist issues impossible. Although concepts such as patriarchy, sexuality and reproduction feature prominently in the work of both radical feminists and socialist-feminists, the latter have set themselves the task of ensuring that such concepts can be articulated with those of Marxism (see Women's Study Group CCCS, 1978; Kuhn and Wolpe, 1978; Eisenstein, 1979).

There is a third branch of feminism which in terms of historical priority, political influence and membership size, has the edge on both the movements mentioned so far. It comprises several generations of campaigners for women's rights and can be termed 'bourgeois feminism' because its goal is to obtain sexual equality within the economic and political framework of capitalism. This is not however to deny its political and theoretical importance. Theoretically, it can be used to point up the contradictions between the principle of formal equality on which capitalism is founded and the realities of inequality as people experience them. Politically, it can press for a number of immediate reforms to alleviate the misery of particular groups without agonizing over the question of whether such reforms obstruct the path of major change.

Within feminist criminology, there is a tendency for the three strands of feminism to become entangled; although the critique of existing theories and policies is clearly articulated, the way forward often remains obscure. Bourgeois feminists are the easiest to identify; they have drawn attention to the denial of civil liberties that occurs within the criminal justice system whenever those who come under its scrutiny are treated differently on the basis of sex. Their goal is sexual equality (women catching up with men); their strategy is to eliminate sexual ideology from the legal system. For American feminists, the campaign for the Equal Rights Amendment provided the focal point of this strategy for a number of years. [7] The failure of this campaign was a severe setback for the equal rights lobby. It also reduced the chances that the long-term limitations of its strategy would be recognized. Erasing sexual ideology from the legal system becomes a symbolic gesture unless we simultaneously attack the structural inqualities that underpin this ideology. Catching up with the men is a vital first step but it should be the beginning and not the final goal of the political struggle. Gains secured under the equal rights banner are inherently fragile as individuals or groups with competing rights claim equal legitimacy. A woman's right to choose an abortion is challenged in terms of the rights of the unborn foetus. Fathers compete with mothers for an extension of rights in relation to their children. Such divisions cannot be resolved within the framework of competitive individualism that capitalism breeds (Cousins, 1980; Eekelaar, 1978; and Bottomley et al., 1984).

Although radical feminists are more strident in their critique of the existing political and economic system than bourgeois feminists, their analysis is even more divisive in its implications. Their major intervention in criminology is on the issue of how to protect women from the more extreme manifestations of male power, particularly domestic violence, rape and pornography. Several thoughtful and well-documented studies in these areas provide a vivid demonstration of the ways in which men oppress women and also reveal the deeply entrenched sexual bias exhibited at all stages of the law enforcement process. The radical feminist interpretation of this evidence is unequivocal: extreme forms of abuse merit an extreme response. The writers of the studies themselves, although they are by no means unanimous in their conclusions and would by and large resist the radical feminist label, also lean heavily towards the introduction of more punitive measures against the perpetrators of these particular crimes (Dworkin, 1981; Griffin, 1981). It is impossible to resolve this dilemma without re-locating the issue of what to do about violent men within the general debate about penal policy. Radical feminists have no interest in such an enterprise. Their analysis of crime is partial and often reactionary; if the criminal justice system is merely an expression of patriarchal power and nothing else, then men cannot be oppressed by it. A feminist criminology informed by radical feminism would simply replace the sex-blindness of Marxism with its own class-blindness.

A socialist-feminist criminology would seek to avoid the pitfalls of both Marxist and feminist criminology by combining the insights of both. At the theoretical level, the obstacles that confront such an enterprise often seem insurmountable; capitalism and patriarchy are presented as two competing and mutually exclusive frames of reference. At the substantive level, however, the prospect becomes less daunting. The difficulties begin to recede as the analysis uncovers the ways in which men and women are both oppressed by gender and class relations. Once this is recognized, an analysis of one without the other becomes unthinkable. For example, the ways in which poor, black women are treated within the criminal justice system can only be fully understood in terms of the material and ideological realities of both class and gender (see Hacker, 1975, Katzenelson, 1975 (quoted in Giordano and Cernkovich, 1979), Klein and Kress, 1976; Young, 1980; and Box-Grainger in this volume).

Towards a non-sexist critical criminology
This paper does not advocate an androgynous criminology that would seek to explain male and female criminality in identical terms, but rather a criminology which has the explanatory power to encompass within its framework an understanding of both. This distinction is important, because 'non-sexist' is not used here to mean that gender relations are to be ignored. On the contrary, the analysis of such relations is a crucial

component of the approach advocated. A non-sexist criminology would be firmly rooted in the distinction between sex and gender, insisting that gender is socially constructed and not biologically given, recognizing that the ideas of masculinity and femininity are extremely powerful in their consequences but refusing to share the assumptions on which they are based. Having successfully challenged those theories which conflate sex and gender in the direction of biological determinism, it is just as important not to collapse them in the other direction, by denying that there are any biological differences at all. The consequences of such an over-reaction are superbly illustrated in the recurring controversy over the relationship between pre-menstrual tension and female criminality.

Menstrual taboos have a long and varied history but are particularly pronounced in societies which have a clear-cut division of labour between the sexes. When women begin to exert pressure to improve their social position, there often seems to be a resurgence of interest in ideas about the harmful effects of menstruation, so that an emphasis on biological difference becomes a vindication of traditional sex role patterns (see Sayers, 1982). Hence the hostile reaction of certain groups within the women's movement in Britain recently when the judiciary accepted pre-menstrual tension as the basis for pleas of diminished responsibility.[8] The data suggesting a relationship between the menstrual cycle and crime was not new, so why were the courts suddenly so receptive? Were they not simply providing additional ammunition for those who wished to exclude women from positions of power and responsibility? The prevailing social meanings attributed to the biological phenomenon of pre-menstrual tension are so powerful, and so patently damaging to the cause of female equality, that the temptation to deny the existence of the biological phenomenon is overwhelming. There is however, evidence that some women do experience considerable pain and distress at certain times of the month. The problem is how to recognize this and respond to it humanely, while resisting the connotations of social inferiority normally associated with this response. This is not an easy position to sustain in a culture which exhibits a general tendency to regard women who step outside the feminine stereotype as requiring medical attention; it is however vital.

Our efforts to demystify notions of femininity and masculinity will be placed in jeopardy if the distinction between sex and gender is not retained. They will also be placed in jeopardy if we fail to recognize that the impact of gender is mediated by class. The medicalization of 'deviant' behaviour is particularly oppressive in its consequences for working class women, both as a diversion from the realities of economic and social deprivation and in terms of the forms of social control which it produces (see for example, Hutter and Williams, 1981 and Greenwood, 1983). Interventionist policies derived from a partial analysis could well make matters worse. To demand formal equality for women while the substantive inequalities remain may in the short run increase the oppression of the most vulnerable groups. If equality means the disappearance of leniency and hence the separation of more female offenders from their children, or even if it means taking drugs away from women who cannot face the misery of their daily routine without them, then such 'reforms' can only be part of a more radical programme of change.[9]

Beyond the criminal law
An analysis of the criminal law provides only a partial understanding of the nature of social control within capitalism. The new deviancy theorists acknowledge this in part by focusing not only on the formal processes of law enforcement but also on the informal control processes (see McIntosh, 1978). Radical or critical criminology challenged the disciplinary boundaries in a different way. This derived initially from a specific interest in corporation crime and subsequently from a more general concern with the rule of law (see for example, NDC/CSE, 1979, Fryer et al., 1981). Legal issues became crucial once again but, no longer concerned with the operation of the criminal law, they raised broader questions about the relationship between the law and the state in capitalist social formations. In order to make sense of the low rate of female crime, we need to build on both these developments in criminology.

Applying a 'new deviancy' approach to the study of gender, we discover that the same stereotypical notions of gender prevalent inside the criminal justice system also operate outside it and are used to control men and women in a variety of ways. The more we know about the informal mechanisms of control, whether they occur within the family, education, medicine, employment or the media, the more we will be able to say about why it is men rather than women who turn to crime. The recent work of Marxist criminologists on the law and the state opens up another important terrain. In order to comprehend the ways in which the law controls working class lives, we have to look beyond the criminal law and consider the economic and ideological implications of other areas of law. In terms of its day to day impact on working class families, legislation relating to marital breakdown, unemployment benefit and social security payments is undoubtedly a more effective mechanism for establishing discipline and reinforcing the sexual division of labour than is the criminal law. Clearly, no single study can expect to examine all aspects of social control simultaneously, but it is important to avoid constructing academic fences around criminology, which would prevent us from recognizing the significance of other work and from formulating interventionist strategies derived from its insights.

From theory to practice

In seeking to devise interventionist strategies grounded in a socialist-feminist criminology, one inevitably starts with a critique of existing penal policies. These regard law-breakers both as inadequates who require medical attention and as the enemies of society who deserve to be punished; incarceration is justified on the grounds that it protects the public from dangerous villains and yet the vast majority of those under lock and key have committed minor, non-violent offences. It is not difficult to draw attention to these contradictions in order to exploit them politically and in doing so, it might prove rewarding to spear-head the campaign with the issue of female prisoners. Policy makers may well be receptive to overtures in this area, precisely because female offenders are not regarded as a serious threat. Furthermore, the contradictions between policy statements and penal practices are particularly marked in relation to women. Thus Victoria Greenwood draws attention to the Home Office prediction that female imprisonment would experience a steady decline from 1970 onwards and compares it with the sharp increase that has occurred in reality (Greenwood, 1983). A concerted campaign on this issue which produced a positive response could provide considerable momentum for a more broadly based decarceration strategy. It would not be the first time that women's issues have been used to prepare the political ground in this way. [10] It is however, vital that a campaign on behalf of female prisoners does not become a strategy in itself; unless it is extended to male prisoners, women will once again be treated as a special case with a consequent accentuation of gender differences.

Within the present criminal law, there is considerable mileage in developing interventionist strategies around the themes of decarceration and decriminalization. They do not in themselves however constitute a comprehensive alternative policy. When we see how crime impacts on women, whether as prisoners or the wives of prisoners, as mothers blamed for juvenile delinquency or as the victims of rape, it becomes increasingly difficult to regard crime as a politically motivated response or to cast it in a romantic light. The freedom of one person too often involves the oppression of another. An essential component of an alternative penal policy would be to devise humane forms of treatment and containment for those instances where neither decriminalization nor decarceration is appropriate.

There is no easy way in which we can 'read off' social policy statements from a socialist-feminist approach to crime; indeed, simple prescriptions should be treated with scepticism. A socialist-feminist approach should, however, ensure that we ask the right questions. The precise consequences of any proposed reforms need to be considered carefully, so that any attempt to equalize the treatment of men and women does represent a genuine step forward for both sexes.

Notes

1. In England and Wales some 6,900 adult males were cautioned for indictable offences in 1981 in comparison with some 5,200 adult females. For men, the figure represents 4 percent of offenders found guilty or cautioned; for women it is 11 percent of the total (Home Office, Criminal Statistics England and Wales 1981, Table 5.4)

2. In the United States, it is possible to challenge discrimination of this kind under the 'equal protection' clause of the 14th Amendment. See Babcock (1973), Singer (1973) and Krause (1974). In Britain, the problem tends to be ignored; see Heidensohn (1981), Greenwood (1983) and Carlen (1983).

3. Table: Offenders cautioned as a percentage of those found guilty or cautioned for indictable offences by age and sex

	10-under 14	14-under 17	17-under 21	21 and over	all ages
Female	87%	60%	5%	11%	31%
Male	68%	35%	3%	4%	17%

Source: Criminal Statistics England and Wales 1981, Table 5.4.

It is interesting to note the sharp drop in the cautioning rate for the 17-under 21 age group for both sexes. Indeed, women over 21 fare considerably better than that age group.

4. Canadian statistics show a higher percentage of girls than boys appearing in court on charges of sexual immorality, truancy and incorrigibility (Barnhorst, 1978). In the United States 70 percent of the girls committed to training school are there for juvenile (i.e. status) offences (Chesney-Lind, 1977). In Britain, over 85 percent of the young people placed on care orders on the grounds that they are in moral danger are female (see Smart, 1976: 12; Campbell, 1981: 9; Casburn, 1979).

5. Juvenile justice campaigns are mostly concerned to establish civil liberties for children of *both* sexes. For a useful discussion of the American case law on this see Wilkerson (1973), particularly the chapter by Stansby on the Gault case. In Britain, the case for juvenile civil liberties is persuasively argued in Morris et al. (1980) and in Taylor (1980). The 1982 Criminal Justice Act was a small step in the right direction, although there is no guarantee that magistrates will interpret the provisions in order to reduce the different treatment of boys and girls. Although attendance centres are to be made available for girls for the first time, it is likely that magistrates will continue to regard the single 'short, sharp shock' approach as more appropriate for males and will continue to use care orders (operative until the child's 18th birthday) for girls in order to 'protect' them. Community Service Orders have been available since 1973 for both sexes, but tend to be used by the courts as a 'male' form of disposal (Matthews, 1981).

6. The contradictory nature of the processes that Willis describes are further complicated by the problem of rising youth unemployment. In the light of these developments some reassessment of Willis's thesis is required. For an excellent account of the ways in which recent social and economic changes have accentuated the absences in youth culture research see Dorn and South (1983). Willis's own reaction to these changes can be found in three *New Society* articles (March–April 1984).

7. See for example Eastwood (1971), Temin (1973), Frankel (1973) and a symposium in the Harvard Civil Rights-Civil Liberties Law Review, March 1971. The proposed Equal Rights Amendment stated: 'Equality of rights under the law shall not be denied or abridged by the United States or by any State on account of sex'. It was approved by the Senate in 1972 but failed to obtain the necessary ratification by individual states, despite an extension of the time limit. (Thirty-five states ratified the amendment, three short of the required number.)

8. In November 1981 there were two cases that attracted a great deal of publicity. In the first, a barmaid was given three years probation after being convicted of threatening to kill a policeman and possessing an offensive weapon. In the second, a woman pleading guilty to manslaughter (she killed her lover by driving a car at him) was given a conditional discharge. In both cases, judges accepted pleas of diminished responsibility after hearing medical evidence that the crimes were provoked by pre-menstrual tension. Representatives from Women's Health Concern expressed strong objections to the verdicts, believing that they would have damaging consequences for women in general (*The Standard*, London, 12 November 1981).

9. For an even more striking example of what happens when middle class feminists assume that particular changes will liberate all women equally, see the 'protective legislation' debate. Although it is true that legislation restricting the hours and conditions of work for women has been used to impede their employment and promotion prospects, simply to remove such legislation and thereby free women to work the night-shift without making any other changes, will not be experienced as liberating! (see Coussins, 1979; Gregory, 1981).

10. It was, for example, no accident that Roy Jenkins presented his 1975 Sex Discrimination Bill to Parliament before introducing the 1976 Race Relations legislation. The two measures were virtually identical; even so, several provisions that passed into law without comment when applied to women became the subject of heated debate when the recipients were to be members of ethnic minority groups.

4

Unemployment, crime and imprisonment, and the enduring problem of prison overcrowding

Steven Box and Chris Hale

Over the last decade there has been a renewed interest in the possible relationships between unemployment, crime and imprisonment. The reasons for this interest are not hard to fathom. We appear to be in the middle of a crime and penal response crisis. For the period 1972–82 the number of unemployed rose from 800,000 to approximately 3.5 million (or nearly 14 percent of the available labour force), and the number of persons unemployed for over one year topped the 1 million mark for the first time since records have been compiled. In addition, the number of recorded serious offences rose from 3,448 per 100,000 population to 6,226 (80 percent), the number of persons under sentence received into prison climbed from 57,739 to an unprecedented 94,377 (63 percent) and the average daily prison population increased from 38,328 to 43,707 (14 percent). In the face of these dramatic simultaneous changes an obvious question was posed: how are they causally connected?

One fairly orthodox answer to emerge from this growing concern was that rising unemployment leads to crime, and this in turn, assuming constant rates of reporting and recording crimes, arrest, conviction and imprisonment sentences, leads automatically to an increase in prison population. Whilst there may be some truth in this view, it has at least two serious flaws.

First, as we show below, the common claim that unemployment leads to crime is theoretically too simple, and at best, the scientific evidence relevant to testing this hypothesized monocausal relationship is equivocal, particularly if applied to the entire population without due consideration for variation amongst different age, gender, class and ethnic groups. Nonetheless, it is clear that many people *believe* that unemployment causes crime and this belief has real consequences, particularly when it affects decisions taken by state officials processing suspected and convicted persons.

Second, the rates of recording, arresting, convicting and imprisoning will *not* remain constant over time and under varying economic circumstances. Indeed, during times of increasing unemployment it is reasonable to expect that: (i) reporting and recording crimes increase partly because the unemployed offenders are more noticeable; (ii) the number of police

72

increase, partly because it attracts some of the unemployed, and this in turn affects the level of recorded crime; (iii) the judiciary *increase* the use of imprisonment, although not simply as a mechanical response to any increase in the numbers convicted; and (iv) the government maintains, defends and extends the judiciary's right to imprison as many offenders as it sees fit, even if this requires the building of more and expensive prisons.

These are reasonable expectations because during a prolonged economic crisis, as has been experienced in Britain for over a decade now, the state encounters a crisis of managing the 'legitimacy' of its major institutions. As far as the criminal justice system is concerned, the state's preferred solution to this 'legitimacy' problem takes both an ideological and control form. Ideologically, it propagates the view that crime, particularly 'street crime' has dramatically increased and that only a 'law and order' campaign, pursued with determination and vigour, has any chance of dealing with this problem and hence protecting the people. This prepares the path for strengthening the forces of social control, particularly police powers and resources, the judiciary's sentencing armoury, and the prison estate's capacity to absorb an enlarged number of prisoners in an ever harsher regime of punishment and deprivation.

In other words, during a prolonged economic crisis, the state is hard pressed to maintain living standards and welfare services, without adversely affecting the interests of capital. This inevitably forces it to shed the mask of consent and expose its more coercive character. Imprisonment, as part of this move from consent to coercion, is used increasingly. The latent effect of increased incarceration rates, as opposed to the judiciary's deliberate intention, is to demoralize, fracture, and eliminate *resistance* to domination. Whether this resistance is real or imagined, actual or potential, organized or unorganized, is immaterial. The important point is that members of the judiciary have to believe this threat exists. The belief alone is sufficient to propel them towards stiffening their sentencing practices.

For these two reasons, the orthodox view outlined above is opposed in this paper. Instead we adopt a radical perspective in which the relationships between unemployment, crime and imprisonment are *not* viewed mechanistically — crime automatically following unemployment, and imprisonment automatically following crime. Instead, the relation- ships are viewed as *dynamic*, reflecting not only class cleavages, but also the *active* contribution played by judicial and State officials in response to intensified class struggle during periods of economic crisis. However, before proceeding to develop our argument in more detail, it is necessary to consider more fully the first flaw in the orthodox position.

Unemployment and crime

Not only has the idea that economic conditions in general, and unemployment in particular, cause crime had a long life in criminology (Bonger, 1916; Mannheim, 1949; Sellin, 1937), but it continues to inspire academic research (Box and Hale, 1984), and in the context of the current economic crisis, causes much concern outside academia. Thus the Select Committee of the House of Lords on Unemployment (1982: 59) stated its belief that 'unemployment' was 'among the causes of...crime or civil disorder'. Lord Scarman (1982) in providing the social background to the Brixton disorders on 10–12 April 1981, was at pains to point out that deprivations do not justify attacks on the police, or excuse such disorders. But at no stage did he deny that these conditions are part of the explanation. Indeed, amongst the deprivations he lists, unemployment figures prominently. It stood at 13 percent in Brixton in early 1981 and 'for black people, the percentage is estimated to be higher (around 25 percent)....' Furthermore, young blacks were even more affected, for 'unemployment among black males under 19 has been estimated at 55 percent' (Scarman, 1982: 27). Malcolm Dean concluded his survey of literature on unemployment and crime by pointing out that most of the authors assert that there is a direct relationship between unemployment and crime (*Guardian*, 1 May 1982: 17). A similar assertion can be found in *Keep Out* (Bulletin No. 5, August 1982) and the *Unemployment Unit Bulletin No. 4* (July 1982: 3). But what evidence is there that unemployment causes crime?

We have located over thirty studies on this possible relationship, and to cut a long tedious analysis very short, the one very clear conclusion is that the findings are inconsistent! Even if those numerous studies which lack methodological sophistication were removed from this list, the remainder still fail to provide an unambiguous answer. Thus, whilst it is not difficult to locate time-series or cross-sectional studies which reveal a positive correlation between unemployment and crime, there are other studies which do not have similar conclusions. Furthermore, even those 'convincing' studies fail to eradicate two obvious problems which plague this type of research.

First, and elementary, in most studies, crime is measured by 'crime recorded by the police'. Numerous factors affect the validity of this measure both over time and also between different places. For instance, the propensity of the public to report crimes changes. It tends to increase as the opportunities expand. Thus, over the last couple of decades the rental of telephones and ownership of cars has increased and these changes have made it comparatively easier for the public to report crimes. Changes in motivation may also increase the recorded level of crime. For example, women are more prepared now than they were previously to report rape or sexual assault. This change is largely a result of the Women's Movement exhorting the victims of sexual humiliation to use the law (and rape crisis centres) to make public this form of patriarchal domination. The incentive to report crimes may also change. Thus as more and more citizens become house owners and seek to insure their property so their preparedness to report burglaries goes up because this is a prerequisite for claiming on insurance policies.

Cross-sectional analyses do not get around this problem of variations in reporting behaviour. Nottinghamshire for example constantly comes out top of the recorded crime league. This is clearly *not* because there is more serious crime in Nottinghamshire than in inner-urban areas of say London, Manchester, Liverpool, Glasgow and Birmingham. Maybe Nottinghamshire citizens have a greater propensity to report crimes; maybe the police have a greater propensity to record reported crimes, or a more efficient method of counting, or double-counting. Whatever the reason, it is clear that the studies on unemployment and crime which rely on recorded crime for measuring the dependent variable, are very suspect. If they rely instead on conviction rates as their measure of criminal activity, they are even more suspect because there is overwhelming evidence that discrimination in the criminal justice system between arrest and conviction adversely affects individuals from deprived, underprivileged and relatively powerless backgrounds (Box, 1981: 180–96).

Second, and even more important, social life is never so simple that a monocausal relationship can exist without being simultaneously affected by other independent and intervening variables. For example, economic inequality, housing market, racial relations, and many other factors may be inter-related with both unemployment and crime, thus throwing into doubt the reliability of any discovered correlation.

A recent attempt to illustrate the problems (Carr-Hill and Stern, 1983) simply included the average annual number of policemen. They considered that more police would mean both that an increased number of crimes would be observed directly, and also that more crimes would be recorded. They found a positive correlation between unemployment and recorded crime for the whole population, but when they added the number of police to their model it cancelled out this correlation. It appeared more reliable to argue that when there are more police there is more recorded crime. Of course there may only be more police because there is more unemployment: the government being more willing to attract recruits through higher wages, and more unemployed succumbing to this temptation.

In addition to these two problems, there is a theoretical difficulty. The *meaning* of unemployment may change over time and between subsections of the general population (Guttentag, 1968). This variation in meaning reflects different answers to such questions as: 'Is unemployment a natural visitation, or the foreseeable and avoidable consequence of government economic policy?'; 'Is it *fair*, or am I unemployed because of the kind of person I am or the social attributes ascribed to me?'; 'Is it a form of

welcome early retirement, or a disturbing sign that my work-life is over?';
'Is it only a temporary setback, or a more or less permanent feature of
my life?'; 'Am I supposed to bear the burden of unemployment alone,
or will others, family and friends, help me cushion its worse material and
psychological effects?'

Clearly answers to these, and other similar questions would not be
randomly distributed throughout the general population, but would tend
to cluster into patterns between groups of people. Thus the relatively
young, and ethnic minorities within this group, might *now* regard unemployment and unemployability as *avoidable suffering*, which casts an
indefinite shadow on their future prospects. Amongst this group of British
citizens, it would be hard for a government to establish the 'legitimacy
of unemployment'. Unemployment is not an experience they would have
been led to expect, or prepared to put up with, during their formative years
when Britain was 'affluent'. Consequently, because of resentment, bitter-
ness, relative deprivation, and sheer material considerations, youth, and
particularly black youth, might be much more disposed towards innovative
behaviour, including criminal, than other unemployed groups, such as
women or elderly middle-class professional people.

Because of these, or similar types of theoretical considerations, numerous
researchers have focused their attention on unemployment and crime
amongst young and ethnic minority males.

Although Glaser and Rice (1959) could find no relationship between
unemployed youth and crime in the US during the period 1932–1950,
Fleisher (1963) reanalysed their data because they 'did not attempt to
account for effects of war or to include a trend variable in their regression
equations' (Fleisher, 1963: 549). After analysing the data for Boston,
Cincinnati and Chicago, Fleisher concluded that 'the effect of unemployment on juvenile delinquency is positive and significant...[although]
...one cannot assert that unemployment is more important than those
factors left out of account' (Fleisher, 1963: 555).

Singnell (1967) examined the relationship between delinquency and
unemployment in Detroit, using both cross-sectional and time-series data,
he concluded that 'at current levels of unemployment a cut in the unemployment rate of 1 percent will lead to a reduction in delinquency rates of from
one-fourth to one-sixth of 1 percent...[a result which seems]...significant
enough to excite hopes for corrective action' (Singnell, 1967: 386).

Phillips and colleagues (1972) analysed data on unemployment and arrest
rates for economic crimes (i.e. larceny, burglary, robbery and auto theft)
for the period 1952–1967 in the US. They also paid attention to non-whites,
because 'by comparison, youth in general and non-whites in particular,
were clearly in a disadvantaged position in our society', both in terms
of unemployment rates, and rates of labour force participation. They
concluded that 'changing labour-market opportunities are sufficient to

explain increasing crime rates for youth.' In particular, they considered that the participation rate (or the rate of exclusion from work) was more predictive than registered unemployment. Consequently they proposed that 'a successful attack on rising crime rates must consider the employment problems facing young people' (Phillips et al.: 503). Two years later Votey and Phillips (1974) reported that youth arrest rates for felonious property offences increased with youth unemployment from 1952 to 1960 in the United States.

These, and other research (Calvin, 1981; Ewing, 1977; Kraus, 1979; Vinson and Hommell, 1975) which gives less equivocal support to the view that unemployment causes youthful crime, were all conducted *outside* the United Kingdom. Of course, there are no good reasons to expect that social relationships empirically verified in other similar industrial countries do not hold here, nevertheless it would be prudent to consider home-based research. Unfortunately, there is little to consider.

There is plenty of evidence that high rates of unemployment exist amongst convicted populations, but there is little substantive research, either of a time-series or cross-sectional type, on a causal relationship between unemployment and crime. Mannheim (1949) found no correlation between unemployment and recorded crime in a number of English cities. However, Brenner (1976) analysed recorded crime rates and unemployment in England and Wales for the period 1900–1970 and reported a significant correlation even when other economic factors were controlled. This research finding might have been conclusive were it not for a substantive criticism (Orsagh and Witte, 1981). Carr-Hill and Stern (1979) conducted a cross-sectional analysis for the years 1961, 1966 and 1971. They discovered a positive correlation between unemployment and recorded crimes rates, but when they introduced other possible explanatory variables into the analysis, this correlation all but vanished. Finally, Stevens and Willis (1979) studied London police districts in 1975 and found that white unemployment levels and arrest for assault, robbery, other violent theft, and other indictable offences were highly correlated. However, this did not hold for the black population. Consequently they interpreted this finding to mean that white unemployment per se was not the important variable. Instead they argued that unemployment was merely an indicator of the general level of economic deprivation in an area and this last factor was a major determinant of crime.

The best available evidence then, does not provide unambiguous support for the hypothesis that unemployment causes more crime, although if such a relationship did exist, it would probably be found amongst young and/or ethnic minority males. Any relationship depends very much upon the particular sub-population studied and the meaning they attribute to unemployment, as well as the potency of other possible criminogenic factors.

This conclusion does not affect our second main argument in the slightest, since, as we spell out in detail below, it is not whether unemployment really does cause crime that is pertinent to our radical perspective, but whether many people, particularly those processing suspects in the criminal justice system, *believe* unemployment causes crime. For if they do, they will act in terms of this belief. The outcome, particularly during times of deepening economic crisis, will be that a suspect's employment status becomes an important factor affecting judicial decisions.

Unemployment and imprisonment

Government penal policy and judicial sentencing practices do not emerge from a vacuum; rather they both reflect changing patterns of social relationships, particularly between those in positions of power and their subordinates (Adamsom, 1984; Rusche and Kirchheimer, 1968). During the last decade, Britain has experienced a deepening economic crisis and this has affected the way governments and the judiciary have criminalized subordinate groups. This crisis has enlarged those groups called 'unproductive elements' by Mathiesen (1974: 77), 'surplus population' by Quinney (1980), and 'problem populations' by Spitzer (1975: 642). Despite these different images, each of these authors echo Marx (1977: 782) who argued that capitalist accumulation 'constantly produces a population which is superfluous to capital's average requirements for its own valorization'. This population 'unrequired' by the productive process becomes a nuisance eligible for state intervention. If they are 'social junk', as Spitzer graphically describes it, they have to be *managed*; if they are 'social dynamite', such as the unemployed, or the unemployable, they have to be *controlled*.

The former groups are a financial drain. They become more problematic to the modern capitalist state during periods of economic crisis because it is increasingly unable to generate sufficient surplus wealth to pay for its welfare programmes (O'Connor, 1973, 1984). In response to this fiscal crisis, governments have attempted to pursue a policy of *decarceration* (Scull, 1977), that is, removing people from mental hospitals and similar institutions, closing them down, and diverting potential inmates by encouraging and legitimating 'community treatment', which is often no treatment at all, but is, of course, comparatively cheaper.

The latter groups — 'social dynamite' — present an acute problem of social control because they are actually or potentially more troublesome. Spitzer argues that this problem population — the able bodied, mainly young unemployed or unemployable — throws into question the ability of the capitalist mode of production to generate enough work and wealth, and this in turn creates a 'legitimacy' crisis. Furthermore, it is just this problem population who can distance themselves from the consent to be governed. As a consequence, they are likely to be perceived by those in positions of power and authority as potentially disruptive, thus constituting a threat to social discipline, law and order. For this reason, this problem population has to be tightly controlled, even by coercive means, in order to preserve ideological and social hegemony.

In this restoration-and-preservation-of-social-order-work, the criminal justice system can be relied upon to play a significant part. With its elastic ability to expand into areas not previously subject to its jurisdiction, its preparedness to parachute forces into this expanded territory and increase the rates of apprehension and prosecution, its apparent willingness to be partially blind to the police force's disregard for law when their violations are against the 'enemies of the state' (Box, 1983; Jacobs and Britt, 1977), and — the issue to be magnified shortly — its capacity to increase the use of prison sentences, it is one of the first line defences available to the powerful. From the existing evidence, mainly but not exclusively derived American data (Box and Hale, 1982; Braithwaite, 1980; Dobbins and Bass, 1958; Greenberg, 1977, 1980; Jankovic, 1977; Joubet et al., 1981; Kellough et al., 1980; Marenin et al., 1983; Reasons and Kaplan, 1975; Scott and Scull, 1978; Stern, 1940; Yeager, 1979), this last hypothesis — that incarceration is positively related to unemployment — enjoys considerable support. This is not to imply that the criminal justice system is merely a puppet dancing to the tune called by its political masters. The view taken here is that the judiciary is a relatively autonomous institution, but at the same time a reliable and trustworthy ally of the ruling class.

The Conservative government is unashamedly aware that its economic policies, like those of its Labour predecessor, are reducing the living standards of large sections of the community. In particular, the government is acutely conscious that unemployment is creating havoc, not only in the lives of 'Boys from the Black Stuff'. Unemployment is very unevenly distributed among regions, social classes, age-cohorts and ethnic groups (Hawkins, 1984; Sinfield, 1981). According to Kellner (1982), data from the government's Office of Population Censuses and Surveys shows that one man in *three* is currently unemployed in Liverpool, Newcastle, Manchester and Birmingham. This contrasts sharply with the one man in *ten* currently unemployed in the South East suburban areas of Surrey, Middlesex and Essex. This broad North-South division conceals wide variations *within* regions. In London for example, the unemployment rate in parts of Islington, Hackney, Lambeth, Southwark, and Tower Hamlets was almost four times as great as in parts of Barnet, Bexley, Croydon, Harrow, Hillingdon and Kingston.

Unemployment falls heaviest on manual workers, particularly the unskilled. Thus in March 1982 the ratio between registered unemployed and notified job vacancies was .004 for general labourers compared with an overall occupational average of .03. The highest reduction of workers was in the manufacturing industries. Between 1978 and 1982 they declined by 20.4 percent compared with 18.4 percent in construction, 6.5 percent in transport and a 1 percent increase for insurance, banking and finance. The average decline in employment for all industries and services being roughly 10 percent.

Long-term unemployment — i.e. one year or more out of work — follows a similar pattern. In July 1979 29 percent of the unemployed were 'long-termers' compared with 38 percent in 1982. The highest concentration was located in the West Midlands and the North, where it reached nearly 50 percent, whilst in the South East and East Anglia, where the rates of unemployed were generally much lower, the proportion of long-termers was more like a third.

Unemployment, falling living standards, and economic marginalization generally, are more acutely felt by the young and by ethnic minorities, many of whom are concentrated in already declining and deteriorating inner-city areas. Thus in October 1982, more than 25 percent of males in England and Wales aged under 20 years were unemployed compared with a 13 percent unemployment rate amongst older males. A similar differential existed between young and older females. And according to a recent Home Office research publication, the black unemployment rate (registered and unregistered) in London in 1975 was about 12.5 percent compared with a white rate of only 5.5 percent.

The government has reason to feel anxious about the possible effects of unemployment's differential distribution. Mrs Thatcher and her colleagues may well argue that unemployment is no excuse for rioting or committing any other crime, but away from the public gaze, they may well ponder whether those bearing the burden of their economic policies can be relied upon to accept it magnanimously. Politics, like sociology, is not an exact science. Increasing people's oppression, by reducing their living standards and imposing intolerable levels of unemployment without compensatory and hassle-free welfare benefits or hopes for a brighter employed future, may not necessarily lead to riotous assembly or criminal mayhem, but it *might*. As Lord Scarman (1982: 34–5) warned: 'to ignore the existence of economic, social and political factors . . . without which the disturbances [in Brixton during early April 1981] cannot be fully understood. . . is to put the nation in peril'.

Glimpsing this haunting possibility, and not being dissuaded by the contradictory research findings on the 'unemployment-causes-crime' thesis, successive British governments, and particularly the present one, have taken prudent precautions. One of these has been to pursue rigorously a policy of non-interference with the judiciary's autonomy, even though Their Honours' and Worships' sentencing practice has exacerbated overcrowding in prisons, a problem many a Home Secretary's heart has bled for — at least on the colour television screen! The government need not interfere with the judiciary because it is an institution of proven, even if unwitting reliability, particularly when it comes to buttering the powerful's side of any conflict (Griffiths, 1977). Under the government's approving sideward glance, the judiciary has, in effect, although not necessarily with intention, set about making its contribution to imposing discipline on the unemployed and unemployables — although not these groups exclusively — thus hoping to nip their criminal propensities where it really hurts.

The depths to which these anxieties run in the stream of government consciousness can only be indirectly plumbed by dipping into Home Office publications, House of Commons and Lords debates, and of course, governmental penal policy, particularly as it affects police powers and judicial sentencing. There is ample evidence in the *Home Office Research Bulletin* (Gladstone, 1979; Smith, 1980), where the demographic characteristics and economic conditions of ethnic minorities were given as strong grounds for predicting a surge in 'black crime' well into the 1980s. The *House of Lords Select Committee on Unemployment* (1982) also shared these fears. And the government's *Observations on the Fifteenth Report of the Expenditure Committee* argued that (1980: 1):

> Between 1968 and October 1979 the prison population rose from nearly 32,500 to 42,500. Earlier this year it rose to 44,800 and continues to be not much below this level... *the main factor in the general year-by-year trend has been the steady increase in the absolute number of offenders coming before the courts. Despite some recent levelling-off in the upward trend in recorded crime and offenders, and* without counteracting policies, *further increases in the prison must be expected.*

Additional signs of anxiety are reflected in recent parliamentary *Acts* and *Bills*. Thus the *Criminal Attempts Act*, 1981, was intended to repeal the widely condemned 'sus' laws. But the strengthened law of 'attempt' can be stretched as a result of this Act, to cover attempted theft of unknown materials from unknown persons, as well as attempt to steal a parked car. This last possibility is particularly pernicious. Mere presence, particularly if your face does not fit or your skin colour is a darker shade of black, in a street with parked cars, could, through an officer's suspicious eyes, constitute an 'attempt'. Through this Act, police discretion has been extended rather than curtailed, and it is the powerless on whom this discretion falls heaviest.

The *Criminal Justice Act*, 1982, also strengthened the state's armoury. This Act hammered a final nail into the *Children and Young Persons Act*, 1969. It not only restored to the judiciary the power to commit young persons to prison, a power the earlier Act had severely restricted — at least in principle — but it also extended the age limit downwards from 17 to 15 years. The new youth custody sentence introduced by the 1982 Act reflects a very strong desire to move wayward adolescents from the 'caring' hands of romantic social workers and sentimental probation officers to the 'calloused' hands of prison officers who at least have the good sense to see evil when it's under their nose.

Finally, the *Police and Criminal Evidence Bill*, which is currently (July, 1984) being processed through the Houses of Parliament will, if passed, represent draconian powers being granted to the police. It not only legitimates most of their current malpractices, particularly their systematic bending and violating the Judge's Rules (Christian, 1983; Hewitt, 1982; McBarnet, 1983), but it also gives them enormously wide discretionary powers of stopping and searching, setting up road blocks, entering and seizing, questioning, detaining and arresting. In other words, the progress towards establishing civil liberties in Britain, as fragile as it has been, will be reversed at a stroke once this Bill becomes law.

When, to all this strengthening of the state's coercive apparatus, is added the 25 percent increase in police personnel during the last decade (from 112,000 to 140,000) the 45 percent increase in prison staff (from 18,500 to 26,800) and now planned to be increased by a further 5,500 or roughly 20 percent — while nearly every other state agency, including the armed forces is shedding labour — and a prison rebuilding programme designed to increase cellular capacity from 38,700 to 49,200 by 1991, then it becomes crystal clear that the state is preparing and prepared for trouble.

In the meantime, the judiciary has been busily responding to the *perceived* threat posed by the growing numbers of unemployed and unemployables, by increasing its use of imprisonment and accepting gratefully the increased powers bestowed upon it by government penal policy. Thus the number of males imprisoned under sentence rose from 55,789 in 1972 to 90,151 in 1982, an increase of 62 percent. Whilst for females there was an even more dramatic increase of over 200 percent, although the absolute numbers, 1,950 in 1972 and 4,226 in 1982 are small. Increases in the numbers sentenced to prison do not simply reflect more convictions, as implied by the government's *Observations on the Fifteenth Report of the Expenditure Committee*, for these rose at a much slower pace — roughly 40 percent — during the last decade. In other words, the judiciary have increased the *incarceration rate*, i.e. persons imprisoned per 100 convicted, and this has inflated prison receptions beyond a level expected on the basis of the increased numbers convicted. For example, during the period 1977–1982, the incarceration rate for all indictable offences rose by 16 percent, which was due mainly to increases in the incarceration rate for persons found guilty of theft and handling, burglary and robbery. Curiously, the incarceration rate for violence against the person actually dropped slightly from 13.58 percent to 13.51 percent.

This does not necessarily mean that during times of rising unemployment the judiciary increase the severity of penal sanctions only against the unemployed; they may well extend imprisonment across the spectrum of persons found guilty, particularly as the majority of these are bound to be working class and/or ethnically oppressed. Nonetheless, when passing sentences, the judiciary are likely to make fine distinctions even within these subordinate groups. If there is judicial anxiety during times of deteriorating economic conditions, then it would be those convicted persons from groups perceived to be actually or potentially disruptive who would feel the harsher side of judicial discretion. It is possible that even within the unemployed population the judiciary would see crucial distinctions.

For example, unemployed males are more likely to be perceived as problematic because in Western culture, work is not only believed to be the typical way in which males are disciplined but it is also their major source of identity and thus the process by which they build up a stake in conformity. Consequently when males are removed from, or denied access to work, it is widely believed that they will have various anarchistic responses amongst which criminal behaviour is likely to figure quite strongly. These cultural meanings of work attributed to males are likely to have adverse effects on how unemployed males are processed in the criminal justice system.

This is not to argue that when it comes to sentencing, magistrates and judges allow the offender's employment status to override the seriousness of his present offence and previous convictions (if they exist). But when they consider sentences for offenders whose offences and previous convictions are similar, they are still forced, because of prison accommodation and court welfare officers' reports, to take other factors into account. One of the most likely extra factors affecting the sentence imposed on a male offender will be whether or not he is employed. If he is not, the judiciary are more likely to view him as potentially more likely to commit other, particularly economic offences, and consequently pass an immediate prison sentence (Bernstein et al., 1977; Carter and Clelland, 1979; Chiricos et al., 1972; Clarke and Koch, 1976; Cohen and Klugel, 1979; Horan et al., 1983; Lotz and Hewitt, 1976; Myers, 1979; Swigert and Farrell, 1976; Unnever et al., 1980). This severe sentence is imposed partly because the judiciary believe it will incapacitate him, and thus marginally reduce the crime rate, but also because this sentence may deter other unemployed males tempted by the possible economic gains of crime. That there is no such simple relationship between incarceration and crime rates (Biles, 1979, 1982, 1983; Bowker, 1981; McGuire and Sheehan, 1983; Nagel, 1977), fails to dissuade the judiciary from using their commonsense notions of crime-causation to guide them in sentencing unemployed males.

In contrast, and again becaue of institutionalized sexism, unemployed females can, and for the most part do, slip back into or take up the wife/mother social role and hence become subject to all the informal controls of being in the family, thus making criminalization and imprisonment, as forms of social control, unlikely resources to be utilized by the judiciary. Furthermore, given the view, held by a large proportion of the population, that female employment leads to delinquent 'latch-key' children, it is unlikely that judges and magistrates will favour imprisoning unemployed mothers, for they will be seen as fulfilling their stereotypical gender-role and hence playing their informal part in delinquency control (Kruttschnitt, 1980, 1982). Removing them to prison would interfere with this vital social service. Indeed, the gender-role of keeping the family together becomes all the more important during times of economic crisis and high unemployment; rapidly increasing the rate of imprisonment for unemployed mothers during such times would jeopardize the 'social reproductive' process, and thus further impair the chances of longer-term economic recovery. Whilst it is unlikely that the judiciary will necessarily be aware of this macro-functional relationship, the aggregation of their individual decisions not to imprison unemployed females unwittingly brings it about!

In addition to making a distinction between gender, the judiciary will also be affected by the offender's age. Thus young unemployed males will be perceived as potentially or actually more dangerous than older males simply because their resistance to adversity will have been less worn away by barren years of accommodative strategies to inequalities in the distribution of income and life chances. They will have experienced less discipline at the work place, and their physical prowess and energy, attributes often considered prerequisites for 'conventional crime', will still be in prime condition. Consequently, it can be expected that the association between unemployment and imprisonment will be greater for a population of younger compared with older males.

Finally, there are reasons why ethnic minorities, particularly young males would be treated more harshly by the judiciary. Not only is the unemployment rate amongst this group two to three times higher than its white counterpart, but their demographic characteristics — they are disproportionately aged between 15 and 25 years old — also signal potentially high levels of criminal behaviour. So, as a group, the British black population are doubly vulnerable, first to higher levels of unemployment and second to higher levels of criminality because that is 'youth's speciality'. In addition, black youth is politically marginalized and therefore unwilling and incapable of attempting to struggle for change of the system from the inside. As Lea and Young argue:

> The growth of a generation of young people in the decaying inner cities, vast numbers of them with little or no experience of work and employment, is...not simply a set of social problems and deprivations, it is also a crisis for the political process. The local networks of trade union branches, trades councils and Labour Party branches, the traditional institutions of organized working class politics, no longer function as channels for the political organization of a generation of young people whose experience of work and production, and the patterns of life that come with it, is minimal (Lea and Young, 1982: 14).

When racial discrimination is added to this cauldron of evil ingredients, and when there have already been urban riots in which unemployed British blacks figured prominently (Southgate and Field, 1982) – a fact blown-up out of proportion in highly sensationalized media presentation – there is a whole bundle of reasons why the government would view ethnic minorities as needing discipline. Indeed, in an article called 'Predicting Black Crime', Stevens (1979: 16) concluded that:

> solely on the grounds of age, West Indian unemployment is likely to increase in the early 1980s; and that solely on the grounds of contraction of manufacture, West Indian unemployment is likely to go on increasing until 1991, and, who knows, after that. The net effect is certain to be increasing West Indian unemployment in the 1980s, even before consideration of the possible effects of any purely racially discriminatory factors in a shrinking job market...[thus]...black representation among the young and unemployed will almost certainly increase, and therefore black representation among those arrested and convicted is also likely to increase, and the absolute numbers of blacks arrested and convicted will increase rapidly in the 1980s and perhaps beyond.

The judiciary would not necessarily have to be credited with this degree of sociological insightfulness! Individual judges and magistrates merely have to view many young offenders, particularly if they are also black and unemployed, as likely to commit further serious criminal acts, and that would justify, in their learned opinion, imposing a sentence of imprisonment. The government then only has to throw up its arms in despair that the prison population is growing, but quietly allow the prison building programme to proceed at a rate of knots so that the swelling number of prisoners can be accommodated. As former Home Secretary, Willie Whitelaw put it, in one of those rare open and frank admissions to the 1982 Conservative Party Conference faithfuls:

> When the courts decide that a custodial sentence is essential, places *must* and *will* be found. So we have launched the largest building and maintenance programme for decades. Three new prisons are now under construction, and seven more are at various stages in their design.

A year later, Leon Brittan, Whitelaw's successor, announced proudly that four new prisons in addition to the ten already planned would be built by the end of this decade. 'This programme of prison building', he boasted, 'far surpasses anything undertaken before in this century.' He did not mention that this costly programme — estimated to be around £250 million — would not end overcrowding. For the evidence from America, where a similar prison building programme was pursued during the 1970s, is that the prison population rises to fill every available space, and more, within two years (APT Associates, 1980; but see Blumstein et al., 1983). Indeed, the more the judiciary believes that there is prison accommodation the more likely they are to imprison offenders.

Our position can now be summarized: as the economic crisis deepens, the judiciary become increasingly anxious about the possible threat to social order posed by 'problem populations', particularly unemployed males rather than females, and unemployed young males rather than older unemployed males, and within this former group, young black unemployed males (although we cannot test this on our available data), and it responds to this 'perception' by increasing the use of custodial sentences, particularly against property offenders, in the belief that such a response will deter and incapacitate and thus defuse this threat. The government, also being anxious, is willing to defend the judiciary's right to impose such sentences, and simultaneously strengthens both the judiciary's and its own coercive apparatus just in case civil disorder and ungovernability increase.

Results of testing the unemployment-imprisonment hypothesis

We have analysed time-series data for England and Wales for the period 1952–1981. For the curious and technically minded reader, the full details of measures and methods of analysis can be found in appendix A, and the results in statistical form can be found in appendix B. In order to understand the results it is essential to realize that the key dependent variable is the annual number of receptions into prison *under sentence* (including borstal and detention centre, but excluding imprisoned fine defaulters). For the purpose of this analysis alone, we were not interested in persons sent to prison on remand, those convicted and awaiting sentence, or imprisoned non-criminals. Our statistical analysis is an attempt to discover whether those sentenced to immediate imprisonment co-varies positively with annual unemployment levels after recorded crime levels and conviction rates, as well as population sizes, have been taken into account. In other words, once the changes in prison receptions under sentence accounted for by these other factors are removed, we assume that the residue can be accounted for by the judiciary's increased use of imprisonment as a response to unemployment and the economic crisis.

The results of our statistical analysis broadly support the above hypotheses. We found that the total population under immediate sentence of imprisonment was sensitive to the level of unemployment even after controlling for crime levels and conviction rates. This effect was stronger for the male population alone and still stronger for young males. One crude and very simplistic way of rendering our results would be to say that as the unemployment rate increased by 1,000 so the number of persons sent to prison over the number expected due to increases in crime levels and conviction rates was eight, for the male population it was eleven and for young males it was seventeen. This does not of course mean that unemployment is the major determinant of imprisonment levels; clearly the crime and conviction rates have that honour. Nonetheless, it is clear that the number of persons immediately imprisoned, and hence the average daily

compares unfavourably with only a 7 percent increase in the average daily prison population.

The *Criminal Law Act*, 1977, removed simple drunkenness from the list of offences punishable by imprisonment. The magistrates responded by imposing fines unpayable by persons inclined to be drunk and disorderly and therefore 'without the wherewithal'. The outcome was that as many persons guilty of being simply drunk in a public place ended up in prisons as fine defaulters.

The *Criminal Justice Act*, 1982, abolished imprisonment for the offence of loitering for the purpose of prostitution. Yet that has not prevented prostitutes being fined the maximum £200. Since those convicted are likely to be the least successful street walkers, these fines, whose total soon mounts up with subsequent court appearances, frequently and predictably exceed their ability to pay. Many of them thus end up in prison as fine defaulters.

Curiously in February 1984 the Home Secretary announced that maximum fines in magistrates courts are to be doubled! Without arguing that magistrates will take full advantage of this increased power, there will no doubt be a substantial increase in imprisoned fine defaulters, the majority of whom will be unemployed or in receipt of supplementary benefit. Whether this outcome is averted by the Home Secretary granting courts the power to impose a community service order on fine defaulters, as he suggested he might in a recent speech to Liverpool magistrates (Dean, 1984a), remains to be seen.

The introduction of the partially suspended sentence, which was introduced under the *Criminal Law Act*, 1977, and implemented in 1982, has also failed to achieve a reduction in the prison population. Home Office researchers examined 600 partially suspended sentences imposed in the fourth quarter of 1982 and concluded that 'possibly up to half these sentences replaced fully suspended sentences of imprisonment or non-custodial sentences' (Dean, 1983). The outcome of this sentencing practice is that more persons are imprisoned than was ever intended by those implementing this alternative to immediate imprisonment.

After the *Butler Report on Mentally Ill Offenders*, 1975, the government urged every Regional Health Authority to build a secure hospital establishment to relieve the prison system of over 1,000 mentally ill prisoners. But even eight years later the number of such prisoners had hardly dropped because the Health Authorities have not been willing to do this, despite considerable financial aid — much of which appears, mysteriously, to have been spent elsewhere (Kilroy-Silk, 1983). In the *Government's Reply to the Fourth Report from the Home Affairs Committee* (1982: 11), it was stated that they were still waiting for one of the fourteen Regional Health Authorities in England to provide plans for establishing secure accommodation. As of mid–1982, one 30-bed unit was open, building in progress would, when complete, provide a further 160 places, and building to begin in 1983 would add another 136 places. By 1985, there are expected to be over 500 places available, but that target may not be reached. Furthermore, there is every indication that the government will have to prevent resolutely any attempt by mental hospital authorities to disgorge their more troublesome patients into these more secure units and thus thwart any attempt to reduce significantly the number of mentally ill prisoners.

A final example of half-hearted and contradictory attempts to ease the problem of prison overcrowding is the executive dictat on parole issued by Leon Brittan during the 1983 Conservative Annual Conference. To appease the howling 'lock 'em up and throw away the key' mob who constitute the Party's backbone, Brittan promised that violent offenders, including drug dealers, serving five years or more would no longer be considered for parole except maybe in the last few months of their sentence. At the same time, he pandered to the liberal component, in and out of the Conservative Party, by reducing the minimum length of sentence qualifying for parole from 19.5 to 10.5 months. Because of administrative delays, this latter measure only came into effect in July 1984 when 2,000 prisoners were released on parole. This one-off reduction in prison population however is dampened by the rise in long-term prisoners who would otherwise have been released on parole after serving one-third of their sentence. Furthermore, since the majority of those released early will be homeless (largely becaue of the Government's moratorium on building hostels for ex-offenders) and unemployed (largely because of this Government's economic policies) many of them will reappear in the prison population in the near future. This simply illustrates how impossible it is to alter successfully one section of the prison system without simultaneously altering conditions outside prison.

The recent history of government attempts to reduce the prison population is a history of 'tinkering'. Each Home Secretary has in turn drawn back from taking the most obvious and practical steps with the disingenuous excuse that they cannot legislate for the judiciary — its independence is inviolable. It can be encouraged, exhorted, informed, reasoned with, but it can never be instructed. The result is that major reforms are completely avoided, and every minor reform is weakened or sabotaged.

For example, in 1981, Whitelaw proposed to reduce the prison population by an estimated 7,000 through granting parole after one-third of a prison sentence. But the Magistrates' Association Sentencing of Offenders Committee strongly opposed this move and threatened to retaliate by committing more offenders to Crown Court for sentence — a move calculated to secure longer sentences to offset early parole. By mid-1982, Whitelaw backed off, the plan was dropped and instead partially suspended sentences created under Section 47 of the Criminal Law Act, 1977, were introduced as a poor and ineffective compromise.

A similar fate will almost certainly await intermittent (or weekend) imprisonment which Brittan has promised to introduce during the 1985/6 Parliamentary session. Although appearing to be a liberal move, reflecting the Home Office's recent sideward glance at the Dutch penal system, it is likely to exacerbate rather than relieve the problem of prison overcrowding. The Magistrates' Association have already made it plain that their members intend to use this sentence as an *extra* custodial sanction rather than an *alternative* to a six months (or less) sentence. The net effect, according to the Association of Chief Probation Officers, will be to increase the total number of persons in prison (Dean, 1984b).

Of course, at the heart of the overcrowding issue is the fact that too many persons are sentenced to prison, and for *too long*. The government could drastically reduce the prison population. It could: remove minor offences from the list of those subject to criminal law (e.g. drunkenness in public, sexual offences between consenting young persons, cannabis consumption); remove some offences from the list of those punishable by imprisonment (e.g. fine and maintenance defaulters, vagrants, beggars, and indeed, all summary offences); prevent the imprisonment of certain types, such as the mentally ill/disordered, the persistent petty but socially inadequate offender, the undefended offender on the *Gideon* principle that the state shall not deprive any person of liberty unless that person's best defence has been presented by a legally qualified or competent person, those awaiting deportation, all first offenders and no one under the age of eighteen, except for violent offences; require the police to caution more suspects and only prosecute after convincing an independent judicial office that this course of action would be in the public interest; increase bail hostels, institute a national programme of registered medical practitioners willing to provide examination of suspects in the community, and provide sufficient funds to speed up the period of time on remand in custody; increase the extent of suspended sentences to cover all periods of imprisonment, with the exception of a life sentence; introduce day-fines, which would in turn reduce the number of fine-defaulters and, by heavily fining those more capable of paying, reduce the pressure to imprison where the present fine level is incommensurate with the offence's seriousness; pressurize the Regional Health Authorities to push ahead more quickly with the provision of more secure units; educate judges and magistrates to realize the limited objective — punishment — prisons can achieve, and to regard alternatives to prison, especially community service orders, probation orders, day centres and weekend attendance centres, as genuine *alternatives* to be used more often for those who would otherwise be imprisoned, and not, as is currently suspected, as an *additional* way of bringing more persons under state control.

In addition, and even more important, the government could introduce new maximum levels of sentencing below the present levels and persuade the judiciary to aim for an average comparable with the present average on a pro rata basis. There is no question that the reason why Britain has a higher prison population per 100,000 of the general population than, say, The Federal Republic of Germany, Luxembourg, France, Denmark, Ireland, Belgium, Italy, The Netherlands or Switzerland, is because the average prison sentence is much longer here than in these other countries (Fitzmaurice and Pease, 1982). Furthermore, in terms of the comparable crime problems or the levels of recidivism, this marked difference in the average length of imprisonment seems unjustifiable. The government could, by directly engineering a shorter average prison sentence, substantially reduce the prison population. If it wanted to act even quicker, because the crisis is now and not in the future, it could activate its powers under the *Criminal Justice Act*, 1982, and grant a six month amnesty to all but those guilty of serious violent offences. The effect, at a stroke, would be to reduce the prison population drastically.

However desirable this goal, it has to be achieved fairly. Justice must not be compromised, the judiciary must not become merely an extension of the governing political party, and the public must not be endangered or ignored.

Justice demands that offenders receive a punishment commensurate with the seriousness of their offence. However, the present tariff level is not inviolable, and is certainly not the only possible interpretation of what constitutes a suitable gradation of punishments for different offences. If through administrative, legislative or judicial reforms, the average severity level of the tariff were reduced, the current judicial interpretation of justice (which one could query) would still be preserved — the established relationship between offence and punishment would be left intact.

The independence of the judiciary is meant to stand between the citizen and the state to make certain that arbitrary or politically inspired punishments are not meted out. Whether this is mere rhetoric or reality is immaterial here, for the fact is this 'independence' is not compromised merely by the state reducing the average length of prison sentence, or providing educational courses for the judiciary on the uses of imprisonment. The judiciary would still be left to conduct its own business of establishing guilt and handing down a just punishment within the law.

The public need not be endangered. It has been documented that the crime rate would not increase as a result of offenders being imprisoned for shorter periods, released earlier than at present, or diverted entirely into some alternative punitive scheme. The public need to be reassured; the evidence needed to achieve this is available, it merely has to be publicized effectively. Indeed, recent surveys and research already indicate that the public is well prepared to accept a lower sentencing tariff for a wide range of offences (Shaw, 1982; Walker and Marsh, 1984). Furthermore, if the government widened its criminal compensation scheme from the current modest figure of £24 million, and made direct victim-restitution more central to our criminal justice system than it is at present, then the sense of public outrage and indignation which might follow the implementation of the above ideas, especially if whipped by by the 'law and order' brigade and its media supporters, might be forestalled.

The means of reducing the prison population exist — indeed they have been presented to various governments ever since Roy Jenkins raised the alarm nearly twenty years ago. Unfortunately, the history of the last decade's penal policy has been a history of government reluctance to do very much constructive, except construct more prisons! Is this because the above reforms are the utopian dreams of barmy radicals or the ivory-tower musings of starry-eyed academics? Hardly, for without exception these reforms come from a liberal consensus consisting of such official bodies as the Advisory Council on the Penal System, the Committee of Inquiry into the United Kingdom Prison Service, the House of Commons Expenditure Committee, and the Parliamentary All-Party Penal Affairs Groups. These have been joined by, or echo the ideas of, the National Association for the Care and Resettlement of Offenders, the Conference of Chief Probation Officers, the National Association of Probation Officers, and the British Association of Social Workers. In addition, such libertarian/reformist groups as the Howard League for Prison Reform, the Prison Reform Trust, the National Council for Civil Liberties and Radical Alternatives to Prison, have joined the chorus calling with passion and urgency for the above ideas to be implemented.

Yet despite this pressure, governments have expressed concern at the problem and sympathy for most solutions, but have remained curiously passive with only an occasional twinge of activity. Have they simply lacked the will? Have they not got the stomach to battle with the judiciary, public opinion or the law and order lobby? It would be easy to infer such cowardice from the actual penal policies governments have pursued, but such an inference would be naïve. An alternative explanation is that they cannot afford to be that interested in reducing the significant contribution prisons make to maintaining law and order and instilling discipline into recalcitrant populations. Indeed, governments faced with a population they perceive to be increasingly ungovernable, and realizing that their economic policies may substantially exacerbate this, particularly amongst certain sections of the community, have not seen any pragmatic sense in alienating such a trusted and loyal ally as the judiciary, or abandoning prison as an iron fist of threat, control and punishment.

Magistrates and judges act as a major form of social control over potential groups of 'resisters', particularly during periods of economic social crisis. They help, unwittingly or not, to shore up the state's domination by weakening the resolve of these resisters. Thus, those who do not benefit from judicial decisions (but are instead sent straight to gaol) are in no position to change them, and those who do benefit, namely the state and those group interests it ultimately serves, have no interest in changing them. Government ministers and Home Office officials allow the judiciary to carry on independently because collectively they agree that the unemployed either have to be deterred or incapacitated, or allowed instead to become socially disruptive. That is why, despite the concern over prison overcrowding nothing significant is attempted to crack this problem. The government is not so much interested in solving this problem as it is in *using* it. Overcrowding occupies a central position in the political debate on prisons because it is an ideological device enabling the recent British government to legitimate its real penal policy, which is to build more prisons. It feels the need to pursue this policy because it is anxious that social order is threatened by the current economic crisis undermining consent amongst those suffering its worse ravages. Consequently, the government is eagerly building more prisons, including converting schools and hospitals closed down as a result of its cuts in public expenditure, to accommodate the increased numbers being imprisoned by a judiciary responding to its own class-linked gut anxieties.

Appendix A

Measures and method

Testing these hypotheses has been difficult because official definitions and computational procedures change over time, thus making strict comparability problematic. Consequently a discussion of the results has to be preceded by the usual cautionary note on the validity of official time-series data.

We collected annual data for the period 1952–81 for males and young males in England and Wales on the following variables:

X_1 *Receptions into prison under immediate imprisonment.* This includes receptions into prisons, borstals, detention centres, and other total penal institutions. Data were derived from the annual publications *Prison Statistics England and Wales* and *Reports on the Work of the Prison Department.*

X_2 *Unemployment.* Figures on the average number unemployed in a given year were obtained from *British Labour Statistics Annual Abstracts.* The only figures available on youth unemployment for the time period covered were taken from August editions of the *Department of Employment Gazette* and refer to the number of those under 20 years of age registered as unemployed in a particular month (July). This would be higher than the annual average because it is swollen by the recent school-leaving population.

X_3 *Population.* Midyear estimates were obtained from the *Annual Abstract of Statistics.* The figures for males refer to those between the ages of 15–65. Those for young males to 15–20.

X_4 *Numbers found guilty of indictable offences* were taken from *Annual Abstract of Statistics.*

X_5 *Indictable offences* recorded by the police were taken from *Annual Abstract of Statistics.*

The technique used for analysing these data is multiple regression (Johnston, 1972; Theil, 1971). The essential result of multiple regression is to allow us to isolate the effects of individual variables by holding the effects of the other (possible) causal factors constant. Since we are using time-series data, we must allow for the possibility of serial correlation. Where the presence of serial correlation was detected using the Durbin-Watson (1950, 1951) *d* statistic, we re-estimated the model to account for this, using the iterative Cochrane and Orcutt (1949) technique.

In an attempt to reduce the problems of multico-linearity likely to arise with time-series, we expressed our data as rates per 100,000 population. Specifically, taking receptions under sentence X_1 as an example, the linear model specified would be

$$x_{1t} = \beta_{10} + \beta_{12}x_{2t} + \beta_{13}x_{3t} + \beta_{14}x_{4t} + \beta_{15}x_{5t} + u_t$$

but we redefined the model by multiplying through by $(100/x_{3t})$ to give

$$\left(\frac{100x_{1t}}{x_{3t}}\right) = \beta_{10}\left(\frac{100}{x_{3t}}\right) + \beta_{12}\left(\frac{100x_{2t}}{x_{3t}}\right) + 100\,\beta_{13} + \beta_{14}\left(\frac{100x_{4t}}{x_{3t}}\right) + \beta_{16}\left(\frac{100x_{5t}}{x_{3t}}\right) + u_t\left(\frac{100}{x_{3t}}\right)$$

Hence our analysis is carried out with variables $x*it$ ($i=1, \ldots, 5$) defined by

$$x*_{4t} = \left(\frac{100}{x_{3t}}\right) \quad x*_{it} = \left(\frac{100\,x_{it}}{x_{3t}}\right) \quad i \neq 3.$$

We should stress here that we are in no way arguing that the estimated parameters of our model may be interpreted in a strict causal sense. We are using multiple regression simply as a technique which allows us to discover whether unemployment accounts for any significant variation in sentencing practices after controlling for other (possibly) important factors. If an increase in unemployment only affects sentencing policy through the increased rate of criminal behavior it induces, then when in multiple regression we control the rate of crime, population changes, and numbers found guilty of indictable offences, it should be statistically insignificant. If, however, this is not the case, this may be taken as support for our argument that unemployment also affects sentencing policy through the ideologically motivated response of the judiciary.

Appendix B

Statistical results

In Table 1 below we present the results for the multivariate regression analyses. A discussion of the technique and a description of the variables used may be found in Appendix A.

TABLE 1
Dependent variable: receptions under immediate imprisonment

	Constant	$X*_2$	$X*_3$	$X*_4$	$X*_5$	R^2	DF
A. Total Population	0.522	0.008 (3.386)	−244.4 (−4.706)	0.077 (2.769)	−0.112 (−2.206)	0.889	24
B. Male Population	0.764	0.011 (3.537)	−165.9 (−4.736)	0.065 (2.188)	−0.009 (−1.956)	0.888	24
C. Young Male Population	0.039	0.017 (2.351)	−0.412 (−0.073)	0.043 (1.996)	0.002 (1.348)	0.573	24

The figures in brackets are t-values for $H_o:\beta_i = O$ against $H_A:\beta_i \neq O$. For a 5 percent significance test the critical value is 2.064 — t values greater than this indicate that the variable has a statistically significant effect upon the dependent variable after controlling for the effect of the other variables.

5

Radical criminology and criminal victimization: proposals for the development of theory and intervention

Alan Phipps

Introduction

The purpose of this paper is to consider the neglect by radical criminologists of the emergence of victimology as a distinct sub-discipline within mainstream criminology, and of its subject-matter, criminal victimization.[1] I will begin with an account of the political context of the emergence of victimology, and go on to examine the areas of knowledge generated through this new area of study. This paper is also intended to be a contribution to the development of the left-realist perspective in radical criminology, and as such will attempt to account for the neglect of criminal victimization in terms of aspects of the development of the radical paradigm. Finally, the paper argues for the serious consideration of the subject matter of victimology as part of a new integration of theory, evidence, and practice in radical criminology.

The discovery of criminal victimization

In order to understand the orientation of radical criminologists to criminal victimization, it is necessary to begin by examining the context of the emergence of concern for this topic within mainstream criminology in the United States, and the subsequent emergence there of victimology as a particularly thriving sub-discipline oriented towards practical policy issues in criminal justice.

Traditionally, the central focus of enquiry in positivist criminology — in its biological, psychological, and sociological variants — has been the criminal offender. This approach has viewed the offender as fundamentally constrained — the locus of various motivating factors and circumstances over which he has little or no control. Depending on the perspective in question, the offender has been held to be biologically or psychologically abnormal, improperly socialized, or else responding normally to the normative pressures of the culture. The commission of crime has, therefore, been seen to be either an irrational expression of the offender's inner problems, or else an expression of dilemmas confronting him as a result of his place in the social structure.

These deterministic conceptions of the origins of criminal behaviour have, I believe, given rise to a view of the *offender-as-victim* — a victim of biological processes, personality disorder, poor parenting, under-socialization, poverty and blocked opportunity, or of criminogenic environments.

The offender-centred nature of criminology has, as has often been stressed, neglected the study of the state, law creation, processes of criminalization, and the structural arrangements of capitalism. These omissions on the part of positivist criminology have also led to an almost total neglect of a number of other issues which, it could be argued, are equally indispensable to a comprehensive understanding of the social roots of crime and the nature of the criminal justice system under capitalism. These neglected issues include the conceptions of 'victim' in the law, the role of the victim in the law enforcement and judicial systems, aspects of the relationship between offenders and victims, social processes of victimization, and the impact of crime on individual victims and communities.

Criminological studies which have sought to discuss victimization as a dimension of the crime problem have been very few. Some notable examples are the early work of Shaw (1930), who was interested in victimization as part of his naturalistic approach to street robbery; Sutherland (1949) who was sceptical of criminology's reliance on the official statistics of crime, and who sought to problematize such issues as the definition of 'crime', 'victims' and 'harms'; and Sykes and Matza (1957) who engaged in a rare attempt to understand offenders' cognitive and moral orientations towards their offences and their victims.

Within mainstream sociological criminology, interest in crime victims continued to be an extremely peripheral concern until the mid-1960s when, for various reasons relating to the internal and external histories of the discipline, there occurred a revival of the concern for the accuracy and utility of the official crime statistics. This concern led a new focus upon the behaviour, characteristics and attitudes of *crime victims*, particularly as these had a bearing upon the reporting and non-reporting of crimes to the police, as part of the process of the creation of official crime statistics.

In the complex history of the relationship of criminology to the criminal justice system, a central problematic for more critically-minded liberal criminologists has been the attempt to develop more reliable measures of crime.

Unlike social scientists working in other areas of social concern, criminologists have had very little control over the data essential to their endeavours. From its very beginnings criminology has based its theoretical generalizations concerning the causes and distribution of crime, and the testing of many of its central theoretical assumptions, largely on data whose collection and compilation it does not control, and which have always been regarded — to one degree of seriousness or another — as imperfect and unsatisfactory.

From the time of the pioneering work of Quetelet in the early nineteenth century, however, criminologists have been able to sustain with remarkable consistency the view that, although the official statistics represented nothing like a complete count of crimes committed, there existed a constant ratio between reported and unreported crime. This belief allowed the criminologist to use the data whilst keeping at bay an underlying sense of unease (see Sellin and Wolfgang, 1964).

At certain times, however, this unease has surfaced and blossomed into open debate. The period of the Wickersham Commission enquiries in the 1920s and the subsequent creation of the Uniform Crime Reports in the United States, was marked by considerable debate within the criminological community concerning the need for crime data to be collected by social scientists working for an agency divorced from law enforcement (Maltz, 1977). From the 1930s through to the 1950s, numerous papers emerged which couched these problems of measurement in terms of what was eventually to become a criminological obsession — the 'dark figure' of unreported crime.

The pace of this debate gathered considerable momentum in the 1960s. Beginning perhaps with the work of Daniel Bell (1962), Kitsuse and Cicourel (1963), Sellin and Wolfgang (1964), and Leslie Wilkins (1964), the period saw a tremendous onslaught by leading figures in American liberal criminology upon the poor quality of official crime statistics. A number of papers also began to argue for the routine collection of data on all aspects of the crime problem, including criminal victimization (Biderman and Reiss 1967; Wheeler 1967; Wilkins 1965).

A turning point in this reorientation of mainstream criminology towards the importance of knowledge about victimization, came with the creation in 1965 of President Johnson's Crime Commission, which — under the influence of the new trend — commissioned the first large-scale sample surveys of crime victims. The largest, and most often cited (Ennis, 1967) produced a number of findings which were to prove important in redefining the problems of crime and its control, in a manner which elevated the crime victim to a central position of concern for criminologists and criminal justice planners.

Ennis' survey showed the size of the dark figure to be particularly large. Also, victims' reasons for not reporting crimes to the police seemed to indicate that the criminal justice system was subject to a crisis of legitimacy. Victims cited their dissatisfaction with the police and a belief in their ineffectiveness, as well as their definition of the offences as a private matter, as the main reasons for non-reporting. The fear of crime was also shown to be a problem in its own right, in that it substantially affected the attitudes and behaviour of individuals and communities. Perhaps the most far-reaching findings regarding victimization concerned its unequal distribution between different sectors of the population. For offences such as forcible rape, robbery, and burglary, rates were highest among the lower income groups; non-whites were also found to have higher rates for forcible rape, robbery, aggravated assault and burglary. Non-whites also felt less safe in their neighbourhoods at night and expressed less confidence in the efficiency and integrity of the police. The findings also demonstrated a fact which has emerged from almost all subsequent studies — that victim-ization is *intra*-racial, rather than *inter*-racial, for robbery and assaultive crimes.

The Crime Commission had much evidence at its disposal to show that victimization is disproportionately concentrated in the slums and racial ghettos. In these areas, it held, physical deterioration and social disorganization combined to create a multiplicity of social problems, of which crime was a consequence.

> Burglary, robbery and serious assaults occur in areas characterized by low income, physical deterioration, dependency, racial and ethnic concentrations, broken homes, working mothers, low levels of vocational and educational skill, high unemployment, high proportions of single males, overcrowded and sub-standard housing, high rates of tuberculosis and infant mortality, low rates of home ownership or single family dwellings, mixed land use, and high popula-tion density (President's Commission 1967: 35)

Not only are slum and ghetto residents brutalized by their conditions of life, said the Report, but also they are involved in a process of transition from the rural existencies from which they have emerged, and the mainstream of American society. This process of transition is, however, effectively held up by discrimination and unemployment which leads to much of everyday crime as a 'blind reaction to the conditions of slum living' (President's Commission, 1967: 37).

Implicitly accepting the reasoning of strain theories of crime and social structure, the Crime Commission extended its analysis, in the spirit of these theories, to see these conditions creating cultural atmospheres which lead to the decline of the quality of interpersonal relationships. This process is seen as leading, in the slums and ghettos, to two related sets of cir-cumstances. Firstly, there is internecine crime in which the oppressed victimize the oppressed; secondly, and more disturbingly for white society, there emerges a new and somewhat politicized variety of crime, in which there is a racially motivated shift towards the victimization of whites outside the ghetto area.

The riots which occurred during the mid- to late 1960s, became viewed from this general perspective as a further indicator of the consequences of injustice and 'blocked opportunity' in American society.

The Report of the Advisory Commission on Civil Disorders — the Riot

Commission (1968: 268) — concluded in similar fashion, that criminal victimization was a scourge of ghetto existence which was directly attributable to the nature of the social and psychic strains which its residents faced daily. Crime not only creates an atmosphere of insecurity and fear, but also causes continuing attrition of the relationship between ghetto residents and the police; this was seen to bear a direct relationship to civil disorder.

Although the ghettos were the areas of the highest rates of serious personal victimization, the Riot Commission found that the high levels of police manpower concentrated there did nothing to reduce the problem. Instead the policies of 'blanket policing' and 'alley justice' led to well-founded beliefs in the existence of police brutality and the feeling that residents of ghetto neighbourhoods were not being given adequate police protection. The police were shown to maintain less rigorous standards of enforcement in ghetto areas, tolerating activities such as drug-trafficking, prostitution, and street violence, which they would not be prepared to tolerate elsewhere. It was also discovered that in some black districts the police took almost four times as long to respond to calls for assistance in robbery situations than they did in white districts.

The discovery of criminal victimization and its implications as it appears in the pages of the Crime Commission and Riot Commission reports, can be explained with reference to a number of different factors.

Firstly, liberal criminology in this period was dominated by theories of causation which located crime and delinquency as consequences of aspects of social disorganization and injustice (e.g. Cloward and Ohlin, 1960). The dominance of this perspective particularly facilitated an alliance between liberal criminology and the social reformism of the Democratic Party during the period of the Kennedy and Johnson administrations.

The Democratic Party, it has been argued, maintained in the 1960s an accentuated commitment to state intervention in the social and economic spheres, and was ideologically committed to a vision — social democratic in all but name – of social justice as a necessary basis for social order (Harrington, 1972, 1976; Davis, 1980). As such, this social democratic reformism found a natural ally in social sciences such as criminology, which provided a rhetoric through which the ideology of state interventionism could be articulated.

The Crime and Riot Commissions provided authoritative expressions of social democratic images of crime and social structure, and established a programme for reforming the criminal justice system towards a more effective 'war on crime' as a necessary corollary of the Great Society programmes and the 'war on poverty'.

Victimization was a most central concern because firstly, it could be seen to stem directly from the human consequences of social injustice; secondly, the failure of the state to protect citizens from criminal depredations could be shown to lead to a situation where communities accept the inevitability of crime and have a low level of confidence in the police and the criminal justice system. This process leads in its turn to a greater reluctance to report crime, a further weakening of law enforcement, with all the consequent implications for social order.

It was in the context of this analysis that the Crime Commission called for a 'scientific and technological revolution' in criminal justice (President's Commission: 245). Part of this was to be a 'data revolution' in which social science research and quantitative statistical methods were to play a key role in identifying problems of crime control and in the monitoring and evaluation of the component parts of the system. Knowledge of the extent and distribution of victimization were thus indispensable to the reform of the criminal justice system, especially in the monitoring of the behaviour and attitudes of those on the receiving end of crime. The regular large-scale surveys of victimization, which the Commission envisaged, would in a sense return statistics on crime to a role approximating that envisaged in the last century by Bentham and the moral statisticians — a social indicator or barometer of social conditions and social order (Sellin and Wolfgang, 1964: 8). Social statistics would act therefore as part of the *rhetoric* of reformism, in that they would identify the extent and distribution of problems, as well as being a guide to intervention.

The findings of the Commission concerning victimization, dovetailed into a strongly persistent theme in social democratic thinking about crime, in which issues of social justice and criminal justice are inextricably linked. Inherent in this thinking is the belief that reform of social conditions through social policy and the reform of criminal justice policy, are necessarily intertwined. In the logic of this position, a certain collapsing of categories of victimization occurs. Conceptions of *social* victimization and *criminal* victimization become merged in a way which renders the creation of a 'strong but fair' criminal justice system a necessary corollary to a 'just society' in which structural disadvantage is eliminated through ameliorative legislation and its enforcement by agencies of the welfare state.

This social democratic conception of the implicatons of criminal victimization is further fed by evidence that the poor suffer disproportionately the effects of crime. The task then becomes one of eliminating bias from the enforcement of the law by the courts and police, and for the war between the poor and the police to be avoided through the provision of adequate protection to the law-abiding majority of the poor, and through securing fuller enforcement through community policing and citizen involvement. The paradoxical feature of this reasoning is that the widespread victimization of the poor is seen as a rationalization for the creation of a more efficiently repressive criminal justice system as a means through which consensus and legitimacy can be renewed, and the integration of marginalized sections of the working class can be achieved. This was a persistent feature of the crime talk of the Democratic Party in the 1960s, and particularly that of Johnson and his Attorney-General, Ramsey Clark (Clark, 1970).

The social democratic image of criminal victimization contains therefore contradictory elements which are addressed more clearly and precisely within the framework of conservative thinking about crime. In the conservative thesis the importance of *order* is stressed as a means through which justice can be achieved, a reversal of the causal relationship espoused by social democrats. It would therefore seem to follow that conservative images of victimization would take a quite different form. Firstly, conservatives reject the notion of victimization as born of the desperation, dehumanization, and the distortion of human values attendant on inequality and injustice. Rather, victimization is seen explicitly as that which is visited on the law-abiding by the lawless. The lawless do not commit their depredations because of inequality or injustice, but because of a weakening of the ties of social discipline and moral authority which results in freely-chosen decisions to prey upon the weak and helpless. [2]

In the conservative redefinition of 'civil rights', it is *criminal* victimization which leads to *social* victimization. The greatest wrong which a citizen may suffer is not social inequality — for this is indispensable to a just society — but the interference by criminals, or indeed the interventionist state, in the harmonious natural patterns of social and economic relationships.

It is an integral part of this position that 'liberalism' and 'welfarism' have contributed to the weakening of social discipline, and that the effectiveness of law enforcement has been hampered by placing the rights of offenders above the rights of the law-abiding to be free from victimization.

As Ian Taylor has recently remarked in his discussion of right-wing criminology:

> The rhetoric of the Right is almost always silent on the specific social context of any crime . . . and tries to displace crime and delinquency from their origins in the social formation itself, and in so doing asserts that the disorder in social relations is unrelated to the accelerating crisis of social reproduction in capitalist society . . . Right wing criminology's essential project is indeed to disconnect the facts of social disorder from the (developing) disorderliness of social relations by remaining silent on the specific social context of crime and by speaking about crime as individual moral defect (Taylor, 1981: 23–4).

In conservative crime talk, criminal victimization is directly referred to in terms of the harms inflicted upon individual victims and the fearfulness of the law-abiding. In the well-documented crime talk of Richard Nixon and Ronald Reagan — during the 1972 Presidential election campaign — there are several predominating themes. These themes have been constantly reiterated in Conservative Party crime talk in Britain since 1979, and in its response to the disorders of 1981. Firstly, there is a concerted attack on 'welfarism' and 'social Keynesianism', in which government expenditure on social problems such as poverty and delinquency is held not only to have fuelled inflation, but also to have failed to prevent ever-higher levels of crime and the spectre of black insurrection. Secondly, there is a continual statement of the basic conservative premise that 'justice' and 'progress' are incidental to order. Thus large expenditure on repressive criminal justice is justified mainly in terms of their benefits to potential victims (e.g. Chester et al., 1969; Taylor, 1981).

The emergence of victimology
As I have noted, positivist criminology has traditionally been offender-centred, and has seen its main purpose as laying bare the secrets of the ætiology of criminal behaviour through the use of the methods of the natural sciences. As such, positivist criminology embraced a concept of the offender as a passive entity. It is arguable therefore, that the neglect of the *victim* as a focus of study, arose in part from an unconscious extension of this aspect of positivism's image of human nature and action. The victim has also implicitly been seen as passive, playing no particular role in the drama and process of criminal behaviour, but merely represent-ing the random focus of the statistically rare criminal event. Although it was taken for granted that the social situation and personal characteristics of offenders were highly relevant to *criminal* careers, the logic of this model of causation was rarely extended to victims.

Exceptions to this general rule have been the various attempts to under-stand the social psychology of offender-victim interactions at the micro level. Most notably these have included the pioneering work of von Hentig (1948) and Schafer (1968; 1977), Wolfgang's studies of homicide (1958), various studies of child victims of sex offences (e.g. Gibbens and Prince 1963), and Amir's well-known work on rape (1970). These studies have been produced by writers operating within a trend in criminological work which is heavily influenced by clinical and psychodynamic tradi-tions, and have contributed to founding victimology as a so-called 'science of victim-offender relationships'.

In the 1970s, the growth of victimology in the United States has been very impressive, both in terms of the sheer volume of work produced and its contribution to shifting the orientation of mainstream criminology from its narrow focus upon the ætiology and treatment of offending, towards a much broader range of issues.

It is possible to distinguish three main trends within victimology. Firstly, there are a number of broad statements aimed at setting a programme for the development of the discipline. The statement by Dadrian (1976) is unusual in that it points in the direction of the development of a social theory of victimization:

1. the extent of the dark figure of crime for the locality, in comparison to the police statistics;

2. the social characteristics of victims as these may be related to their exposure to certain types of crime;

3. the social characteristics of offenders — if known — and their relationship to victims;

4. the characteristics of offences, their frequency and distribution;

5. the impact of victimization on individuals, households, and neighbourhoods;

6. the impact of victimization upon subsequent behaviour and attitudes of victims;

7. the behaviour of the police towards victims and groups at risk;

8. public assessment of policing priorities and the seriousness of crime;

9. the assessment of the needs of crime victims in relation to the type of services available or desirable;

10. priorities for immediate intervention by the police and the local state for victimization prevention.

More detailed knowledge of these and other dimensions of the crime problems of localities would have three clear advantages for a practical radical criminology. Firstly, it would permit radicals to move away from guesswork and intuition to a more informed basis for understanding the origins and forms of criminal victimization. Secondly, there would be a clear basis from which to formulate demands concerning policing and aspects of local social policy having a direct bearing upon victimization patterns. Thirdly, there would be a firm basis for transitional socialist programmes for crime prevention. In these three respects, the reintegration of theory, evidence, and intervention, which the use of local victimization surveys may facilitate, is analogous to the approach already adopted by socialists in the area of health, and the provision of health services.

As mentioned earlier, local victim support schemes exist, of which there are now approximately forty in Britain.[6] They are largely supported by private and temporary state funding, cover about 150 localities and operate the only specific services for victims of crime. Although the number of schemes is growing constantly, and helping in excess of forty thousand people annually, there is no question of their being able to respond to the mass of largely hidden need, given their present level of operation. Part of the task of victimological research at the local level should be to arrive at an estimate of the type of need which exists in given localities and how best those needs might be met. Such information could then be incorporated as part of local demands for services, fully funded by local authorities.

Lastly, there is the question of restitution by offenders to the victims of crime. At present restitution, reparation, and reconciliation schemes, by which essentially local disputes and problems are dealt with in the community, are regarded with considerable suspicion by radicals in the criminal justice field. What is most required is a thorough debate on the basis of present theory and research (see Harding, 1982; Wright, 1982) in order to consider an agenda for a series of demands for the democratization of justice, and for the development of alternative concepts and frameworks for justice (see Christie, 1978).

Conclusion

This paper has outlined the development of the study of criminal victimization and has argued that victimology has — in the past decade — enlarged the scope of our understanding of the social roots and consequences of personal crime. I regard the failure of all but a minority of radical criminologists to engage in the study of these matters to have resulted in the one-sided development of radical perspectives on crime. The direction of our theoretical and empirical work should now address questions concerning the impact of crime on individuals and communities, and investigate the possibilities of fighting back against this aspect of the distortion of human relationships under the present social system. In so doing, radical criminologists may seize the opportunity to bring back crime into the scope of their general analysis of the socially generated, but non-criminalized harms of social relations under capitalism.

Notes

1. I have chosen to use the term 'radical criminology' as a convenient label to denote trends which, since the late 1960s, have been variously known as the 'new', 'alternative', 'critical', 'left-wing', 'Marxist' criminologies.

2. By far the most comprehensive conservative statement on victims of crime is that by Carrington (1975).

3. Very few victimization surveys were carried out in Britain before 1981. The most important of these was that conducted by Sparks et al. (1977). In the wake of the British Crime Survey local surveys have been conducted in the Midlands and Merseyside and are planned for various London boroughs.

4. Victimization surveys are notoriously poor at uncovering unreported instances of violence to women, sexual assaults and rape. The British Crime Survey (BCS) uncovered only one (attempted) rape. The methodology and hidden assumptions of the BCS have come in for well-deserved criticism from feminists. Betsy Sanko (1983) has argued that the apparent gap between women's reported fear of crime and actual reported instances of criminal victimization, lies in the fact that much crime to women remains hidden from official authorities, police and researchers alike. She contrasts the findings of the BCS with other studies, and with the level of self-reported victimization by women to rape crisis centres and women's refuges. A survey of violence to women reported by Hanmer and Saunders (1984) seriously examines definitional and methodological issues in the attempt to uncover this aspect of victimization. A further important paper in this respect is that by Hilary Graham (1983).

5. The British organization Radical Alternatives to Prison is engaging in an important internal debate on these issues, (see Box-Grainger, 1982; Phipps, 1981). See also the paper by Platt (1978) for an examination by a radical criminologist of issues arising from street-crime in American cities.

6. One important example of local surveys in Britain of criminal victimization is the Merseyside Crime Survey which was conducted in 1984. It was based on interviews with a sample of 3,800 people throughout the county, including 1,400 in five small dissimilar areas, one in each of the five metropolitan districts of Merseyside (see Kinsey, 1984; Kinsey and Young, 1983).

6

Black young people and juvenile crime: some unanswered questions

John Pitts

This chapter considers whether young black people are treated differently from young white people in the British criminal justice system. It considers firstly how conventional academic debate and government policy have failed to squarely address the racial dimension in juvenile justice. It then considers the limited evidence which exists concerning the involvement of young black people in crime and the formal responses to this crime. It considers the subjective experience of being a young black subject in the juvenile criminal justice system and concludes by raising some issues which must be addressed by those claiming to take young black people in trouble seriously.

The juvenile justice debate

From social action to social reaction
From the mid-1960s onwards the academic discourse on juvenile crime gradually abandoned its concern with the causes of law-breaking by the young in favour of an analysis of the capacity of the apparatus of justice and control to generate crime and compound nascent criminal careers. This changing focus emphasized the ways in which the justice system selected and identified its subjects, how it processed them, and the consequences of such processing for future offending and personal identity. The preoccupation with social reaction, with the ways in which an inept apparatus inadvertently worsened the problem it aimed to solve was paralleled by a growing scepticism in the academy about the possibility of developing initiatives within the welfare or penal apparatus which could 'rehabilitate' the offender. This abandonment of conventional criminology's central project, 'the decline of the rehabilitative ideal', as it came to be known, signalled a changed focus, away from causation and the site of primary deviation to a preoccupation with the more effective management of social reaction.

Now the academic reformist was to correct the apparatus of justice rather than the criminal. The quest for a technology of human manipulation had given way to the quest for a technology of system manipulation. This technology was to address not the mistakes made by offenders but the mistakes made by probation officers, judges, and policemen. According to Thorpe et al.:

> it was the decision-makers — policemen, social workers, probation officers, magistrates and social services administrators who effectively abandoned whatever potential for reform the 1969 Children and young Persons Act contained. Quite simply, cumulatively these disparate bodies of professionals made the wrong decisions about the wrong children at the wrong time (Thorpe, Paley and Green, 1980:3).

The technologies which developed eschewed considerations of the state, the causes of crime and importantly, the attempt to understand the motivation of deviant actors, which was at the core of the American social reaction theories which the new technologies of system manipulation took as their theoretical rationale. The offender emerged as the inadvertent victim of a control apparatus which had misrecognized and mishandled what was in fact merely innocuous culturally patterned adolescent behaviour. That the offender might be a social critic, albeit an inarticulate and misdirected one, and that social reaction might have a deeper significance, was lost in this new formulation. Matza, commenting upon a previous generation of social reaction theorists, writes:

> Their contributions were to be absorbed into a tradition of enquiry whose first premise was the separation of crime and state; thus the absorption was not without a certain measure of distortion or misfit. Left unassaulted, the historic misconception of the positive school — the separation of crime and state — could remain the cornerstone of a sociological study of deviation that heeded the possibility that the correctional system's effects sometimes boomeranged. But as long as the misconception was maintained, such a possibility could be regarded as easily rectified, instead of a profound irony lodged in the very nature of the intimate relation between crime and the state (Matza, 1969:144).

Social reaction theory was adopted pragmatically in an attempt to develop a technology of delinquency management which would lead to a more humane rational and cost-effective apparatus of control. These initiatives were opportunistic in as much as they traded upon growing anxieties within the Home Office and local authorities about the mounting costs of, and the impending crisis within, penal and other correctional institutions. The assault upon clumsy social reaction was however modest in its selection of targets identifying social welfare and social work as the major threat to the liberty and authenticity of the control system's unwitting victims. This assault upon welfare which grew to a clamour by the end of the 1970s in the academy emanated from the left, right, and centre, and coincided precisely with attempts by government to limit expenditure on welfare in particular and the social wage in general. Thus the orthodoxy of 'minimal statism' was established and drew support from the entire political spectrum (see Cohen, 1983). Similarly the repudiation of welfare concerns within the juvenile court and the demand for a reversion to due process for juveniles ('back to justice') which came from the same quarter coincided with a series of right-wing law and order campaigns which strove to achieve precisely the same ends but for profoundly different reasons (see Morris and Giller, 1980).

By the end of the 1970s we had witnessed a convergence in the debate about juvenile crime in which there appeared to be an agreement between left liberal academics and the Home Office, that social workers' power should be limited, that the injection of welfare resources made little or no impact on crime levels, that due process offered more justice to the juvenile and to the aggrieved community, and that the development of harder headed community alternatives would serve to alleviate the financial and control problems in the British penal and correctional apparatus. This was a convergence, the rhetoric notwithstanding, which agreed that the problems of juvenile crime were essentially problems of the management and physical deployment of a deviant population.

What we witnessed, then, was a vulgarized version of 1960s social reaction theory, finding a remarkable level of accommodation with a vulgarized version of 1970s utilitarianism. The Home Office emerged as the delinquency manager par excellence. The meaning of juvenile crime for those who perpetrated it meant little, its political significance even less.

Because, in the orthodox academy which was part of the new convergence, the question of the relation between crime and the state could only be asked in terms of the relation between particular offenders and particular 'soft policemen', social workers, or probation officers, and the impact of the actions of the latter upon the former, the possibility of understanding changing patterns of juvenile crime in relation to the radically changed political landscape of Britain in the late 1970s and early 1980s was precluded. The bland acceptance within this debate of an over-simplified version of Durkheim's observation suggested that since juvenile crime, like the poor, is always with us, then its form need not tax us unduly. By accepting juvenile crime as an undifferentiated monolith to be managed more humanely it becomes irrelevant to ask why, in a particular place at a particular time, people choose, are impelled towards, or are implicated in, the trangression of particular laws. Truancy in Scunthorpe or street crime in Lewisham may both be described as juvenile crime but it is hard to believe that their origins as pieces of deviant behaviour do not have distinctively different roots and different meanings for their perpetrators. They certainly have different consequences for the neighbourhoods in which they are enacted. As Rock has observed:

> The beings and groupings that inhabit crime's bestiary are apparently thought to be simple unchanging discrete and analytically transparent. Work on juvenile

delinquency for instance has been managed as if it were a single prolonged assault on one essential problem (Rock, 1979:57).

Yet while conventional academia laboured to conceptually reconstruct the apparatus of justice and control, youth unemployment in general and black youth unemployment in particular, soared. The police reorganized themselves for the more effective containment of the 'unemployed ghetto' and a right-wing populism emerged which implicitly and sometimes explicitly strove to identify the young, the poor and the black as a major component in the forces threatening to undermine the social order. And here too, ten years on, the radical new criminology of the early 1970s was, it seemed, converging with social reality. According to some commentators and some young people black youth crime might not just be inadvertent, the possibility was raised that it might be a mode of resistance to racial oppression and over-zealous policing. The inarticulate social critic and the inadvertent delinquent as well as the conforming young black people who constituted the overwhelming majority seemed to be developing new meanings for their experience. Here was a group of people acting back upon perjorative labels and the deviant behaviour of some black young people was (seemingly) separating itself conceptually from the 'monolith' of juvenile crime. The legitimacy of the social order was in question and the questions were being asked in a new language with a new urgency. And if this crime was in fact crude survival dressed up as resistance then it was an even greater challenge to that order. In the main these young people had not read Matza and therefore did not know that they were living in Hobbes' Leviathan but growing numbers came to believe that they were living in Garvey's Babylon.

As Lea and Young (1984) have argued, a major factor in this changed understanding lay in the experience of relative deprivation. A realization born of an appreciation and acceptance of socially valued goals and an experience of the barriers constructed out of racial discrimination led to the achievement of these goals. As Cloward and Ohlin have observed:

When pressures from unfulfilled aspirations and blocked opportunity become sufficiently intense many lower class youth turn away from legitimate channels, adopting other means beyond conventional mores which might offer a possible route to success goals (Cloward and Ohlin 1960:105).

The juvenile crime which emanated from a rising generation of Afro-Caribbean youth was distinctive in many ways. Firstly, it was far greater than the crime which was perpetrated by the parental generation, a remarkably law-abiding section of the population. Secondly, it was localized, instrumental, and opportunistic concerned with procuring small amounts of money — what have been described as crimes of poverty. Thirdly, its meaning came to be reconstructed by many perpetrators and most commentators as resistance (see Pryce, 1979; Gilroy, 1982).

Understandably the phenomenon of black juvenile crime has been almost totally ignored in the current debates within the new orthodoxy, for nowhere in its repertoire is a set of questions which have any relevance to the phenomenon. Even when it became clear that young black people were heavily over-represented in arrests, court appearances and custodial institutions, the only possible rejoinder could be that through ignorance and stupidity the system was rounding up and penalizing the wrong people. This inability to come to grips with the involvement of young black people in the juvenile criminal justice system is endemic to a perspective which denies the necessity of a historical or political dimension to its analysis and maintains an untheorized notion of the state as a large, somewhat inept, but ultimately benign bureaucracy. For in truth the attempt from the Heath government onwards to ideologically transform the economic crisis into a moral one had the effect of locating the Afro-Caribbean and to a lesser extent the Asian populations as parasitic and potentially subversive to cultural stability and social order. Thus in the second half of the 1970s the police did not just make a mistake or overreact in their policing of black neighbourhoods. They were deployed as a response to crime but also in anticipation of social disorder. These important decisions about the deployment of manpower and resources were made at the highest levels of the police bureaucracy (see Hall et al., 1978). The state was not benign nor crime meaningless and the police and the black community understood this much more clearly than the orthodox academy. The borderland between policing and the black community was 'sus' and the successive indiscriminate sweeps of black areas by special squads of police. The consequences of such policies were to transform all black people effectively into suspects and all police officers into racists, irrespective of the wishes or intentions of the individuals involved. The extent to which this served to legitimate their actions and thus project some people policed in this way into illegal activity can only be guessed at.

Black juvenile crime, its perpetration or construction by predatory and pre-emptive interventions on the part of the police is peculiar. To be understood it must be separated off from the monolith of juvenile crime and located in time and place.

The new orthodoxy fails lamentably to do this. By addressing only one aspect of one part of this complex equation, 'social reaction', usually in the form of the responses of welfare personnel, it offers no possibility of grasping the social realities which give rise to the involvement of young black people in crime. On the other hand by persisting in a particularly myopic view of 'social reaction', by failing to trace it back to its roots, by divorcing it from the state, it offers only a partial and limited possibility of understanding the tortuous confrontation between the state and its control apparatus and young black people.

I shall now consider why black young people appear to be treated more harshly than their white counterparts when they break the law or are suspected of breaking the law. In such a discussion the following questions usually emerge.

1. Are the offences young black people commit different and more serious?

2. Are they processed differently by the police and welfare agencies in the juvenile criminal justice system?

3. Are the backgrounds of young black people different and is their understanding of the significance of their offending different from that of their white counterparts?

4. Are young black people subject to higher levels of incarceration than whites?

Are the offences young black people commit different and more serious?

If it were true that young black people simply committed a greater volume of more serious offences than whites, then the question of their apparently harsher treatment in the juvenile criminal justice system could be easily resolved for we could explain it as a normal response to abnormal behaviour. But the problem is not so simple.

This particular issue characteristically has the protagonists of the right arguing that young black people are making the streets unsafe for the (white) law-abiding citizen while the defenders of young black people cite the abuse of the law of 'sus' now transmogrified into 'criminal attempts' as the mechanism whereby black youth are made the subjects of false attributions of criminality. The problem with this debate is that it is no debate at all and has the contenders standing, as it were, back to back arguing about different things to quite separate audiences who already agree with them anyway. Given the high levels of arrests of black young people for both 'street crime' and 'criminal attempts' it becomes important to try to move beyond rhetoric.

Stevens and Willis (1979) have argued that the apparent over-representation of young black people in the criminal statistics may be accounted for in large part by the age structure of Britain's black population. In central Lambeth in 1978, for example, 40 percent of the secondary school population was black, while the Runnymede Trust notes that in 1971 90 percent of black Britons were aged less than fifteen years. Thus when we consider the heavy over-repesentation of young black people in the crime-prone age group fifteen to twenty-five who are moreover located overwhelmingly in a crime-prone social class and are required to live in traditionally low-income crime-prone areas we might, Stevens and Willis imply, gain some solace from the fact that the phenomenon of black youth crime, which we confront, is almost normal. Indeed Stevens and Willis are at pains to stress its normality:

in London for instance, Camden and Tower Hamlets, with low proportions of West Indians had higher recorded crime rates than Lambeth and Hackney with high proportions of West Indians. . . The analysis shows that the presence of West Indians or Asians in a community is irrelevant to recorded indictable crime rates (Stevens and Willis, 1979:40).

On the issue of age group and social class they conclude that:

the differences between White, Black and Asian arrest rates have therefore been largely, but not wholly, statistically accounted for by demographic and socio-economic characteristics (Stevens and Willis, 1979:41).

Beneath this surface of (almost) statistical normality, however, lurk some nagging social doubts. Lambert (1970) has noted the tendency for levels of crime amongst immigrant groups to rise over a period to crime levels already pertaining in the neighbourhoods in which they settle. As we know, Afro-Caribbean settlers in this country have of necessity settled in the most impoverished areas of the inner city and thus a rising generation of young black people has been placed at risk of levels of offending far in excess of those of their remarkably law-abiding parents. Clearly this finding must alert us to the contribution of racially discriminatory policies of housing zoning to the production of future delinquency. The statistical normality of which Stevens and Willis write does not take account of the fact that for reasons which will be explained later, crimes committed against black people tend to be substantially under-reported. Furthermore, evidence suggests that black citizens are very likely to be the victims of crime perpetrated by black offenders.

Mugging
In the media and in much popular discussion the problem of street crime has come to be viewed as synonymous with the problem of black youth crime. In London, perhaps inevitably this has led to a concentration upon what happens in Lambeth. In looking at Lambeth we see, for example, that while in 1979 Lambeth supplied 15 percent of all reported robberies and thefts in the metropolis it constituted only 4 percent of the population. This might be accounted for by the fact that Lambeth has a high proportion of young people in the crime-prone age group. Indeed 75 percent of those arrested in that year fell into the 10–20 year-old age group (see Pitts and Robinson, 1981). All commentators agree with Stevens and Willis that coloured assailants are disproportionately involved in assault, robbery and other violent theft but as they suggest, the heaviest concentration of 'coloured assailants' was in the least serious offences in this category (Stevens and Willis, 1979). This highlights the contentious nature of the offences which are broadly termed muggings or street crime since they cover anything from purse snatching or pickpocketing to serious assaults

followed by robbery. As Pratt (1980) has argued and Scarman (1982) accepted, while street crime is a reality it tends to be comprised of offences committed frequently by small numbers of young people in the 12–18 age group and as such should point to an outcome in which a small number of defendants would, if apprehended, be sentenced for a large number of offences and as such would not serve to swell the penal population in any significant way. Black young people in the juvenile criminal justice system are not treated harshly because they are 'muggers' though perpetrators of street crime are usually treated harshly when apprehended (cf Hall et al., 1978).

But 'mugging' as Hall et al. (1978) have argued, has a significance beyond its immediate impact. The 'mugger', they argue, emerges as a folk devil, as the manifestation of all that is unsafe in the world, as the object of social anxiety.

On Wednesday 10 March 1982 Assistant Commissioner Gilbert Kelland of Scotland Yard in revealing the crime statistics for the metropolis spoke of 'the violent year of 1981' and was at pains to identify the contribution made to the mounting level of crime by young black people. The statistics and the manner of their presentation was not a little contentious. The *Daily Express* readily grasped the point:

> Publication of these grim statistics will certainly lead to renewed demands for a fresh look at the consequences of Lord Scarman's report on last year's Brixton riots (*Daily Express*, 11 March 1982).

The publication of the 'black crime statistics' was generally regarded as a rejoinder to Lord Scarman and as a vindication of Swamp 81, the police operation which had triggered the Brixton disturbances in the previous year (see Hall, 1982). Here we had the 'black crime statistics' being used as a central prop in a political power play. Mr Jim Jardine, the erstwhile chairman of the Police Federation, in a similar vein blamed rising crime upon the official reaction to the riots suggesting that 'they' (young black people) were laughing at the law. A few days later the Police Federation launched an extensive and expensive media campaign which anticipated the imminent free vote in the House of Commons on the return of capital punishment. The half-page advertisement read:

> Today there is widespread public concern over the sharp increase in violent crime. The Metropolitan Police announced last week that robberies in Greater London increased last year by 48 percent. Firearms were carried in 1,415 cases compared with 767 in the previous year. Other large cities are reporting similar increases in violent criminal offences. Last year for the first time, more than 100,000 violent crimes occurred in England and Wales (Jardine, 1982).

The advertisement implies that the alarming increase in the use of firearms was in some way connected with the purported increase in street crime. Assistant Commissioner Kelland had bemoaned the doubling of offences in which firearms were used and also stated that robberies of shops, post offices and banks had increased by 83 percent in the previous year. In fact, in only one in four cases were victims of street crimes threatened with a weapon and in no case was it reported that the weapon had been a firearm. Nonetheless it was street crime committed by young black people which was the major focus of Mr Kelland's presentation since, as he said, 'Beyond all doubt the crime causing most concern and disquiet is robbery and other violent theft.' He noted that of those 18,763 'robberies', 10,399 were committed by coloured assailants, 4,967 by whites, 704 by groups of all races and 2,693 by those whose colour had not been identified by victims (Davis, 1982b).

These statistics posed considerable problems since they conflated purse snatching with serious assaults. They were based upon reports made by victims and recorded by the police raising queries about the perceptions of a frightened victim and the police interpretation of that perception. They are also a record of offences and not offenders, and as we have already noted one offender may well be responsible for many offences. In presenting his data Mr Kelland acknowledged in his interview that 'statistics are difficult' but Gareth Pierce replied that the real message of the figures was that:

> 'muggings' were not the figure of 19,000 quoted last week by Scotland Yard but instead under 6,000; that the victims were never for the most part elderly and white, but in the main between the ages of 21 and 30 and on Home Office statistics 36 to 50 percent more likely to be West Indian or Asian; that the percentage of alleged perpetrators crudely classified as black was derived from a questionable categorization that included many different ethnic groups (Pierce, 1982).

'Sus' criminal attempts

Landau notes that 90 percent of charges for being a suspected person were made in Area 1 South London (Lambeth). His study was conducted in four inner London and two outer London boroughs. Other data suggests that Area 1 Lambeth is second only to Toxteth in Liverpool in terms of the numbers of 'sus' charges made. The new charge of 'criminal attempts' has given greater potency to a police intervention which has long been a source of conflict between the black community and the police. Demuth writes:

> Sus cases fall into two distinct categories — tampering with car door handles and loitering with intent to steal from handbags. Of the cases examined defendants in the first category came from a wide variety of backgrounds; some of them pleaded guilty. In some cases the informant was a member of the public, although in the majority it was the police.
> In the second category most of the defendants were black. They were picked up in certain streets and underground stations particularly in the West End, and very few of them pleaded guilty. The informants in all cases were the police,

usually in plain clothes, and the evidence in each case was in format, if not in points of detail, identical (Demuth, 1978:53).

Appearances at Balham Juvenile Court in 1979 clearly demonstrate the substantial over-representation of black young people charged with 'sus'.

Defendants	White	Black
Attempted theft	54	26
Burglary	80	14
'Sus'	11	89

Source: Pitts and Robinson (1981:7).

Stevens and Willis (1979) note that the chances of young black people being arrested for the offence of 'other violent theft' and 'being a suspected person' were 14 and 15 times (respectively) the chances of a white young person. In a masterpiece of Home Office caution they write:

> These ratios are so much higher than might be expected that they give rise to the question whether arrest rates are accurate indicators of relative white and black involvement in crime and if not whether some of the difference may be accounted for by the possibility that suspicions of policemen bear dispropor-tionately on blacks (Stevens and Willis, 1979:33).

Yet as Lea and Young contend, if such an over-representation were merely a construction or fabrication born of police prejudice why should it be that young black people are under-represented in other categories of crime. We are left with the possibility that the statistical over-representation of young black people in street crime and criminal attempts may well represent an actual over-representation but one which is not however as great as the statistics imply because these young people are subjected to more intensive levels of surveillance and are demonstrably the subjects of false attributions of criminality by the police.

Are they processed differently by the police and welfare agencies in the juvenile criminal justice system?

Sivanandan has argued that: 'Black youths could not walk the streets outside the Ghetto or hang around the streets within it without courting arrest' (Sivanandan, 1982:108). He goes on to note that in 1975 in response to anxieties about street crime the Metropolitan Police Special Patrol Group moved into Lewisham and stopped and interrogated 14,000 people on the streets. At the time a young black man gave his account of the experience:

> To drive a car anytime in Lewisham or New Cross is a big joke, you might as

well walk, and when you do that you might as well stay inside, and me no 'fraid of the wicked. I driving through Lewisham to New Cross and get stopped three times, the whole place full with road blocks, transit vans, police cars, the lot — curfew in this town (CIS, 1976:10).

As Lea and Young (1984) have pointed out, the issue of street crime and offences which arise out of confrontations with police on the streets are related. They argue that while the dimensions of street crime may be exaggerated or distorted by the media it is nonetheless a reality and as such is a source of great anxiety to the police and the public. Street crime is extremely difficult to police in that it happens quickly and sometimes, as in the case of purse-snatching, unbeknown to the victim. As an opportunistic crime related to an immediate need for cash it is unpredictable. A response developed by the police has taken the form of successive 'sweeps' of neighbourhoods in which these offences occur by large numbers of plain-clothes and uniformed police officers whose job it is to identify, stop, and search people who look like 'muggers'. Lea and Young quote from an instruction document issued to police officers prior to the operation Swamp 81 in Brixton:

> The purpose of this operation is to flood identified areas on L district, to detect and arrest burglars and robbers. The essence of the exercise is therefore to ensure that all officers remain on the streets and success will depend on a concentrated effort. . . based on powers of surveillance and suspicion proceeded by persistent and astute questioning (quoted from Lea and Young, 1982:63).

From Friday 3 April to Friday 10 April, 1,000 stop and searches were conducted by the police. These yielded 100 arrests. None of those arrested was charged with burglary or robbery but some people were charged with possession of marijuana, insulting behaviour, and carrying an 'offensive weapon'.

These sweeps and the more routing procedure of moving-on or stopping and searching groups of young black people have served to heighten antagonisms between the police and the black community, since policing of this type tends to identify large numbers of black people who have no involvement in crime. Such policing also generates its own crime.

Figures collected by probation officers in the Midlands indicate that the second highest category of offences for which young black people are charged arise out of confrontations with the police on the streets. These offences would include criminal attempts, assaults on the police, public order offences, and insulting behaviour. In short, these offences had not occurred until after the police arrived.

'Criminal attempts', as stated above, offers the police a more flexible instrument with which to contain crime than the 1824 Vagrancy Act. The 'sus' controversy concerned the use of the law as a means of harrassing black young people but 'sus'/criminal attempts has other consequences.

In Lambeth for example a young person charged with 'sus' would seldom if ever, as a matter of local practice, be offered the opportunity of being referred to the juvenile bureau who, if the charge is admitted, are empowered to issue a caution. Young people charged with 'sus' were normally charged immediately as a matter of course which meant that they had to appear in court. In court the complainant and the witnesses were almost invariably the police. Upon conviction the young person's name would be added to the 'recidivists' list, which meant that if at some future date he or she was apprehended, for whatever charge, no referral to the juvenile bureau could be made and the young person would be charged immediately. This has the effect of projecting those young people so charged deeper into the juvenile criminal justice system and further up the tariff of penalties.

Landau's study (1981) already cited above, noted that 'sus' was the offence for which there was the greatest difference between races. He noted that black young people were up to 50 percent more likely to be referred to the juvenile bureau for this offence than their white counterparts. While it might be argued that this discrepancy may be accounted for by the fact that black youngsters so charged had a larger record of previous offences, Landau shows that black first offenders were subject to an immediate charge decision significantly more than whites. He also noted that the police tended to see black young people as more antagonistic to them than whites and suggests on the evidence of the studies of Piliavin and Briar (1968) and Cicourel, (1976) that this may be a significant factor in the decision whether to charge immediately or refer to the juvenile bureau. In conclusion he writes:

> As to ethnic group, the main finding was that blacks involved in crimes of violence, burglary, and public disorder are treated more harshly than their white counterparts (Landau, 1981:44).

What is suggested here is that young black people are subject to higher levels of policing, that such policing will generate further offences, and that upon apprehension young black people are less likely to be diverted out of the mainstream of the system to the juvenile bureau.

It is usually at the point of the court appearance that the young black defendant will first encounter a social worker or probation officer. Here a difference between white and black defendants appears for there is growing evidence that a majority of young black people who become involved in the juvenile welfare criminal justice system do so at a later stage than their white counterparts. Whereas many white juvenile defendants and their families may have been known to welfare agencies for many years, the involvement of young black people tends to start around the age of fourteen or fifteen. Put another way — a distinctive feature of the criminal careers of many young black people is that they are not characterized by prior involvement with welfare agencies concerned with other social or family problems. They are not in the main drawn from families who have previously been a cause of concern to welfare agencies. Observations of young black people in penal establishments tend to support this in that they have a broader spread of academic abilities and tend in many ways to be more socially and academically able than their white counterparts. They are also much more likely to be drawn from 'respectable' rather than 'disreputable' families. [1]

What we are not seeing here is the apparently inexorable unfolding of a criminal and institutional career which may be traced back, sometimes over generations, but rather a rupture, a departure, from a previously conventional mode of existence by a group of young people, many of whom had until shortly before their first court appearance been successful conforming schoolgirls and schoolboys. These observations steer us back towards issues of differential policing of blacks and whites on the one hand and the question of differential access to legitimate opportunity on the other.

This said, where social welfare agencies intervene with younger black children in trouble, these children will tend to be made the subjects of care orders (i.e. an order which allows the local authority parental rights and the power to place the child in a community home with education (the erstwhile approved school) at an earlier age than their white counterparts. This tendency has fuelled the controversy about the tendency of white social workers to act pre-emptively in their dealings with black families. Black protagonists in this controversy argue that because of their failure to understand Afro-Caribbean child-rearing patterns and their misinterpretation of parents' responses to the child's offending white social workers will resolve their anxiety by the removal of parental rights. Whatever the rights and wrongs of these situations it remains the case that the imposition of a care order, particularly upon a child, will have some serious effects if that child continues to appear in court.

Wendy Taylor (1982) has shown that in the Crown Court black defendants are two to three times more likely to receive a custodial sentence than whites. These custodial sentences have very little to do with the nature of the offence but correlate most closely with whether the defendant is homeless, jobless, or was previously the subject of a care order. As will be shown later, young black people experience extremely high levels of homelessness, they are much more likely than whites to be unemployed and their predicament is seriously worsened if they have previously been the subject of a care order. This inequitable sentencing is not merely reducible to the racial prejudice of those meting out the sentences since offenders, black and white, appearing before a court with no visible means of support and no fixed abode have traditionally been much more vulnerable to custodial sentences. The problem is more serious than this however because these defendants are victims of structural inequalities which affect the black population in general but Afro-Caribbean young people in particular. It seems that these young people are being sentenced three times over; firstly for their offence, over which they have some control; secondly for a set of social, economic and cultural circumstances which have dramatically limited their options and over which they have no control; and thirdly because there exist few, if any, legitimate means whereby they might escape from these circumstances (see Taylor, 1981).

What this study also showed was that black offenders were substantially less likely to be offered the option of probation than whites. Indeed most black offenders made their first contact with probation officers while serving detention centre (DC) or borstal sentences. This contact was statutorily necessary since the probation service is responsible for supervising the post release DC or borstal licence. Thus the question was raised as to why young black offenders were not being offered probation as a non-custodial alternative. There are clearly three possibilities; either the magistrate or the judge did not remand prisoners for probation reports; the remand was made but the probation officer did not recommend probation; or probation was recommended and the offenders decided not to avail themselves of the option.

As a response to this situation the Handsworth Project was established. This project aimed to support the courts and the probation service in order that they might begin to use the probation order as a non-custodial alternative for black offenders, those offenders who by dint of their social circumstances were being condemned to custody. The project offered help with homelessness and employment and ran a literacy project. Project workers attended court and worked closely with probation officers in order that they were aware that this support existed and would therefore be encouraged to recommend and offer the option of probation. The first year of the project revealed some perplexing results. Probation orders for black offenders increased by over 100 percent but this was paralleled by a decrease in other non-custodial sentences — fines, bind-overs and discharges. More alarmingly there was also a substantial increase in custodial sentences given to black defendants. In the second year of the project's operation the same tendency to increase custodial sentencing of young black people has continued. The behaviour of probation officers has changed, so has that of the magistrates and judges but in the latter case the change has been paradoxical. What we do not know yet is whether the increase in the use of probation means that offenders who would previously have been subject to lesser non-custodial sentences are now being made subject to the more serious probation order thus pushing them closer to the gates of the prison if they are apprehended for further offences. Here we may be witnessing another sad example of an initiative which attempts to influence the functioning of the justice system being confounded by the apparently profligate and unfettered behaviour of the bench and the judiciary. Unfortunately the situation is likely to worsen since the 1982 Criminal Justice Act handed new powers to the magistrates to make a Youth Custody sentence of up to a year. This resulted, in the first year of its operation, in the numbers of young people subject to these or analogous sentences increasing by 67 percent (Dean, 1982). Given that we are unable to establish significant correlations between levels of recorded crime and the use of custody but that the correlation between custody and levels of unemployment is a remarkably close one, we might reluctantly conclude that by increasing the magistrates' power to imprison we will increase the likelihood of black offenders entering those prisons.

Even prior to the enactment of the 1982 Criminal Justice Act the black subjects of the magistrates' courts were wary of it. In an article Wendy Taylor (1982) noted that whereas only 11 percent of white young people charged with indictable offences opted for trial by jury in a crown court, 43 percent of black young people did. They claimed that the magistrates' courts were 'police courts' and there you only get 'white man's justice'.

A sentencing survey undertaken recently suggests that 'white' 'black' and 'other' defendants appear to be treated equally by the courts. The survey points to higher levels of unemployment amongst the black group but does not tell us if unemployment has, as other research has suggested, had a bearing upon sentencing. It notes:

> In only a third of cases in the black group is the offence known to have resulted in any loss in terms of the value of goods stolen or damage caused compared to nearly half the cases in the other two groups (Cave and Crow, 1984:416).

It also notes that the black group was twice as likely (12 percent against 6 percent) to have been convicted of drug offences. Interestingly, in this survey, only 8 percent of black defendants had been charged with robbery as against 14 percent for the other groups. We are not told, but we may ask on the basis of this data, whether in fact a higher proportion of black defendants were in court for public order offences; offences which often occur after the police have arrived.

The big question left hanging by this survey is why, if the findings are representative, are penal establishments for young offenders filling up with black young people. The overall trend for incarceration to follow levels of unemployment is clearly a complex one. However, the survey has not explored this possibility (see Taylor, 1981 and Box and Hale, 1985 in this volume).

The Handsworth experience raises the question of whether young black people in trouble are offered alternatives to custody in the same way, and with the same frequency as whites. In 1982 an investigation was undertaken into the ways in which intermediate treatment projects in an area of London with a high ethnic minority population was responding to the needs and the predicament of young black people in trouble (West London Institute of Higher Education, 1982). What became immediately evident was that although arrest rates for black youngsters were quite high very few were finding their way through the system to intermediate treatment (IT). The two Afro-Caribbean boys who were at one centre had already spent a period in a detention centre whereas the white young people, by contrast, were there largely as an alternative to the detention centre or the community home with education (CHE) Intermediate treatment workers interviewed said that the referring agents — social workers, probation officers, education welfare officers, and the police, seemed reluctant to refer young black people and as a result a disproportionate number were finding their way into custody. They also ventured the opinion that many welfare workers seemed to assume that because of the influence of strict Afro-Caribbean child-rearing patterns, black youngsters would understand the detention centre in a way that they would not understand the more relaxed and 'person-centred' regime of IT. If this was in fact the process at work, then the possibility emerges that stereotypical, indeed caricatured, perceptions of a culture may seriously worsen the black young person's chance of being diverted from custody. We shall return to this stereotype later.

The investigation also showed that, with some honourable exceptions, projects which offer alternatives to care and custody have often failed to attract a black clientele. The major pressure for places at community homes (with education) is from social workers attempting to place young black people who are made the subjects of care orders as a result of their offending. We also know that many of these institutions operate a racial quota system which attempts to prevent the proportion of black residents rising above 20 percent. The quota system is, it is argued, necessitated by the problems of management posed by Afro-Caribbean young people when they are together in substantial numbers. This parallels exactly the complaints of the police, prison officers, and to a somewhat lesser extent field social workers and probation officers; 'they band together'; 'they speak their own language'; 'they intimidate other residents or members or prisoners'; 'they are insolent to staff' (see WLIHE, 1982). Yet this is not a universal experience and while this is not the place to examine institutional dynamics we know enough to know that when people feel threatened, devalued or misunderstood in institutional or group settings, they will often develop collective defences around what is known and what is shared. In such circumstances what is individual, special, and unique about people becomes subordinated and this is as true of those in positions of authority as it is of their subjects.

The quota system has created a log-jam of young black people in remand, observation and assessment centres, the institutions which assess young people for placement in community homes (with education). Indeed

Stamford House, a major London remand and assessment centre for young offenders currently holds a black population of approximately 60 percent. [1] the economics of child care has led many local authorities in recent years to develop community alternatives to residential care because of the crippling costs involved. Ironically this pressure and the inability of the CHE system to absorb these young black people may yet give the impetus to local authorities to address their disproportionate institutional confinement and search for alternatives in the community. This will however involve a major intervention with professionals and administrators who at present seem reluctant to find or create suitable resources for young black offenders in the community.

Are the backgrounds of young black people different and is their understanding of the significance of their offending different from that of their white counterparts?

It is often assumed and sometimes asserted that Afro-Caribbean young people face peculiar problems in relation to their families and their schools. Indeed, this is an operational fairy tale, plausible in detail, dubious in its entirety which has in my view informed a great deal of intervention in the lives of black young people over the past fifteen years. In essence it asserts that:

> The Afro-Caribbean child is born into a family which offers clear and rigorous injunctions about propriety and authority resembling in some measure Durkheim's state of mechanical solidarity. This stands in marked contrast with the more relaxed and relativistic moral ethic of the school and the home of the white indigenous child whom, it is implied, has made the leap to a state of organic solidarity. The Afro-Caribbean child will therefore experience confusion, we might say anomie, at school since whereas the home experience of social relations of the white child is congruent with the relationships he or she maintains with the staff, the Afro-Caribbean child experiences a disjunction. This problem is compounded by the tendency of some Afro-Caribbean families to leave children in the West Indies with relations until they are 'on their feet'. Thus culture shock, emotional stress, and anomie all conspire to lead the Afro-Caribbean child to infringe rules and to become embroiled in family conflict at adolescence. Afro-Caribbean families will often respond to this situation in a punitive way sometimes expelling the child from the house. In Britain unlike the West Indies these young people are not picked up by the extended family but are instead projected into a growing deviant street culture made up of young people experiencing similar problems. This subculture offers identity for those suffering from anomie and illegitimate opportunity structures to those who have no legitimate opportunity.

This view is seldom articulated, although Roy Kerridge's article *How Many Lies to Babylon* (1983) comes close, and yet it seems often to act as the meta-theory or ideological backdrop for much research and social intervention. While it has absurd features, hardly any black teenagers today started life in the West Indies, and few white working class school age adolescents in inner-city schools experience the schools as a benign and welcoming institution; this account does weave together certain realities (see Willis, 1977).

It is, for example, the case that young black people have serious problems of homelessness and that some of them have been thrown out by parents. Without wishing to perpetuate an unhelpful stereotype it is important to recognize that, for example, in 1981 in the area between Brixton and Lewisham a local authority survey estimated that 300 young black people were sleeping rough or squatting in derelict houses. One west London homeless young people's hostel reports that it currently deals with up to 40 percent of young black people from this area while south London hostels have even higher proportions. [1] It should be noted however that many of them are homeless as a result of having to leave local authority care. A survey of homelessness amongst young black people in Moss Side produced similarly alarming results. Of the clients dealt with by the Handsworth Alternative Scheme, a scheme for black young offenders, most had housing problems and many were actually homeless. What is missing from the usual accounts of expulsions from home or homelessness amongst black young people is any reference to the housing conditions in which their families actually live. Afro-Caribbean families in Lambeth occupy the most crowded accommodation and as such these families must cope with the combined stresses of unemployment, low pay, substandard housing and social amenities.

In such circumstances conflict between family members will disturb everybody's peace of mind and create pressure to expel the deviant member. It should be noted that unemployment which is particularly high amongst young black people will fuel such conflict. The persistent presence of a bored and frustrated adolescent in an overcrowded home who is forced into a state of financial dependency upon his or her poorly paid parents is hardly a recipe for family harmony. If we set this against the picture of homelessness amongst young people in general, irrespective of race, we must recognize that it is precisely these circumstances which lead to family conflict with consequent homelessness for its adolescent members. Homelessness has important consequences for young people. As a homeless person it is all but impossible to claim supplementary benefit. Beyond this, employers, even if they have jobs to offer, are unwilling to offer them to young people who have no permanent address. As we have seen from Wendy Taylor's work (1981:1982) cited above, within the juvenile justice system homelessness and unemployment, which affect young black people disproportionately, has even more serious consequences.

The lack of a home and a job clearly affects sentencing but to what extent can high levels of homelessness and unemployment explain the development of black street culture?

The emergence of a street culture amongst black young people has given rise to a heated debate which has thus far suffered from a lack of precision on all sides. The problem of identifying this culture has dogged the debate with the right seeing it as a source of crime and ignoring the fact that street cultures are not necessarily organized around a focal concern with crime, and that even if they were young people would participate in them in different ways and with different levels of commitment to such core values (see Hebdige, 1975). Some will affect only a style of dress and speech, while others may, as Pratt (1980), suggests be heavily involved in crime. Paul Gilroy (1982) correctly castigates commentators like Brown (1977) who weave together family breakdown, homelessness and Rastafarianism as components of, or factors militating towards the construction of a criminal subculture. It remains the case that where such street cultures exist they may well recruit from a growing band of homeless black young people. It may, as Hebdige (1979) suggests, to be a culture constructed out of imported reggae records but its main task is to develop meanings and explanations of the predicament of its adherents. As such it acts as a vehicle for the construction of an identity for a group of young Britons who have been offered few materials with which to construct a positive identity for themselves which is different from that of a deferential parental generation and a white society with which they no longer wish to identify. Street culture is then more than a simple anti-social reaction to inappropriate parenting or schooling for it is a milieu in which contemporary problems of discrimination and inequality are explored and given meaning. Something does happen at school which predisposes young people to an affiliation with this culture. At school the Barbadian child, the Bangladeshi child and the Ghanaian child come to see both the myth of white racial superiority and the fact that what unites them is that they are not white, that they are defined negatively by their blackness. It is no surprise then that in adolescence they unite to turn the pejorative label 'black' into a property or quality to be asserted, celebrated and elaborated. The street culture is a place, one of the few places, where they can do this, Black protagonists in the debate about black youth subcultures have tended for strategic reasons to stress that these subcultures are not subversive and do not merit the suspicion of the police and the white establishment. What we confront, they assert, is just a manifestation of difference, an innocuous style. While recognizing that much suspicion may be ill-founded and exaggerated we should also accept that these groupings are actively subversive to meanings and attributions placed upon them and they are actively engaged in an attempt to redefine themselves and their situation. This process may however, as some commentators have suggested, lead to active norm violation and crime. Dodd observes:

The welfare state is seen on the street as another means of keeping blacks helpless and dependent. It leaves nothing to risk and provides no structure for action — except in designing schemes to manipulate it advantageously. It is just another white man's game for which the black man must, as always, invent his own response. The problem is how to construct a serious identity outside the roles that are offered — a problem of meaning as well as survival. Well, there is meaning in ganja and there is meaning in crime. For increasing numbers of black youth in Great Britain those are the only real options — listen to Junior, 'police and thieves' is the biggest game in town (Dodd, 1978:25).

Here Dodd argues, and it is not clear upon what basis, that black young people are constrained by circumstances to search for meaning in crime. It is as if a process of drift occurs in which encircled by a hostile world black young people are constrained to adopt illegitimate means to assert an identity. Lea and Young (1982) have pointed out the process whereby the policing of the black community serves to blur the distinction between resistance and assertion and criminal activity. 'High profile' policing, they suggest, tends to antagonize large numbers of people who have no involvement in crime whatsoever and so they grow resentful of the suspicion and surveillance of the police and the indignity of the stop and search. Thus the public, in this case the black public, become disinclined to furnish the police with information about law breaking which leads to the substantial under-reporting of crime by the black community referred to above. In these circumstances the police intensify their military-style activity since they have less and less access to information which would allow them to police black neighbourhoods in a conventional manner (see Dodd, 1978). By creating an ambivalent or hostile response to the police amongst a black public the legitimacy of the police is called into question and the belief that the police are acting as an arbitrary oppressive and racist force becomes more deeply entrenched. This has a number of consequences. Writing in 1979 Pryce was at pains to distinguish between the quite distinct adaptations to the 'internal colonization' of Afro-Caribbean people in the UK. He presents 'the expressive disreputable orientation' and 'the stable law-abiding orientation', two groups: the former with a fierce commitment to criminality and resistance, the latter locked into a pattern of over-conformity. Pryce presents these adaptations as caricatures, a kind of subcultural id and superego. He writes:

The perspective of the expressive disreputable orientation stands in radical contrast to that of the stable law-abiding orientation. The expressive-disreputable orientation differs essentially from the behaviour of stable law-abiders in that it is the most uncompromising of the postures that has developed in the West Indian community in response to the crisis of late capitalism in Britain and the wage slavery of blacks in the labour process. In particular, the orientation is wageless, being fundamentally antagonistic to 'slave labour', and adherents of the life-styles on which the orientation is based have consciously chosen the criminal path of survival as an expression of their contempt for the system that 'puts them down' (Pryce, 1979:276).

What Dodd, and by implication, Lea and Young, suggest is that such radical differentiation, if it existed, is being broken down in the face of saturation policing since this has served as a unifying force. Crime, conformity and resistance become blurred for the older and younger generation alike and this blurring loosens the moral bind and eases the transition from a conventional to a deviant mode for some young black people faced with problems of identity survival and status frustration. Crime then assumes the character of a struggle against the concrete manifestations of oppression — the police.

Piven and Cloward have noted that:

> sometimes however the events that create disorder are accompanied by a repudiation of the rules. Disorder is then likely to spread and worsen for the disorderly act comes to be defined as morally proper, as the appropriate response of a victimized group to their victims. Thievery is one way of surviving but it may sometimes come to be justified on the ground that whites have always stolen from blacks so reparations are due (Piven and Cloward, 1972:P228/9).

Lea and Young have argued that what we encounter is not crime 'politicized' into resistance but an emergent culture of poverty created from multiple deprivations. Gilroy (1983) by contrast sees in the activities of black young offenders the expression of a culture of resistance which is both intact and developing, passed down from the time of slavery and representing a clear and conscious expression of resistance by working class black youth to imperialism.

Pratt (1980) however finds no solidarity or meaning here, explaining black street crime with reference to Downes' *Delinquent Solution* (1966) as the individual pursuit of excitement rather as Baden-Powell once did. Indeed Pratt's solution resembles that of Baden-Powell in that it involves individual black offenders being provided with the wherewithal to engage in sport. One is left with the suspicion that he is advocating a pre-verbal activity for a pre-social being. His solution is both demeaning and romantic with more than a shade of the tough ethnic minority kid boxing his way out of the ghetto to fame and fortune.

While the foregoing accounts stress the ways in which the contemporary predicament of black young people propels some of them towards crime in general and violent street crime in particular, Cashmore and Troyna argue that black street crime is both widespread:

> We accept that the hustling street crime type of existence is commonplace amongst black youth and this type of activity is attracting recruits as regularly as young blacks drop out of school, and that is regularly

and culturally pre-determined:

> There is a penchant for violence within the West Indian culture, possibly stemming from the days of slavery when the only method of retaliation was doing physical damage to the overseer agent or even a slave master (Cashmore and Troyna 1982:32–3).

Have they not heard of Luddism, football hooliganism, the Indian mutiny and the regular massive gang fights in Dalston between the Jewish gangs and the Italian gangs, we must ask? Pearson's lively and perceptive study of the history of disorder and violence amongst white working class young people in the UK (Pearson, 1976) gives us far more evidence than Cashmore and Troyna deploy to argue, if we should be so hasty, that 'there is a penchant for violence within the white British working class'. They cite the 'almost incredible enthusiasm of black youth for movies in the Kung Fu idiom' as evidence of this penchant for violence. One wonders how they would explain the fact that the present author has now watched *The Magnificent Seven* and *Butch Cassidy and the Sundance Kid* nine and five times respectively! More seriously their account does not square with facts. Even allowing for the dark figure of unreported crime perpetrated by black young people the fact is that most of them simply don't do it. In a letter to his father from prison, George Jackson offers a more balanced and more comprehensible view of the predicament of working class black people.

> You know our people react in different ways to this neoslavery. Some just give up completely and join the other side. They join some Christian cult and cry out for integration. These are the ones who doubt themselves most. They are the weakest and hardest to reach with the new doctrine. Some become inveterate drinkers and narcotic users in an attempt to gain some mental solace for the physical deprivation they suffer. I've heard them say 'there's no hope without dope', some live on as janitor, bellboy, redcap, cook, elevator boy, singer, boxer, baseball player or maybe freak at some sideshow and pretend that all is as well as possible. They think since it's always been this way it must always remain this way, these are fatalists; they serve and entertain and rationalize.
>
> Then there are those who resist and rebel but do not know what, who, why or how exactly they should go about this. They are aware but confused. They are the least fortunate because they end where I have ended. By using half-measures and failing dismally to effect any real improvement in their condition they fall victim to the full fury and might of the system's repressive agencies (Jackson, 1971:70–71).

Are young black people subject to higher levels of incarceration than whites?

In England and Wales this 'full fury and might of the system's repressive agencies' is expressed through imprisonment.

We have already noted the massive over-representation of young black people (up to 60 percent) in remand and assessment centres and the pressures upon CHE's to take greater numbers. When we look at those parts of the juvenile criminal justice system administered by the prison department of the Home Office, we find a similar pattern emerging. Martin Kettle (1982) notes that an assistant governor at Wandsworth jail monitored the daily intake to that prison by colour and discovered that 23 percent of the intake was black. Of the broader picture he writes:

> In April this year according to the Home Office 50 percent of the population of Ashford remand centre was black. Brixton (another remand prison) and Aylesbury prisons were between 25 percent and 35 percent black. So were Rochester, Dover, and Hewell Grange borstals and Blantyre House detention centre. Others with more than 10 percent black inmates were Wormwood Scrubs, Parkhurst, Albany, Wandsworth and Reading prisons and Wellingborough, Bullwood Hall and Feltham borstals (Kettle, 1982:535).

What we note then is that as we move down the age range so the proportion of young black inmates confined in custodial or child-care institutions increases. As Radical Alternatives to Prison argued recently, while the overall black prison population was 20 percent, in young prisoners' wings this rose to 37 percent and as Kettle (1982) has noted in some borstals (now youth custody centres) the figure is as high as 50 percent. When we recognize that the proportion of black people in the population of the United Kingdom is only 3 to 4 percent we realize the seriousness of the problem.

This is stark enough but we have to recognize an additional trend which is that the fastest growing section of the penal population is in the fifteen to twenty-five age group. Indeed the Young Offenders White Paper 1980 and the subsequent 1982 Criminal Justice Act was in large part a response to this fact and its apparent commitment to the development of community alternatives to prison is explicable in that the 'crisis in prison' is nowhere more acute than in the institutions for this age group. If we recognize that young black people will over the next few years constitute an ever-increasing proportion of this population we must argue that a very significant component in the crisis in the prisons is the increasing confinement of young black people. Beyond the bald statistics however we must also ask what we are doing to a generation of black British young people. On 1 November 1981 the TV programme 'Skin' televised a feature on young black people in borstal. It was suggested in this programme that if current trends continued then by 1991 50 percent of all black males under twentyfive would have spent some time behind bars.

**Being young and black and in
trouble with the law**
What does seem evident from the little we do know about the social predicament of young black people who break, or are suspected of breaking the law, is that like their conforming contemporaries they face formidable barriers in their attempts to make their own way in the world.

The disadvantages they confront are cumulative, and when they fall foul of the juvenile criminal justice system these cumulative disadvantages appear to accelerate their progress towards the correctional institution or the prison. This is not to argue that what happens to young black people is totally distinct or different from what happens to whites but it does have distinctive features.

Firstly, there is a quantitive difference. A larger proportion of young black people are involved with the apparatus of crime control than their white counterparts. Secondly, young black people bring to this encounter an experience of what being black in a white society means. Once again they confront a bureaucracy in which the power and control rests in the hands of whites and where the subjects of this power and control are black. This I would contend has resonances for them of other experiences, usually experiences of failure and the equation of 'white = power' is not lost upon the unwilling victims of the system. In my own experience of working with young people in a borstal institution it was the white inmates who were able to say stoically 'you did the crime now do the time' while for many of the young black people the relationship between crime and punishment was more complex and often involved the additional dimensions of a critique of predatory policing of a hostile or indifferent social welfare apparatus and a racially prejudiced judge. I would argue then that the necessary truce which exists between the apparatus of control and its subjects is more tenuous in the case of its black subjects. The collective understanding of these young people is a different, more critical and potentially more antagonistic one. The quantitative change in sheer numbers of young black people passing through the system seems to have yielded a qualitative change in the ways in which this progression is understood by its subjects. This different understanding may be dismissed as a rationalization in which individual guilt and blame is avoided by projecting the fault back onto the apparatus of justice. Yet what we know about the processing of these young people through the juvenile criminal justice system suggests to us that at many points this collective account accords with social reality.

It seems that in early adolescence these young people come to gain an experience of what it is to be poor and black. It is an experience of educational, occupational and social disadvantage. A process of entrapment in which they are cajoled towards success by their educators and a broader social world while the wherewithal to achieve this success is withheld. They must find a meaning for their predicament. They can blame themselves, or they can tune in to the emerging critique of the position of poor black people in a relatively prosperous white society which is developing simultaneously within the subculture and amongst the black intelligentsia. They must account for the absence of opportunity and the presence of a police force which at times resembles an army of occupation. They must in short deal with *alienation*. Alienation occurs in two senses. In the first they must deal with the ways in which their social product, the wealth produced by themselves in the present and by their predecessors back to the times of slavery, is appropriated, re-shaped, and visited back upon them as oppression. This finds its clearest expression in saturation policing. In the second sense they must deal with the broken promise, a promise made first to their forebears that as British subjects that are not only equal before the law but would have equal access to opportunity and economic security. But the promise has been broken and as we know from psychiatry, broken promises may make us mad (insane) or mad (angry). In this second sense the alienation is a process in which the promise is reneged upon and these young people are separated off in political discussions from the mainstream of British society. It is a process in which, fixed as aliens by a social and political rhetoric, they must find new meanings and new ways to assert and elaborate that which is distinctive and valuable about themselves and their lives, a process moreover which is fuelled by anger. Robbed of one identity they must set about constructing a new one with precious few materials and one of those materials may, for some of them, from time to time be crime.

As Lea and Young (1982) have argued, the increasing economic marginality of the Afro-Caribbean population in this country is compounded by political marginalization, a lack of access to the established mechanisms of political expression. This *marginalisation* means that there are few if any means whereby the experience of alienation and marginality may be expressed in a public form. This is of course doubly true for the young.

Beyond these two features of the predicament of young black people in trouble in this country, is a third — *expulsion*. The evidence we have suggests that increasingly the control apparatus is expelling young black people in trouble to the institutions which mark the boundaries of civil society. We have already noted the correlation between offending, unemployment, homelessness and penal confinement and the evidence is alarmingly clear that we are increasingly dealing with what Mathieson (1974) calls surplus populations by expulsion. Mathieson argues that advanced capitalist societies routinely rather than inadvertently damage, spoil and waste sections of their populations which no longer have an economic function and that they then expel them to institutions. We have sufficient grounds for arguing that we see this process at work amongst young black people in trouble.

The reason for attempting to identify what the experience of being young and black and in trouble means to the subject is to suggest that this experience should offer clues or sketches to personnel within the apparatus of justice, or to those who would reform it, about how they might proceed. While this chapter has concentrated upon problem finding rather than problem solving, some tentative observations may be useful.

Systems management initiatives are important. The attempt to monitor system inputs and outputs does yield valuable information about our treatment of young people in trouble and the points at which we might make an intervention. Thus far, however, these endeavours have been colour blind and an overall picture in which the populations of community homes with education is dwindling masks the fact that the black populations of these institutions is probably increasing. Only when the variable of race is included in this monitoring will we be able to develop anti-racist initiatives in the juvenile criminal justice system.

The recent government initiative to develop community alternatives to custody makes no mention of the fact that young offenders' establishments are attracting larger and larger black populations and that as the unemployment levels amongst these populations grow it will continue to do so. What this initiative also ignores is that unless controls are placed both upon the judiciary and the magistrates, the situation will undoubtedly worsen, This government has recently extended the powers of magistrates. It must be asked by opposition MPs and pressure groups what these increased powers have meant for unemployed young black people in trouble.

The contemporary debate about the management of juvenile crime acknowledges that the juvenile bureau could be more effective as a mechanism for diverting young people in trouble from the mainstream of the juvenile justice system. It does not however address the fact that young black people are offered this option significantly less than white young people and that this significantly worsens their predicament if they are apprehended. This fact, picked up by Landau (1981) has yet to be addressed by the police.

The debate about police accountability has made no effective impact upon the debate about juvenile crime yet we know that the predatory policing and harassment of young black people is a crucial factor in both the construction of offences and the projection of black offenders into the juvenile criminal justice system. Unless those concerned with what happens to young black people in trouble in the system are prepared to enter this contentious political area then a 'systematic' approach in relation to these young black people remains a nonsense.

The contemporary orthodoxy in the debate about juvenile crime strives to distance itself from the preoccupations of a previous generation of reformers with social need and the capacity of welfare initiatives to ameliorate human suffering, Such initiatives are sometimes dismissed as a 'needology' which served to implicate larger populations in the apparatus of crime control (see Thorpe, Paley and Green, 1980). This argument is not without its merits yet we now confront a situation in which young black people who live in the most crowded homes, whose parents have the lowest incomes, who go to under-resourced schools and have the poorest educational and employment opportunities, are engaged in crimes of poverty. Can we therefore continue to sustain the notion that social circumstances have no bearing upon the nature and extent of offending. If we cannot, then we must move from a bland critique of welfare as a manifestation of creeping state control to a critical discussion about the ways in which public resources might be most effectively employed to create opportunity and the means whereby a dispossessed generation of young black people might be offered some resources with which to construct a life which is not just concerned with bare survival.

Social workers and probation officers have had difficulty engaging with young black people in trouble. The general low level of probation orders or referrals to intermediate treatment projects testifies to this. The problem as seen from the professional end revolves around the question of resistance on the part of black clients, yet initiatives like the Handsworth Project, the paradoxical results notwithstanding, have demonstrated that probation officers can be encouraged to become engaged and that if they are offered a relevant resource they will often use it. There is clearly a great deal of work to be done at the level of provision of resources but also in in-service training for welfare personnel which asks them to confront their own racial attitudes and anxieties about perceived or actual hostility from black clients.

Not an exhaustive list. The tasks of developing initiatives which will transfrom the juvenile criminal justice system into a system which delivers either social or racial justice lies ahead. What we confront at present is a system which penalizes young black people because they are young, because they are black, because they are working class, because they are poor, because they are often unemployed, because they are often homeless but also because they are beginning to understand all this and therefore appear resistant. The hazards which these young citizens confront are different for those encountered by young white people, their understanding of these hazards may well be different and yet the personal impact of this collision with the might of the state upon them is probably no different. As Claude Aveline has said 'white, black and yellow men — they all cry salt tears'.

Note

1. There is not, as yet, any published material on these matters. The figures which are quoted here are drawn from personal experience and personal communication, as well as research in progress.

7

Police racism: some theories and their policy implications

John Lea

It might seem tedious to ask why, in a society in which racism, sexism, and other forms of bigotry proliferate, a particular institution such as the police engages in racial discrimination. Like other public institutions the police can be expected to share the general prejudices and forms of behaviour common in society and to carry them into effect in their own particular ways. However, an attempt to understand the specific dynamics of police racism serves two purposes. First, it helps to clarify the existence of distinct types of racist activity, located at different levels of individual or institutional behaviour, and not reducible to explanation in terms of some general theory of racism. Secondly, if racial discrimination in society is to be overcome then strategies must be developed which are adequate to the task of combating the specific forms of racism in particular institutions. It is no good, for example, screening applicants for work in the police for racist attitudes if those applicants are about to be socialized, irrespective of their original attitudes, into a powerful subculture whose dynamics are quite independent of individual personality structures.

In this chapter I shall attempt to develop a classification of different types of racism and the theories and explanations which are brought to bear on them as they apply to policing. I shall try to indicate the type of policy orientations toward the combating of racism which follow from these theories. I shall stick to the use of the term racism as a general description of the phenomenon I am talking about. The distinction between attitudes and behaviour, between racial prejudice and racial discrimination already presupposes a certain view, not the only one, of the topic. Where I use that distinction it will therefore be in a specific context. But before proceeding to a discussion of racism and its nature and causes in police work it is useful to begin with a brief survey of the extent of the problem.

The extent of police racism

There are various ways of observing the relations between the police and the black community. Some aspects of this relation are readily amenable to social survey methods. But the results of such surveys of 'the state of police—community relations' as well as other forms of (e.g. participant) observation, are not, of themselves, indications of the extent of police racism. A high level of alienation from the police in the black community might, conceivably, be due less to any specific activity on the part of the police than to the general state of race relations in society. The police might simply be regarded by many members of the black community as a visible symbol of an oppressive society. Conversely, high levels of police racism might co-exist with the relative absence of feelings of estrangement in the black community if a subservient and acquiescent mood prevailed in the community bearing the brunt of police racism. We need therefore to look for evidence that feelings of alienation from the police prevailing in the black community are related to police behaviour and practices.

In the United States the riots of the late 1960s prompted a good deal of research into the state of relations between the police and the black community. A major survey of fifteen American cities (Campbell and Schuman, 1968) found that one third of black Americans were critical of the police. Such general statements as these are of course highly ambiguous. Firstly, how they are read and the significance attached to them is determined by what might be called the 'polemics of presentation'. As the American criminologist James Q. Wilson remarked: 'one could report it as saying that "two thirds of blacks were not critical of the police" or as saying "fully, or a whopping, one third of blacks were highly critical of the police"' (Wilson, 1972: 54).

Wilson went on however to conclude that the figures from these surveys offer little support for the view that 'the great majority of blacks are seething with resentment against the police on grounds of injustice or abuse'. But on the other hand he admitted that the overall figures do not tell the whole story. A breakdown by age is revealing. Thus 55 percent of blacks in the sixteen to nineteen age range (compared to 24 percent of whites) believed that the police used insulting language. This contrasted with 26 percent of blacks and 9 percent of whites in the fifty to fifty-nine age range. Likewise while only 26 percent of blacks, and 6 percent of whites, in the fifty to fifty-nine age range believed that 'police rough people up unnecessarily', the figure rises to 49 percent of blacks, and 25 percent of whites, in the sixteen to nineteen age range. So although for all age ranges blacks were more critical of the police than whites in these surveys, and intensity of criticism varies inversely with age, it is in specifically the young age ranges that the proportion of blacks who are critical of the police approaches half.

Fifteen years later a very similar situation has been revealed in Britain. In 1981 the London Metropolitan Police commissioned the Policy Studies Institute to conduct a survey into major aspects of police work and relations with the public. According to the report, published in 1983, 70 percent of Londoners felt that the police were 'fairly' or 'very' success-ful in 'getting on with people'. A similar result came from a London poll conducted by National Opinion Polls Ltd in the summer of 1983 which revealed that 72 percent of Londoners felt that the police were 'doing a good job locally'. This prompted the press relations division of the Metropolitan Police to engage in the polemics of presentation with style. Kenneth Newman, the new police commissioner, was engaged in implementing a new style policing strategy for the metropolis and these surveys were held to show his success. 'The findings provide new evidence that the strategy presently being implemented by Sir Kenneth Newman is on target.' The findings of course showed no such thing. Leaving aside the question of whether 30 percent of Londoners disapproving of the police as regards 'doing a good job' or 'getting on with people' can be read as indicators of success, it is perhaps curious that such complacent conclusions should have been drawn from surveys aggregating the opinions of all Londoners, black and white, inner-city and suburban, old and young, when the origin of the concern about police—community relations in London lay in the disturbances involving young blacks in the Brixton area of south London and the subsequent report of inquiry by Lord Scarman. It was well known that the crisis in relations with the black community centred on relations between the police and young blacks of West Indian origin. Yet when the Policy Studies Institute figures were 'unpacked' they revealed precisely a very alarming deterioration in the relations between police and young blacks in the inner-city areas.

According to the Policy Studies Institute (PSI) report, only 43 percent of black Londoners (black is used throughout to indicate West Indian origin) felt that the police were fairly or very successful in getting on with people compared to 73 percent of whites holding this view (Smith, 1983: 222). The PSI report gives a number of more detailed indicators of police—community relations which reveal a massive scale of disaffection with the police on the part of young blacks. While only 21 percent of Londoners as a whole thought that the police stop people (on foot) 'sometimes without sufficient reason' when this is broken down by ethnic group we find that 20 percent of whites and 52 percent of blacks hold this view. When age is taken into account the problem increases. For the fifteen to twenty-four age range we find that 32 percent of whites and 66 percent of blacks hold this view.

In a similar vein 10 percent of whites and 42 percent of blacks felt that the police use 'unreasonable violence in police stations' and for the fifteen to twenty-four age range 20 percent of whites and 56 percent of blacks hold this view. But from our point of view probably the most significant finding of the PSI survey was that which correlated the percentage holding negative views of the police with the frequency of actual contact with the police. Thus 60 percent of people who had been stopped by the police three or more times in the previous year believed that the police stopped people on foot without sufficient reason compared with 15 percent of people who had never been stopped. Likewise 44 percent of people stopped three or more times felt that ethnic minorities were not treated fairly by the police compared with 17 percent of those who had never been stopped. Of those stopped three or more times 45 percent believed that the police used unjustifiable violence at police stations compared with 8 percent of those never stopped. When it is taken into account that young black males are the category of the population most likely to be stopped by the police then this sort of evidence corroborates the view that attitudes to the police held by the black community are based on the reality of police practices and not simply a general response to the police as symbols of an oppressive society. The general opinion of the police held by young blacks was graphically brought out in the participant observation section of the PSI study:

> Everyone in the group held unfavourable or highly unfavourable attitudes towards the police force ranging from deep bitterness and resentment to feelings of hatred and animosity. It would be fair to say that a rigid stereotype of the police force has developed among the group which portrays most police officers as condescending and contemptuous, unhelpful and uncooperative and hostile or brutal in their actions towards the black population in this country (Small, 1983: 109).

The causes of police racism

Why does such a state of affairs exist? It is important to begin by making ourselves aware of the different types of discrimination and racism that exist and that different explanations of racism are frequently focusing attention on one type to the exclusion of others. A useful classification of types of racism can be obtained through the combination of two polarities: direct as opposed to indirect racism and institutional as opposed to individual racism. The direct-indirect polarity contrasts actions which are overtly and consciously racist, such as deliberately turning down an applicant for a job, arresting someone, or abusing them, because of their ethnic background, with actions which have the *effect* of treating people in a racist way irrespective of the original intention. Examples of the latter might be an irrelevant language test for job applicants which had the effect of excluding some ethnic minority candidates, police officers requiring particular forms of behaviour from the public in possible arrest situations in a context in which ethnic minorities were not familiar with these forms. The institutional—individual polarity is concerned with the level at which the action originates. Racist actions may be built into the policy or mode of operation of institutions irrespective of the attitudes of the individuals who carry out the activities of the institution. A set of racist immigration laws may be administered by officials and police officers irrespective of their individual attitudes to immigrants. Conversely racist practices may originate at the level of individual behaviour irrespective of the formal policies and the general operations of the institutional framework within which the individual is operating.

Combining these two polarities gives us a very useful classification of the major types of racist activity:

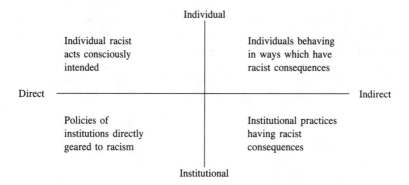

In the remainder of this chapter I shall attempt to illustrate, using this classification, four approaches to police racism. The importance of this classification will, I hope, become clear. For example if the problem of police racism is seen as a question of individual police officers engaging in abusive or discriminatory behaviour towards black people then explanations for the problem may well be sought at the level of the presence or absence of prejudiced individuals in police forces. Such an approach might ignore completely a situation in which, although police officers did not treat blacks markedly different from whites in individual encounters, nevertheless the institutional practices and policing methods in widespread use would lead to the disproportionate targeting and arrest of blacks.

The psychology of prejudice — the 'bad apple' approach

There has been a general predisposition in Britain until quite recently, to define the problem of racism precisely in terms of individual actions consciously intended. The anti-discrimination legislation of the mid 1960s was framed around remedy at law for individual intended acts and this was one of its main weaknesses (Lea, 1980). The distinction between intended and unintended discrimination only appears in law with the 1976 Race Relations Act. This Act also allowed some guarded moves — but did not compel them — in the direction of 'positive action' strategies to improve the position in society of blacks as a group. But there has been nothing on the scale of the 'affirmative action' programmes popular in the United States. It is not surprising therefore to find that the problem of police racism has traditionally been formulated as a question of individual direct racism; of racist officers in the force ('bad apples') getting the force as a whole an undeservedly bad reputation by their idiosyncratic acts which clash with the best traditions of police work. From this standpoint it can be argued that it is only normal that the police, like other public bodies, should be landed with their 'fair share' of prejudiced individuals which is an inevitable result of the widespread nature of racial prejudice in British society and not something for which the police as such can be held responsible. A version of this view was put by the Political and Economic Planning Organization in its evidence to a House of Commons Select Committee investigating the West Indian Community in Britain in the mid-1970s.

> The extent of discrimination by the police is not established but since it can hardly be supposed that they do not share the host society's prejudices it is difficult to believe that these do not influence the police in their duties (PEP, 1977).

The argument lifts the explanation of the dynamics of police racism onto the level of explaining social attitudes about race in general in society at large. There is nothing specific to be said about police racism except that it certainly exists. The Political and Economic Planning Organization is now the Policy Studies Institute. It is not without interest and consequence, as we shall see, that this conception of police racism defines the terms of the 1983 survey mentioned above.

A stronger and more sophisticated version of the 'bad apple' approach focuses on the personal characteristics of the types of individuals who are attracted to the police as a career. The study of police recruits by Coleman and Gordon claims that:

> It seems reasonable to conclude that the police force tends to attract to it people who are more conservative and authoritarian than those of comparative socio-economic status in other professions (Coleman and Gordon, 1982: 185).

This approach is found also in much of the American literature. Some writers have argued that a 'police personality' characterized by an authoritarian character structure is typical of the social strata from which police forces heavily recruit (Macnamara, 1967; Bayley and Mendelsohn, 1969). This character structure is excessively concerned with status and insecurity and is to be found, typically, in the lower middle class. Unlike the blue collar working class which tends to accept a lack of social mobility the lower middle class shares the general middle class view of society as a ladder of opportunity for social mobility and hence feels an insecurity because it is at the bottom of this ladder. A police career can therefore be seen as especially attractive to the lower middle class as a way of compensating for insecurity and gaining a type of artificial social mobility through the symbolic authority and public respect commanded by the police uniform and other aspects of police work. This type of personality is prone, as some classic studies (Reich, 1970; Adorno, 1950) have suggested, to develop racial prejudice. Thus police recruits, according to this stronger version of the argument, do not simply *reflect* the prejudices of society, they may be expected to contain a disproportionately large number of prejudiced individuals.

Seeing the problem of police racism as a question of prejudiced individuals engaged in racist actions towards black members of the public such as abuse, excessive violence, intolerance etc. has certain direct policy implications. These are reasonably clear. The road to eliminating police racism will be that of adopting policies which either filter out prejudiced individuals at the recruiting stage, or retrain, through 'race awareness' training programmes the prejudices of serving officers. Such measures could be backed up by making racially prejudiced actions a disciplinary offence under police regulations. In Britain the recently passed Police and Criminal Evidence Act (1984) includes such a provision and race, or 'human awareness' as it tends to be called by the police is developing in training programmes. It is not my intention here to discuss the implementation of such programmes but simply to point out that their usefulness is predicated on the assumption that police racism is, at least to a significant extent, a product of the prejudiced activities of individual officers. How far is this in fact the case?

In the United States one of the most important tests of the whole 'bad apple' theory of individual prejudice as an explanation of police racism can be found in a study conducted for the President's Commission on Law Enforcement and the Administration of Justice (Black and Reiss, 1969). In this study participant observation of police officers in three cities showed that over 75 percent of white officers working in predominantly black areas were rated by observers as 'prejudiced' or 'highly prejudiced' in views held about black people. Yet, curiously, only 2 percent of police–black encounters were rated as 'obviously prejudiced', 6 percent were rated as 'somewhat prejudiced' and 11 percent involved 'brusque or hostile speech'. There is of course the obvious problem of officers 'containing themselves' if they feel that participant observers are, or are likely to be, present. Nevertheless the discrepancy is large in these studies.

A very similar set of conclusions about the dynamics of police racism emerged from the PSI report:

> Our first impression... was that racialist language and racial prejudice were prominent and pervasive and that many individual officers and also whole groups were preoccupied with ethnic differences... At the same time on accompanying

these officers as they went about their work we found that their relations with black and brown people were often relaxed or friendly and that the degree of tension between them and black people from day to day was much less than might have been expected from either their own conversation or from accounts in the newspapers and on television (Smith and Gray, 1983: 109).

The PSI researchers explained this discrepancy in terms of the distinction between the individual psychological needs fulfilled by racial prejudice on the one hand and the operational needs of policing on the other.

> racialist talk...helps to reinforce the identity, security and solidarity of the group against a clearly perceived external threat...when police officers actually come into contact with members of minority groups a different set of needs comes into play: very often the officer is forced to look on the person as a person — as someone whose support is required or who must be manipulated — rather than as a member of a particular ethnic group (Smith and Gray, 1983: 127–8).

There are problems with this view. Firstly, it is being argued that racialist talk, in the canteen or wherever, acts to reinforce group norms and provide a sense of solidarity. The obvious question is why should it be racialist talk that fulfils this function? Other forms of culture could, presumably, have served as the content of an 'esprit de corps'. Why racialist language? One is led to the view that there is something in the structure of the relationship between police and black communities irrespective of individual attitudes, that explains why it is that racialist language is the necessary content of group solidarity. The PSI report is itself ambiguous about the level at which it considers racialist attitudes to be caused and reinforced:

> Someone who is basically sympathetic towards black people can come to adopt racialist language in order to conform to the expectations of the group which are set by a minority of racialists (Smith and Gray, 1983: 115).

So on the one hand the report talks about group needs and on the other hand about racists being in a minority. It is difficult to see how a minority of active racists could set the expectations and culture for the group as a whole if their activities and talk did not correspond to more basic pressures at work within the police as a group. We are thus led from the study of individual attitudes to the dynamics of police 'occupational culture'. This will be considered in the next section.

The second problem arising from the PSI view concerns the fairly clear opinion that police institutional rules and practices act as a check on racist behaviour. It this is the case then of course it follows that a poor opinion of the police by blacks cannot be based on their experience of police activity. But here again the PSI report is buried in ambiguities.

The hostility of West Indians (and young West Indians in particular) cannot be explained by the way in which they themselves are treated by the police in specific circumstances though it may be explained, at least in part by the large *number* of contacts they have had and the very high *proportion* of such contacts in which they are being treated as offenders or suspects rather than getting help or advice (Smith and Gray, 1983: 333).

The notion that experience of the police has not contributed to opinions of the police by young blacks does not rest easily alongside the evidence, mentioned above, that opinion of the police of a negative nature increases with the frequency of being stopped. The notion that relations between police and young blacks may be influenced by the number and nature of contacts rather than special characteristics of police behaviour opens up a new line of inquiry into the nature of police racism. As we shall see, the PSI report fails to follow this lead precisely because it remains within a framework defining racism as the characteristics of individual actions rather than institutional practices.

Defending the occupational culture

What might be termed the 'occupational culture' thesis locates the dynamic of police racism in the norms and values through which police officers define their roles and the legitimacy of their activities. Individuals will be socialized into group norms, the adherence to which has racist consequences irrespective of the original prejudices or personality structures of police recruits. The occupational culture approach is still concerned predominantly with the behaviour of individual officers but is concerned to see racist behaviour as a result of adherence to group norms which are not of themselves explicitly racist. Initially such norms are concerned with group cohesion and a general suspiciousness of 'outsiders'. Police encounters with the black community are thus structured in terms of a particular way of dealing with outsiders which may have racist consequences as far as black people are concerned. As a consequence of these structured encounters police develop racist attitudes towards blacks which are then incorporated as part of group norms.

One of the clearest accounts of contemporary British police occupational culture is that provided by Holdaway, for whom the central organizing principle of police culture is the concept of 'ground' or territory.

The diffused and sometimes conflicting elements of the police role are rationalized as a coherent identity within this defined territorial area of the ground. Clearly related to territory and identity is the relationship between territory and task. Claim to a territorial imperative imposes a unity on the myriad tasks which constitute police work (Holdaway, 1983: 37).

The ground or territory is regarded as police controlled. The police see themselves, Holdaway argues, as the single agency preventing the territory they police from descending into chaos and disorder. The fundamental definition of the police task in the occupational culture of police officers is this defence of the area against chaos. From the standpoint of this assumption police officers evaluate the social groups and other agencies with which they come into contact

> in the light of their relevance to policing and the power structure of the local community. Key considerations are their actual or potential lack of control, the degree to which they may enhance the excitement or challenge of police work, their power to dissolve and demystify the occupational culture, particularly the secrecy and interdependency of that culture and, finally, the power to call officers to account (Holdaway, 1983: 66).

Black people are viewed, then, in terms of their capacity to threaten the premises of the occupational culture. The threat they present is perceived as characteristics such as violence, disorderliness, a proclivity to crime, and a tendency to exploit grievances. This threatens the police culture insofar as

> control, having been established as central to that culture, the truculence attributed to blacks justifies the perceived necessity for continual vigilance and use of all the available subcultural techniques of routine policing (Holdaway, 1983: 71).

But why are blacks labelled as disorderly, violent and predisposed to crime in the first place? Is this not simply racial prejudice on the part of police officers again? The key to occupational culture explanations is that the labelling of blacks in this way itself stems from certain characteristics of police culture itself irrespective of, though certainly in tune with, the general attitudes prevailing among whites. In an earlier discussion Lambert attributes the negative evaluation of blacks by police officers as a variety of culture clash based on the confusion of role expectations in encounters between police and black people:

> with the English middle class the police can be effective if circumspect through a manner of approach that implies deference; with the lower class a deal is struck by a number of techniques of bombast, bonhomie or old fashioned paternalism...But with coloured immigrants there is no traditional manner of dealing and the old ways may be thought irrelevant (Lambert, 1970: 193).

In this account police officers in their 'normal' relations with the public defend the integrity of their occupational culture through techniques such as deference on the part of the police towards the public which is then reciprocated by the latter. These practices have the indirect effect of discriminating against blacks who do not share the cultural expectations within which these techniques are situated. Police encounters with black people are thus fraught with difficulty and misunderstanding and thus blacks become labelled as troublesome. Once this happens then additions and elaborations of the stereotype to include violence and a disproportionate involvement in crime can develop.

This type of approach to police racism has some advantages over the 'bad apple' approach. It is able to understand racism as an aspect of group norms without assuming that these norms are established simply by prejudiced individuals. It is able to grasp the process of socialization of individual officers into existing group norms. Coleman and Gordon (1982) whose research was mentioned above, while arguing that the main roots of authoritarianism among police officers lay in the types of recruits attracted, nevertheless concluded that 'socialization into the police sub-culture seems...to foster hostile attitudes towards coloured immigration'. The policy implications are also clear. The issue is less to develop techniques for rooting out prejudiced individuals than to change those tenets of police culture that produce difficulties in interaction with black people leading to the development of negative stereotypes of the latter. The maximization of community liaison panels and opportunities for police officers to engage in dialogue with various sections of the public is needed, especially the black community. This will enable them to reach an understanding of black culture which would eliminate this as a source of confusion in the interaction between police and black people.

However the occupational culture approach throws up some severe problems. These occur not at the point of establishment of a police occupational culture but in the assumption of a culture clash between that culture and the expectations of black people. There is an element of 'blaming the victim' in the notion of the 'excitable black' unable to conform to the norms governing police–public interaction. In addition such culture clash explanations have an increasingly dated flavour when applied to the study of the relations between police and a generation of young blacks predominantly born and brought up in this country. Added to this is the evidence that the police belief that young blacks are engaged dispro-portionately in street crime has become strengthened not by cultural differences but alongside the emergence of a culturally assimilated second generation. The contemporary subcultures of black youth are no less made in Britain and indeed partly grow out of relations with a hostile police force, than are those of white youth.

The occupational culture approach fits most easily with the notion of individual indirect racism: individual officers engage in practices sanctioned by occupational culture, such as requirements of deference from the public and this has racist consequences for black people because, ultimately, of cultural expectations. Various theories of institutional racism, to which I now turn, have a decided advantage. They can explain the existence of the racist elements of police subculture, not in terms of some sort of culture clash between other components of police culture and that of black people but as a reflection of material institutional practices characterizing police work which culminate in the identification of the black community as requiring more policing than other sections of the community. Individual acts of racism either direct or indirect will be seen, in these accounts, as derived from, and secondary to, a massive institutional racism characterizing the structure of police work in British society.

State racism — the political role of the police
The first version of institutional racism that I would like to consider is a form of direct racism. That is to say that racism is embodied in the conscious policies and practices of the police as an institution. A current illustration of this type of argument is to be found in the discussion of police racism by Gilroy and others (Gilroy, 1982).

The argument starts from the assumption that policing the black community has become, in contemporary British society, a particular type of political question: 'policing the blacks' has become linked, by the state, the ruling class, and the media with the need to 'maintain the rule of law' in the crisis conditions currently prevailing in Britain. The black community and particularly the young, have become among the first sections of the working class to fight back against the consequences of the capitalist recession: the increase in unemployment and deprivation, and the demands of governments for reductions on living standards. The fundamental aim of the state, acting on behalf of the ruling capitalist class, is to criminalize forms of class struggle now developing. The police, as a branch of the state apparatus thus have the explicit role of portraying political activity by the black community, and its youth, as crime. It is not in anyway incompatible with the argument that other sections of the working class are also finding themselves in a relationship with the police that construes their political activity as a threat to law and order and hence on the frontiers of criminality. At the time of writing the policing of the miners' strike in Britain provides an obvious example.

As far as the policing of the black community is concerned, there seem to be two elements to the argument. Firstly, black political struggles *for* civil rights and *against* the consequences of racial discrimination and economic crisis have become defined by police and media as forms of criminality, such that the forms of activity regarded by the police as crime

> are experienced from the other side as battles for black civil rights and liberties. They cannot be explained away by the cavalcade of lawless images — of stowaways, drifters pimps, and drug dealers — whose procession extends into the present in the form of muggers, illegal immigrants, black extremists and criminal Rastafarians (dreads) (Gilroy, 1982: 145).

Secondly, containing black crime has come to be seen as not just one component, but the fundamental content of the maintenance of law and order under present conditions. The threat to the rule of law has become clearly identified, by the state, media, and ruling class as black political rebellion portrayed as crime. Hence the strengthening of coercive forms of political control of the working class in Britain is linked to the question of race; 'the construction of an authoritarian state in Britain is fundamentally intertwined with the elaboration of a popular racism' (Gilroy, 1982: 9). This elaboration of a popular racism takes the form, then, of the criminalization of black political activity such that the notion of black crime

> has a twofold effect. First, it acts as a signifier for the threat of social instability and a change to which 'law and order' is the only antidote. Second, it rationalizes new forms of control over the black communities at a time when their political traditions and the additional burden of racial oppression mean that they are the first fractions of the working class to give spontaneous opposition to the pressures of the crisis. We focus on criminalization as an instance of this struggle, but it must not be viewed as its entirety (Gilroy, 1982: 152).

Firstly, let us examine the proposition that the policing of black areas in British cities is primarily concerned with the criminalization of black struggles for civil rights in the mid–1980s. An attempt to redefine struggles by the black community against racial oppression as forms of criminal activity is clearly understandable for a ruling class determined to maintain such oppression. If political struggles by the oppressed can be made to appear as crime then other sections of the population, and world opinion, will not associate itself with them precisely because such opinion condemns mindless violence and already has a conception of crime as harmful, antisocial activity.

In certain historical and contemporary situations such processes at work are clearly visible. Struggles against apartheid by black liberation movements in South Africa are, for example, presented to the world by the white minority government of that country as the activity of criminals and terrorists in the hope of thereby isolating such struggles from support both inside and outside South Africa. In these and other cases the mechanisms whereby political struggle is redefined as criminality can be readily seen. Military-style policing, the banning of demonstrations, the imprisonment of civil rights activists on trumped up charges derived from catch-all 'anti-terrorist' legislation or ordinary criminal law are processes which can be investigated and documented. In addition, other forms of 'redefinition' of critical activity exist besides criminalization. Activity critical of the existing political arrangements may be portrayed by the state as 'mental illness' and political oppositionists locked up in mental asylums. Here, public support for critical thought is neutralized by redefining its exponents as 'not in possession of rational faculties' in the hope that the public will come to see the ideas expounded as themselves irrational. At one end of this spectrum is the locking up of political dissidents in psychiatric hospitals in the Soviet Union. At the other end, the treatment of naughty school children as medical cases of 'hyperactivity' requiring treatment with drugs has occurred in western democracies (Box, 1980).

The argument of Gilroy and his colleagues that the crime control activities of the police in mainland Britain constitute the effective criminalization of civil rights struggles by black youth is much harder to evaluate. Certainly, episodes such as the 'riots' in Brixton and other inner-city areas in 1981 in which black and white youth took to the streets to demonstrate in the only way open to them, their resentment at a decade of police harassment, were treated by both police and media as outbursts of criminality. In fact such events have to be seen as indeed forms of political protest by young people marginalized from the institutions and organized channels of political representation and influence in our society (Lea and Young, 1984).

Here Gilroy and his colleagues are undoubtedly correct: a form of political protest was being presented as crime in a simple unmediated sense. No doubt the 'riots' of 1981 involved many individual acts of a criminal nature being committed but that does not detract from their significance as demonstrations of suppressed frustration to which existing channels of political expression had become insensitive. But what is much harder to argue is that the decade of police activity against which they were protesting was *itself* one of the criminalization of struggles for civil rights rather than the harassment of young people in the context of police operation against street crime. The elusive nature of Gilroy's argument is rooted in the absence of any clear definition of either crime or political activity. But such clear definitions are essential if the criminalization of politics hypothesis is to be sustained in the face of the fact that young blacks in the inner cities were not, in the main, being hounded by the Special Branch and anti-terrorist squads or charged under the Prevention of Terrorism Act, but being subjected to intensive stop and search operations, arrested under the vagrancy or 'sus' legislation and by various means associated with certain types of street crime such as robbery and violent theft. The fact that young people were being charged with offences arising out of street crime in no way disproves the argument that in reality they were being politically oppressed but it does place an onus on those, like Gilroy, who wish to argue that the police were criminalizing black political activity to show the precise mechanisms whereby such activity — clearly identified as such — had become presented, by the police as simply, common street crime. Gilroy and the authors of *The Empire Strikes Back* give little in the way of guidance as to how the distinction — if there is to be one — between politics and crime, is to be constructed. Other writers in the same tradition are, however, less circumspect. Thus Paul Gordon in a recent contribution:

The police have consistently tried to de-politicize black struggles and black activity and have tried to portray them instead as mere criminal activity. This has been true, for example, of the...Spaghetti House siege when three black men held up a restaurant in Knightsbridge, London, to raise funds to establish black schools and self help groups (Gordon, 1985: 171).

This passage evidences an important confusion. It may well be the case that the degree of racial discrimination in British society is such that individual members of ethnic minorities are driven, so they may feel, to such desperate strategies as holding up a restaurant in order to draw attention to their situation. But if they do feel driven to engage in such dangerous and antisocial actions as holding people hostage at gunpoint it can hardly be regarded as *evidence* of police racism that they treat such events as criminal activity. The social significance of such events may well lie in the racism endemic in British society. But, as with the street riots of 1981 the significance of such events as evidence of the oppression of ethnic minorities and their marginalization from channels of effective political influence does not allow us to regard as racist activity the fact that the police acted to control and contain such events.

An alternative interpretation is possible. The economic and social crisis in Britain today has contradictory impacts on working class communities, including the black community. On the one hand there is a rise in traditional forms of class politics, centred around trade union struggles, black struggles for union organization etc., coupled with the emergence of newer forms of community politics, often centring on battles around welfare issues at a local level. On the other hand there has been an increase in social deprivation, poverty, homelessness and unemployment, community decay, and their consequences include an increase in those forms of street crime into which the young, almost permanently unemployed, can so easily drift. Due to racial discrimination in all areas of social and economic life, black youngsters face a disproportionate share of these deprivations. Types of policing policies employed in deprived inner-city areas serve to magnify and exaggerate the degree of involvement of black youngsters in street crime and this is then periodically seized on by the media and elaborated into a concept of innate black criminality. This periodic panic about black crime has the effect of steering public debate away from the issues of economic and social decay towards themes which attribute social problems to 'the presence of alien cultures'. In other words the causal sequence protrayed by Gilroy and his colleagues can be turned on its head. Rather than politics being presented as crime, it is crime that is being presented as politics. *This* is the real content of media and political distortion.

This latter interpretation has the added advantage that it appears consistent with the main dynamics of police–black relations in inner-city areas which centre around certain types of minor crime rather than any recognizable form of mass political struggle. That is not to rule out future changes. Nor is it to suggest that the concept of direct, conscious institutional racism has no relevance to a discussion of policing. An investigation of the policing of the immigration laws would be an obvious example of the police quite explicitly, in their normal work of law enforcement, along with other state officials, notably immigration officers, engaging in racist practices. What is being suggested here is that as far as relations between the police and black youth are concerned, it would be more fruitful to investigate those forms of police racism embedded in the normal processes of seeking to control street crime.

Occupational stereotypes and crime control

There is no limitation on police discretion. Only reasonable suspicion is required, and this can be interpreted very loosely. 'Police officers have to be prejudiced and discriminatory if they are to do their work properly', a senior police officer told a seminar in Oxford. A detective superintendent of the West Yorkshire police, he said that checking long haired youths in bedraggled clothing would result in a seizure of drugs, and checking West Indians 'wearing short jeans, T-shirts and multi-coloured tea-cosy type hats who hover around pedestrian precincts, walkways and subways in city centres will detect outstanding handbag snatchers and what has become commonly known as street mugging'. The superintendent said 'that is the sort of discrimination and prejudice we want from police officers' (Alderson, 1984: 62–3).

This passage taken from the recent autobiography of the former chief constable of Devon and Cornwall, John Alderson, underlines a crucial fact about the normal methods of police work, namely, that generalizations concerning the proclivities of certain sections of the population for involvement in certain types of crime is a normal aspect of police procedures such that it would be difficult to imagine a police force which did not admit to such prejudices making any impact in crime whatsoever. If, for every offence committed, police directed their attentions and suspicions equally to all sections of the community, then no crime would ever be solved. This is the starting point for an understanding of the dynamics of what I have called indirect institutional racism, racism that follows as a consequence of normal operating procedures deployed in police work.

One of the major obstacles in the path of developing this approach to understanding the dynamics of police racism is that the exercise of the sort of 'discrimination and prejudice' described by the superintendent from West Yorkshire would not, in very many discussions, be regarded as a fact relevant to the study of police racism at all. This is partly because it is virtually identical with a description of the normal procedures of policing whereas of course racism is looked for as a deviation or an aberration. Lord Scarman, in his report on police community relations in Brixton (Scarman, 1982) at least recognizes the distinction between direct and indirect institutional racism:

> it was alleged by some of those who made representations to me that Britain is an institutionally racist society. If by that is meant that it is a society which knowingly, as a matter of policy, discriminates against black people, I reject this allegation. If however, the suggestion being made is that practices adopted by some public bodies as well as private individuals are unwittingly discriminatory against black people, then this is an allegation which deserves serious consideration and, where proved, swift remedy (Scarman, 1982).

However, Scarman was unable to locate his perception that some public bodies engage in practices which have the effect of discriminating against black people in any discussion of police work. Racism has to be seen as a *departure* from normal operational practices.

> It may be only too easy for some officers faced with what they must see as the inexorably rising tide of street crime, to lapse into an unthinking assumption that all young black people are potential criminals. I am satisfied however that such a bias is not to be found amongst senior police officers (Scarman, 1982).

But of course it might not matter too much what senior officers think. They are not involved in the day to day processes of policing like the experienced police constable who told the PSI researchers:

> How does an experienced policeman decide who to stop? Well, the one that you stop is often wearing a woolly hat, he is dark in complexion, he has thick lips and he usually has dark fuzzy hair (Smith and Gray, 1983: 129).

If one side of the blindness towards institutional racism in police work is the assumption that racism must constitute some sort of intrusion into normal police work, the other side of the coin is to see the adoption of race as an indicator of criminality as quite rational on the part of police officers — and hence nothing to do with racism — because blacks do, after all, have a higher crime rate than other sections of the population. This view was clearly taken by the PSI report:

> Some aspects of policing behaviour seem to be clearly correlated with colour, though not necessarily with racial prejudice. For example one criterion that police officers use for stopping people (especially in areas of relatively low ethnic concentration) is that they are black. . . In two senses this does not seem to be very closely related to racial prejudice on the part of the police. First, it is not only or mostly the officers who express prejudiced views who behave in this way. Secondly the chance of getting a 'result' from a stop may, in fact, be higher if black people are stopped. Thus the survey of Londoners shows that in about one third of cases people who have been victims of crime in the past year can describe the offender and in 24 percent of *these* cases they say the offender was black. Police stopping behaviour and the reports of victims are, therefore, roughly in step (Smith and Gray, 1983: 110).

If we take this view and add that police methods such as stop and search are inevitable in high crime areas then we can only join the pessimism of James Q. Wilson:

> There are very few strategies by which police can reduce crime rates...but such strategies as they have require them to place a community under closer surveillance and thus to multiply the occasions on which citizens are likely to feel themselves unreasonably stopped, questioned, or observed...Indeed, seeing the police–ghetto problem in the context of the central police mission and its incompatibility with the freedom of all persons to come and go as they please cannot make one optimistic about how much improvement is possible at all in police relations with blacks. So long as crime and disorder are disproportionately to be found among young lower class males and so long as blacks remain over-represented in (though by no means identical with) such groups, blacks, especially the young ones — and the police are going to be adversaries (Wilson, 1972: 63–7).

This is however a shortsighted view. The analysis of both Wilson and the British PSI report ends precisely at the point at which the main dynamic of institutional racism emerges. The dependence of police work on criminal stereotypes provides the institutional framework for the emergence of a particular type of racism which consists in the *exaggeration* of the actual involvement of black youth in street crime as a result of police practices.

In order to understand how this process of exaggeration takes place it is useful to draw a distinction between 'prejudice and discrimination' on the one hand, and 'generalization' on the other. The mistake of the superintendent from West Yorkshire and the PSI Report is that they do not clearly distinguish between the two. Racist stereotypes are generalizations but they are not generalizations conducted on the basis of simple inductive reference to experience.

The PSI report for example clouds the issue. On the one hand, in the passage quoted above from the Smith and Gray volume of the report it is argued that police stopping more blacks proportionally than whites is no evidence of racism because the statistical chances of getting a 'result' from a stop may be higher. This implies that stopping by police officers is a highly rational process carried out on the basis of statistical generalizations — presumably regularly revised and updated in the light of empirical evidence! Yet further on in the same volume the researchers report that:

> In a substantial proportion of cases where stops were reported in the survey of police officers, the officer did not give what we judge to be a 'good' reason for making the stop. We could see no good reason for the stop in one third of the cases recorded in the course of our observational work, and, closely in accord with this, the survey of Londoners shows that for 38 percent of stops the person involved thinks the police had no good reason for making the stop (Smith and Gray, 1983: 321).

It can hardly be consistently argued that a higher rate of stops for blacks is a rational response to black crime rates and at the same time that as much as a third of stops are without good reason. If a sizeable proportion of stops are being made without good reason they cannot be said to have a rational relationship to generalizations about the relative involvement of different social groups in crime. They are neither confirming nor falsifying any generalization of such relative involvement. The PSI found that only a small proportion (as low as between 3 and 5 percent) were actually resulting in arrests, although a quarter of arrests originated in stops.

So the difference between generalizations about the relative involvement of different categories of the population in crime, which are an inevitable and necessary aspect of police work, and racist stereotypes is this: a generalization will act as a statistical hypothesis but one which will not interfere with the existence of genuine criteria for suspicion in an individual case. A generalization to the effect that blacks are disproportionately involved in certain types of crime will guide a police officer in where to look, but before stopping any individual black the police officer will ascertain whether there are good reasons to do so in the individual case. This will enable the generalization to sustain its rational basis. If for example the generalization states that blacks are over-involved in crime but only in a minority of cases are there any good reasons for stopping individual blacks then at some point the generalization will be disregarded as no longer serving a useful purpose. But if stops are, in any case, not being conducted for good reasons and few of them are resulting in arrests then the 'generalization' is not functioning in any rational way as a critical guide. On the contrary it is functioning as a prejudiced stereotype.

A second aspect of the difference between 'generalization' and prejudiced stereotype concerns the way in which the boundaries of the targeted group are drawn and defined. The effect of racism may well be to lump together all members of an ethnic minority group. The consequence of this is that while the police may be quite precise about what sub-groups of the white population they regard as being involved in particular types of crime, they may be far less precise in the case of blacks seeing them involved in crime as a racial group while in fact it is only particular groups of blacks, like particular groups of whites, who are disproportionately involved in specific types of crime. The labelling of an ethnic group as crime-prone, or even a large section of it such as young males, facilitates the adoption of general policing strategies oriented towards stopping blacks in those areas of the city with a significant black concentration, or in central shopping areas where *any* black youth becomes suspected of theft. The culmination of this process is a situation in which the labelling of an ethnic group as crime-prone rapidly leads to a disproportionate number of members of that group being stopped or arrested. This amplifies the original involve..ent of the group in crime. This magnification process, reflected in police arrest statistics, serves to act as a confirmer of police stereotypes of criminality, leading to further concentration of policing resources deployed against the group and further artificial magnification of its arrest rates. This process has been described in detail by Lea and Young (1984).

Conclusion

In attempting to understand the specific dynamics of police racism it is necessary to avoid two extremes: on the one hand to see racism as simply the importation of prejudiced attitudes from the wider society or, on the other hand, to see racism as the direct result of normal methods of police operation. The latter view, besides functioning to give police racism a spurious rationality, leaves little in the way of policies for reform apart from the abandonment of policing as such. However, a careful inspection of the differences between 'generalization' based on empirical observation and critical evaluation of the degree of involvement of social groups in crime, and the racist stereotypes which may in fact guide police action towards minority groups, shows an interrelation between normal police work and racism. Necessary generalizations about group involvement in specific types of crime provide an organizational framework in which racist stereotypes, derived from the wider society and reproduced in police occupational culture, can function in particular ways. These, it has been suggested, concern the exaggeration and distortion of, and the creation of self-fulfilling prophecies concerning, ethnic minority crime rates. And because what is taking place is the exaggeration and distortion of quite normal methods of operation, many commentators, notably the PSI researchers, seem to have avoided altogether any such identification of racism in these areas.

It follows that the most effective policies designed to combat racism in police work will be those designed to minimize the opportunities for such distorted generalizations to act as a guide to police practice. It may seem at first sight that certain aspects of the Police and Criminal Evidence Act 1984 move in this direction. For example in stop and search operations the requirement upon officers to state the reasons for searches and make a record to which the person searched has a right of access might act to reduce the large volume of stops not based on any reasonable suspicion. This would, it could be argued, in turn reduce the scope for stops based more on racist stereotypes than on empirical generalizations about crime involvement. However, as Kinsey and Baldwin (1985) point out:

the opportunity for officers to sidestep these provisions is effectively built into the legislation itself. The Act demands not that any search should be recorded but only 'a search in exercise of any such power (under the Police and Criminal Evidence Act s. 1)'. Thus the recording procedure is always avoided when a person allows a search voluntarily — knowing perhaps that if he or she dissents, more rigorous formal powers will be used. If a searched person asks for a copy of a search record and this is refused because 'you allowed the search voluntarily' or because 'it was not practicable to record the search — we were too busy', there may be little comeback (Kinsey and Baldwin, 1985: 95).

A more practical reform might be to adandon the use of stop and search operations altogether. These operations are well known to be most inefficient at catching actual offenders and produce maximum alienation from the police of precisely those sections of the population which hold most information about crime. Such operations provide the opportunity for a vast number of stops motivated by nothing other than racial stereotypes. The lack of community willingness to offer information to the police only serves as the occasion for more of these operations.

The more detailed information about crime that the police receive from the public the less will be the reliance on stereotypes and generalizations as guidelines in investigation. In an urban setting generalizations concerning the crime activities of social groups can never be entirely eliminated but their scope and the ease with which they can be elaborated into racist characterizations can be constrained by measures designed to increase the flow of information from public to police. The main arguments for a greater degree of police accountability to local government have been rehearsed elsewhere (Lea and Young, 1984). A central theme of the argument for accountability is that it would do more than any other imaginable change to restore community confidence in the police. Such an improvement would undoubtedly result in an increased public willingness to co-operate with the police and an increase in the number of situations in which the arrest or apprehension of individuals by police officers took place on the basis of reliable evidence rather than bigoted stereotype. Such policies will not solve the problem of racism overnight and their implementation is a matter for those in government and in police leadership who are genuinely concerned to combat the blight of racism in our society.

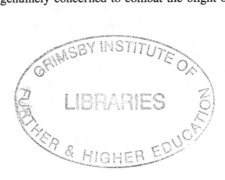

8

Irregular work, irregular pleasures: heroin in the 1980s

John Auld, Nicholas Dorn
and Nigel South

Introduction

The recent period has witnessed a real and substantial increase in the use of heroin, particularly among young adults and those in their late teens. Rather than being injected, the drug has also become more typically smoked or snorted (although a relatively small proportion of recent new users are injecting). A wide variety of social groups are involved; several street agencies report seeing many more women users than in previous years. And, of course, heroin is now being used in circumstances very different from those that prevailed in the 1960s — the last time when there occurred a major upsurge of illicit drugtaking among this age group.

As far as its social and economic structure was concerned, that earlier period was characterized by three main spheres of life: waged work, its associated consumption practices outside the home, and work and consumption within the home. The various forms of deviant behaviour, correspondingly, were defined primarily in terms of the extent to which they were seen as representing challenges to, or illegitimate departures from, established and hegemonic conceptions of normalcy then prevailing within these three spheres. Addiction, for example, was a complex concept developed at the intersection of the sick role (defined essentially in relation to wage work: see Parsons, 1951), of conceptions of unearned pleasure and unacceptable hedonism (defined in relation to consumption norms: see Young, 1971), and of conceptions of masculinity and femininity. This and other forms of deviancy were developed in concrete practices within sectors of the economy that were closely linked to the formal world of wage work. Whether working in a regular fashion or not, the drug user moved in a world in which wage work and a labour market characterized by full employment for males provided the common reference point. Very little of this helps us to understand drug use today, however.

Throughout the post-war period there has been an apparently expanding and diversifying informal economy (Henry, 1982; South, 1982). In the 1950s and 1960s the informal economy was in a subordinate, service role in relation to the expanding formal economy. Although socially marginal drug users were involved in the cultures and economy of the streets and

166

the 'demi-monde', it is only since the late 1960s that parts of the informal economy have become significant for large numbers of men and women, employed as well as unemployed. It is within these informal economies that heroin distribution and consumption has been and continues to be expanding.

In this paper we attempt to demonstrate how the use of heroin and the services which it generates and feeds upon have expanded within a sector of the informal economies that we refer to as the *irregular economy* (Ferman and Ferman, 1973). We examine the scope offered by mass unemployment for the development of new styles of *episodic* heroin use — a consumption pattern which mirrors other features of the irregular economy. We show that the lowered cost of heroin available today has facilitated the development of modes of administration — specifically, smoking and snorting — that lack both the negative connotations and physical dangers of injection, thus adding a further stimulus to drug's appeal. Sexual divisions are discussed in terms of their consequences for the patterning of drug involvements by young males and young females, with the focus of our discussion upon ways in which young men use heroin as a means of extracting emotional servicing from girlfriends and mothers. In the remainder of this paper we attempt to analyse the nature of and the links between these various aspects of 'the problem'. In the process we hope to go some way towards formulating a perspective which may be applied to two aspects of prevention policy — that is, prevention of use and prevention of harm — that have been accorded central significance in the most recent government report on drug abuse.

Heroin, markets, mode of administration and masculinity

The quantitative dimensions
Evidence of the increased use of heroin and other drugs in the UK comes from four principal sources:

(i) evidence relating to international trafficking and seizures;

(ii) criminal and health services statistics of persons apprehended or reported as being involved with heroin;

(iii) local prevalance studies, ranging in quality from the systematic to the frankly inane;

(iv) experience of practitioners and self-help groups in the fields of welfare, advice work, unemployment projects, etc.

A consistent picture emerges from these various forms of evidence. Whilst there may be a 'moral panic' over heroin (following an earlier one over solvent sniffing) and whilst that panic may distort our view of heroin use today, there is no doubt that more people in Britain today have used heroin than ever before. Perhaps the only rough parallel in quantitative terms would be the nineteenth century, when large proportions of the population used the plant extract, opium. Admittedly, they would have been eating it, drinking it as tea or taking it as part of patent medicines rather than smoking or snorting the stronger manufactured derivative of opium, heroin (Berridge and Edwards, 1981). Nevertheless, what this comparison brings out is the common feature of consumption via mouth or nose, with injected use being the practice of a minority. The changes that have occurred in the dominant mode of administration in more recent times will be considered in some detail presently. Suffice it to say in the present context, however, that many more persons in Britain are familiar with opiate drugs today than has been the case for about a century. The next few paragraphs summarize some of the quantitative evidence supporting this claim.

(i) The total international trade in opium (from which heroin is made) has been estimated as amounting to thousands of tons, with profit levels running into hundreds of billions of dollars (Halper, 1975 and RCMP, 1983). Elsewhere, we have argued that part of the explanation for third world cultivation of plant drugs, including opium, should be sought in the pressures of maintaining both personal income and the payment of interest on national debt in circumstances where there is a lack of alternative profitable crops or sources of income (Auld et al., 1984). However, we agree with the staff of the Drug Indicators Project when they state that whilst supply has increased, 'it is not being suggested that supply in itself created demand. There were a number of domestic factors which meant that increased supply would find a ready market' (Hartnoll et al., 1984: 24). We examine some of these 'domestic factors' that have provided a market for heroin in Britain and other western countries later in this paper. But production and supply also have their own dynamics. For example, competition between cultivators in various third world regions has led to shifts in the international division of production, as a recent Royal Canadian Mounted Police report records:

Although record opium crops continue to be harvested in Southeast Asia's Golden Triangle region (three successive crop years have produced estimated annual yields of approximately 600 tons), the world heroin market began to polarize after the narcotics trade had begun to develop in the Golden Crescent region of Southwest Asia. Since the dramatic rise in SWA heroin production after 1978, SEA heroin has lost a sizeable percentage of its markets in both Europe and North America. This development has resulted in Southeast Asian trafficking syndicates concentrating on supplying markets in the Far East. The bumper opium harvests in SEA over the past three years have led to stockpiling in the Golden Triangle region, with prices falling to record low levels. The decline in prices is seen as an attempt by SEA syndicates to win back markets lost during the low harvest years between 1978 and 1980. India, the world's largest supplier of licit opium, is increasingly surfacing as a transit country for illicit opiate narcotics originating from both Southeast and Southwest Asia and is coming to the forefront as a source country for narcotics supplies destined for the world market. An estimated 10 percent of the licit 585 ton annual yield is believed diverted into the illicit market. In addition, the stockpile of unsold legal opium, although down substantially from last year, is still estimated to be as high as 1,000 tons (RCMP, 1983: 3).

The point is made, then, that there is no lack of supply to meet western demand. Without some means of recouping the profits made upon sale of heroin in western countries, the international businesses that link cultivator and consumer would not be able to operate at all. Happily for the trade, though, there are a variety of licit and semi-licit financial institutions that have grown up around the needs of elite political and economic groups. As the same Canadian report says of 'drug money flow, tax haven countries and international money laundering':

> The use of tax havens has grown in popularity in recent times as one of the few means of placing funds beyond the reach of tax collectors. This guarantee of financial privacy became attractive to a wide variety of individuals, including those whose primary interest was not necessarily to avoid taxes. They became popular to fast rising dictators and public officials who wanted a so-called 'guaranteed pension plan' that was beyond the reach of their successors or the public. It was not long before the criminal organizations as well as individual criminals found the sanctuary of tax havens too inviting to ignore. With the development of multinational banking systems and international business and commerce it became easy to develop sophisticated laundering systems that were designed to move money, that was obtained directly from criminal activity, into the foreign banks that were protected from intrusion by concerned law enforcement officials. For the criminal this financial privacy is an indispensable aid in concealing the proceeds of crime. There are a great many countries and territories that currently provide this type of protection (RCMP, 1983: 72).

The preface of this report suggests that 'the laundering of these profits of course abuses our commercial institutions and investing in them undermines commerce', but we would question that this is wholly true. One does not have to endorse heroin to recognize that it provides a means of profit-making and capitalization for investment in a variety of business interests, some of which may be part of the licit, formal economy of western countries. This is just what previously happened in the United States during the prohibition era. Indeed there are signs that the British tax authorities have recognized that here there is scope for bringing aspects of the lucrative activity of drug smuggling more into the formal economy by pressing suspected traffickers for undeclared income tax (*Observer*, 17 June 1984). This is a point to which we shall return later under the heading of prevention policy.

(ii) As regards national statistics recording aspects of the functioning of the state's various control agencies, the figures of increasing numbers of persons notified to the Home Office as receiving some kind of treatment for drug (generally heroin) addiction may be regarded as consistent with an increase in the much larger pool of ever-users of heroin (i.e. persons who have used heroin once or more) from which the addicted few are drawn. There are now over 5,000 notified addicts, and there has been a fairly consistent upward trend over the last decade (Home Office, 1984). What is particularly interesting about the figures is the apparently accelerating increase in numbers of persons notified as receiving treatment for addiction who were 'not previously known'; rising by about 10 percent per annum in 1973–4 and by 50 percent per annum in 1982–3, the figures indicate that over the course of the decade as a whole there occurred a substantial increase in the number of 'new addicts'. Significantly, the total 'no longer recorded' *also* rose substantially, due mostly to people either leaving treatment voluntarily, being refused further treatment of a kind acceptable to them at Drug Dependency Units (drug clinics), or entering prison. [1] Far from being a static one, then, the overall picture as reflected in these Home Office figures is one characterized by the rapid movement of persons labelled as addicts through the health care and control system. This is consonant with the proposition that there has developed a relatively large pool of episodic and recreational heroin users, the majority of whom do not seek to occupy the 'sick role' on a long term basis. Other Home Office figures made available to the Channel 4 television programme *A Week in Politics* indicate that the greatest numbers of new addicts were recorded in Cheshire, Greater Manchester, Lancashire, Merseyside, Sussex, West Midlands, Lothian and Borders, Strathclyde and London (with the latter topping the list for 1982). These numbers may partly of course, reflect the availability of general practitioners and drug clinic psychiatrists who are ready to accept and notify persons as receiving treatment for a heroin habit. But, in any event, the figures refer only to the small minority seeking treatment for problems arising in relation to their drug use. As far as the majority are concerned, none of the available official statistics come near to giving an accurate idea of the extent of episodic use.

Enforcement statistics — based on convinctions for Misuse of Drugs Act offences — are of equally limited usefulness, relating as they do to only a small proportion of users, as observed by this ex-user quoted in *Police Review*:

> At first there was not much hassle from the police [he recalls]. The local police knew the regular users, those that had been taking heroin for the last ten to fifteen years. But once the police caught on that there were lots of people taking it regularly, there was lots of hassle, although they didn't catch many. Now although the local drug officers have a good idea who does it, I'm sure they've no idea of just how much heroin is around.

This man estimated that of the hundred or so users in his town, only two or three would be notified to the Home Office as being addicted:

They would register because they'd been done and wanted a good court report or because they'd heard [that] a particular doctor was easy to register with and would hand out methadone or other heroin substitutes (*Police Review*, 15 June 1984).

It is clear, then, that the official statistics — whether relating to the health system or to the apparatus of law-enforcement — are of little relevance to the task of estimating the overall numbers of persons using, exchanging and selling heroin in Britain. They are suggestive as to the *fluidity* of the situation but that is all.

(iii) Government estimates of the prevalence of drug use in Britain rely on a series of unpublished reports based on detailed local studies, especially in north London (Drug Indicators Project). By weighting the results of these studies so as to fit what is known about the situation in other regions of the country, the government has produced estimates suggesting that there were between 25,000 and 40,000 *regular* users of heroin and other opiate-type drugs in the early 1980s (ACMD, 1982: 24 and Hartnoll et al., 1984: 23). Since that time heroin use — particularly irregular or episodic smoking and snorting — has considerably increased, and it would probably be safe to say that numbers of ever-users of heroin exceeded 100,000 by the mid-1980s. This estimate of 100,000 or more people in Britain who have ever tried heroin is, it must be stressed, no more than a 'guesstimate', or an 'order of magnitude' figure. It has been arrived at by doubling the 1982 estimate of a minimum of 25,000 then regular users to reflect increasing numbers approaching statutory and non-statutory agencies for help and advice and to reflect increases in Customs seizures, and then doubling again to get a minimum figure for the numbers of ever-users (assuming that for every person who uses heroin fairly regularly there is *at least* one other who has used it but does not do so regularly at the present time).

(iv) The experience of practitioners and self-help groups in the fields of health, welfare and advice work, as well as those involved in unemployment projects, bears out media reports that smoking and snorting are the main forms in which heroin is now taken by new, young adult users. The widest information networks on what appear to be quite new patterns of heroin use are provided by community organizations such as tenants' groups, parents' groups and unemployment resource centres. Workers at Merseyside Trade Union, Community and Unemployed Resource Centre, for example, have observed that increasing numbers of local white teenagers and young adults are involved to varying extents in smoking and snorting, and that the latter do not see this as their primary problem — or even a particular cause for concern at all. [2] A consistently reported feature is that although both middle class and working class white young people are involved with heroin in areas where there is a thriving irregular economy, black people currently make up a very small proportion of users (as has indeed always been the case in this country).

Specialist drug agencies such as drug dependency treatment clinics and rehabilitation hostels are seldom familiar with this new situation. Where expertise does exist it tends to be situated in and around community resources such as street agencies, unemployment centres and self-help groups. In the following section, we explore this new phenomenon of circulation of heroin in the context of the informal and irregular economies.

Irregularities: informal economies and heroin

Throughout the 1970s there developed a growing body of literature which discovered or, more accurately, re-discovered a variety of activities that seemed hidden from the official purview of the formal economy (Laite, 1982). Such activities are highly diverse. Some take place within the sphere of waged work, others in and around households, local communities and informal exchange networks. Some of the minor perks, fiddles and benefits associated with them are basically legal, others clearly not, whilst there are a number of other activities which occupy a great area of the law. In the absence of agreement over the matter of precise conceptual definition, we can employ the term informal economies as a means of referring to these activities. Our present concerns focus upon more unambiguously illegal patterns of thieving, dealing and exchange involving a variety of commodities and centred primarily on streets and housing estates and best described, we believe, as the *irregular economy* (Ferman and Ferman, 1973). We suggest that it is within the context of a degree of involvement in this irregular economy that the bulk of heroin use among young people is currently taking place. The irregular economy provides multiple conduits for the distribution and exchange of drugs, and for a variety of other goods and services, prostitution, the disposal of stolen goods, and so on.

Activity within the irregular economy has as a defining characteristic a temporal sense of irregularity. It takes the form of a bunching together of intensive periods of work (buying, selling, contacting, getting money together, etc.). In between these intensive bursts of activity the business of survival requires one to be always searching for further opportunities, and to be on the look-out for potential dangers. Patterns of irregular and even sometimes 'chaotic' styles of drug use mesh with the irregularity of this economy and the subcultures that it underpins.

This perspective carries implications for the way in which one approaches two issues with which the use of heroin (and indeed illegal drugs in general) has traditionally been associated — namely, ill-health and crime. The issues of health care and 'harm minimization' are briefly considered in the closing sections of this paper. The following remarks are addressed primarily to the issue of the relationship between heroin use and criminality.

The question of crime

The involvement of drug users in the irregular economy, where stolen goods also circulate, necessarily makes an important contribution to current stereotypes of drug users as being not only sick but also criminal, being pushed into crime in order to support their expensive habits. As Helmer observed of the typical response in the United States, the 'approach to the narcotics problem is the same one today as it has always been; narcotics cause crime' (Helmer, 1975:12). In London, a senior police officer discussing the rising use of heroin in a BBC news interview (19 June, 1984) ventured the opinion that while there were no official figures which proved a link between rising heroin use and crime, nonetheless a substantial source of income is required to sustain the use of heroin, and he felt quite sure that this income was not coming from the welfare state: the clear implication being that drug users must be stealing in order to get money to supply themselves with drugs.

We would agree that there are links between widespread heroin use today and criminality. However, the nature of these links is mystified in the statement that heroin causes crime. Our argument is very simple. Social security benefits and youth training allowances are at too low a level for satisfaction of basic needs — for housing, clothing, heating and food — let alone buying much in the way of intoxicants. It is partly in order to secure a standard of living better than mere survival that people get involved in aspects of the irregular economy, and it is through their involvement in this partially petty-criminal economy that they may come to buy, exchange, sell and consume heroin. There is a sense, then, in which crime can lead to heroin use: the very opposite of the conventional view. One implication of this might be that a shift in economic policies that reduced the extent to which the irregular economy permeates increasing numbers of inner-city and other areas would reduce petty crime, and with it much heroin use in its presently expanding forms. A direct assault by law enforcement agencies against episodic heroin users, by contrast, would do relatively little to dent the criminal aspects of the irregular economy in which they play only a part.

How one responds to the activities of importers and large-scale suppliers of drugs such as heroin is another question. Organized crime of this kind is by no means new, and has been the subject of lengthy discussion elsewhere, especially with regard to the context of the USA (Timmer, 1982; Chambliss, 1978). Here in Britain, at the same time as the street level irregular economy has significantly expanded, there have been changes in the organization of drug supply at national and regional levels:

the illicit market has become more organized and has attracted the attention of criminal groups who, a few years ago, would not have been willing to become involved in drugs. This is particularly true of cannabis and in the past two years of heroin (Hartnoll et al., 1984: 24).

The large-scale importation and supply of drugs have always been a lucrative source of income — in this respect the illegal market simply reflects that in alcohol, tobacco and pharmaceuticals — and the combination of a ready international supply of heroin and a ready irregular market in Britain makes large-scale pushing even more attractive to established criminal organizations. What is of note is that even here — as on the lower level of the street and local community — *existing* patterns of large-scale criminal and petty criminal activity are expanding to incorporate drugs.

We move now from consideration of the socio-economic to the socio-cultural aspects of heroin use, and discuss the significance of changes in the mode of administration of heroin.

Modes and meanings of administration
Although sample survey evidence is as lacking on this matter as it is on the issue of the total numbers of young people involved, it has come to be widely accepted that the bulk of heroin use amongst those whose use began during the last few years takes the form of either smoking or (less commonly) snorting the substance. Rather than being injected, in other words, the drug is heated and the smoke fumes thereby given off are inhaled.

There are a number of reasons for thinking that this particular mode of administration makes an important contribution not only to the intrinsic compatibility of heroin use with the structural features of the irregular economy, but also to an understanding of why the now widely used description of the rate of increase in the activity among young people as an epidemic might be a particular misnomer. The first and arguably most important one connects with the distinction between the categories of 'sickness' and 'irregularity' referred to earlier. Throughout the 1960s and early 1970s there was a labour market quite favourable to white males in many parts of Britain, offering opportunities for considerable freedom of movement between jobs and, significantly, ease of movement out of the labour market and back again. The adoption of the sick role (see especially Parsons, 1951) in the manner made possible by being officially labelled and treated as an addict provided an important vehicle for such movements in and out of the labour market, and offered other rewards besides. The role of 'addict' was one which — provided one played one's cards right by both acknowledging the undesirability of one's predicament and at least appearing to accept the kind of technically competent medical treatment then being offered by drug treatment clinics — one might have a good chance of occupying indefinitely. There was, of course, a certain price to pay: specifically, an acceptance of the moral stigma which conventional society tends to bestow upon those whom it views as being unavoidably or irresponsibly dependent upon its beneficence, and a corresponding obligation to conform with the stereotypically defined role.

For many young people today, however, the distinction between being either 'inside' or 'outside' respectable society and the formal economy has become very blurred. They cannot easily *choose* whether to be 'in' or 'out', the choice already having been made for them. For those effectively excluded from wage employment there is little advantage to be derived in adopting the sick role, since the primary benefit of the sick role is that it allows one to temporarily evade the obligations of waged work. There is a sense, then, in which the market itself has diminished the appeal of sick/addict styles of involvement with heroin, and in doing so has undermined one possible rationalization for injecting drugs. Injection is an unappealing prospect for most people, but one that can be 'made sense of' within the context of an acceptance of oneself as a 'junkie' or addict. Injection is made less acceptable when circumstances weaken the rationale for adopting the sick/addict role.

The practice of smoking heroin, by contrast, has a number of relatively positive aspects. In the most straightforward sense, of course, it is simply easier at a psychological level to relate it to and view it as an unproblematic extension of more conventional pursuits such as the smoking of tobacco or, in the case of some young people, cannabis.

However, it is also necessary to consider certain consequences arising from the contemporary supply situation. The fact that the bulk of heroin currently entering this country is of high quality, low in cost and easily obtainable (at least in many urban areas) has been a recurrent theme in the expressions of alarm being made by the various agencies concerned with trying to deal with the problem. But it ought to be recognized that the widespread availability of cheap, good quality heroin makes the practice of smoking it a considerably more rational activity than it would have been in former times when the supply situation was not such a favourable one from the consumer's point of view. Only when the drug is relatively plentiful and cheap can the user contemplate letting some of it quite literally go up in smoke.

It should also be pointed out that smoking has certain health advantages in comparison with injection. Firstly, infections, sores and vascular problems sometimes associated with injection of heroin and other substances are not risks run by the smoker. Secondly, smokers may be less likely to overdose. With injection, it is sometimes difficult for the user to calculate precisely how much of the drug to inject in order to achieve the desired effect — a matter of practical inconvenience on many occasions and death by overdose on some. Smoking, by contrast, is a more easily controlled and safer mode of administration.

Summarizing our discussion so far, we suggest that the easing of heroin supply on an international level, the shift to the new modes of administration (most commonly smoking) that this facilitates, and the relatively casual (non-needle/non-addict) and episodic styles of involvement that emerge in the context of a more general involvement in the irregular economy, may reasonably be described as contributing to a quantitative increase in the numbers of heroin users, and to a qualitative shift towards less dangerous patterns of use. Putting it in fewer and plainer words — Britain has acquired rather more of a slightly less bad thing. We take up some of the practical implications of this new situation at the end of this paper.

Boys' talk: masculinity, exploit
and the claiming of care
Turning now to the final element in the overall perspective which we are trying to develop, we attempt to link the living out of *sexual divisions* to patterns of use of heroin in and around the irregular economy.

Although women made up an increasing proportion of injecting drug users as the 1960s turned to the 1970s they remained an absolute minority of those known to helping and enforcement agencies, and most observers in the early 1980s agreed that most of the new young smokers of heroin were male. This perception may of course partly have been the result of biases in referral practices and in the problem categories employed in the recognition of drug users, and partly the result of the fact that drug advice and rehabilitation agencies were particularly dominated by masculine cultures.[3] From 1983 onwards, agencies reported seeing more women users coming forward for help, though the overall impression remained that the majority of users — amongst those seeking help and amongst the far greater pool of users who see no reason to — were male. Whatever the present balance between young male and female heroin users, there are some specific cultural impediments to use of 'heavy' drugs by young women — impediments that may both restrict women's drug use and shape it in particular ways. Sexual divisions also have significance for young males' drug use, as we shall show.

In relation to women, McRobbie suggests that:

> So intransigently male are the mythologies and rituals attached to regular drug taking that few women feel the slightest interest in their literary, cinematic or cultural expressions — from William Burroughs' catalogues of destructive self-abuse and Jack Kerouac's stream-of-consciousness drinking sprees to Paul Willis's lads and their alcoholic bravado. It would be foolish to imagine that women don't take drugs — isolated young housewives are amongst the heaviest drug users and girls in their late teens are one of the largest groups among attempted suicides by drug overdose. Instead I'm suggesting that for a complex of reasons the imaginary solutions which drugs may offer boys do not have the same attraction for girls. One reason is probably the commonsense wisdom deeply inscribed in most women's consciousnesses — that boys don't like girls who drink, take speed and so on; that losing control spells sexual danger; and that drinking and taking drugs harm physical appearance. A more extreme example would be the way that the wasted male junkie can in popular mythology, in novels and films, retain a helpless sexual attraction which places women in the role of potential nurse or social worker (McRobbie, 1980: 46).

This last point will, in a modified form, be central to our argument about male heroin use. But first we want to take up McRobbie's more general point about girls, and to add that the impediments to girls getting involved with heavy drugs are not purely cultural ones related to stereotyping, but are also brazenly economic, insofar as males tend to monopolize the opportunities thrown up within the irregular economy amongst themselves. Girls tend to be excluded from all systems of exchange and trade except those which revolve around one commodity: their bodies. However, prostitution is a role difficult for many young women to combine with an identity as conventionally decent and feminine.[4] Since prostitution is the main avenue of access into the irregular economy for women, the majority of young women, whether waged or not, are channelled away from direct involvement in the irregular economy,[5] and hence away from the consumption practice that we are discussing here — episodic heroin use. For the minority of young women who are directly involved in the irregular economy in the role of prostitute, involvement with alcohol and drugs may be affected by the attitude of pimps. For women who are not much involved in the irregular economy in this or any of the other generally subordinate roles open to them, the initial style and meaning of their involvement with drugs will be mediated by the social circles through which the drugs are supplied. The drug involvements of those who continue to use will probably also be shaped by their general circumstances and concerns; as a street agency worker put it to us in respect of drug use by a number of young women with children, 'they are lonely and have to cope with their own problems as well as those of their kids'.

However, for young men having access through the irregular economy to heroin, sexual divisions have a significance identified by McRobbie as providing — at least in their imaginations — 'helpless sexual attraction which places women in the role of potential nurse or social worker'. It is this placing of women that at least partially explains the appeal to men of residual ideas about addiction and sickness — ideas that still surround their use of heroin to some extent, to be called up selectively as the occasion demands. In this case, we suggest, the occasion is the desire of young men not simply for sexual servicing, but rather to be attended upon or pandered to in a totally exclusive and caring way. Few girls — and few mothers — will normally act the role of 'nurse or social worker', but the declared state of 'having to come off' heroin gives males an emotional lever of use to them in their dealings with women.

Heroin is an active pharmacological agent,[6] and has a spectrum of definite and recognizable effects that may be selectively amplified according to the expectations and needs of the user as brought to the fore in the circumstances of use. Similarly, the condition of not recently having used heroin (or other intoxicants) is a resource in the construction of male identity during those extended periods when the drug is not an available commodity in the irregular economy immediately surrounding the person. Both conditions – being stoned and being straight – are constructed as experiential states through the mediation of sexual identity and social relations.

Masculinity and intoxication

We have already pointed to the essentially episodic aspect of this consumption practice, framed as it is by the irregular 'production' characteristics of those parts of local economies in which heroin circulates. Like the various 'street trades' with which they are intertwined — fetching and carrying, doing favours, seizing all available opportunities to acquire property, and a range of criminal and quasi-criminal activities — the acquisition of heroin and its consumption are enmeshed in a meaning system that celebrates masculine prowess and exploit. There is nothing novel about this depiction of the culture and concern surrounding heroin use. As noted by Margaret Tripp, one of the first psychiatrists to attempt to 'treat' young working class men who came along to the Drug Dependency Units (drug clinics) when these were first opened in the late 1960s, they closely corresponded to:

> the stereotype of the kind that gets nothing from school in the working class area. Truancy, then petty stealing, a joy ride in a car, typically at least one appearance before a magistrate. Then drugs, any and all that were available, including heroin when it came on the street (Tripp, in Judson, 1973: 47).

What is new is the greater extent to which the quasi-criminal irregular economy has expanded, thereby permitting this masculine celebration of the values of that economy to be expressed through one of its commodities, heroin, for a much greater number of young men.

To put it simply: it's *tough* to take heroin! At least, it is as far as your mates, and the world in general, are concerned. However, things are a little different in the domestic sphere.

Masculinity and 'coming-off'

(a) *Girlfriendly help*. It is upon the experience of having been straight for some time, and of actively experiencing this state as an unwelcome departure from the reaffirmation of masculinity made possible by intoxication, that we want to focus in understanding the interaction that places girlfriends (or mothers) of users in the role of 'nurse and social worker'.

The feelings of deprivation that are produced by the *lack* of a commodity that is a potent pharmacological agent, a valued consumption reward for irregular work done, and an important vehicle for the promotion of masculinity are clearly likely to be very strong ones which, if played out in the context of a belief in the addictive qualities of the drug, may be experienced as traumatic and as undermining important aspects of social identity. However, one way whereby a young man can adapt to — and benefit from — this situation is for him to play out and manage such discomforts by coming off heroin within the context of the domestic, or *private* sphere. Within this sphere a man may feel safe enough to explore the temporary dent in his masculinity that results from cessation of drug consumption, to recognize (indeed luxuriate in) feelings of lack, vulnerability and need that are normally unacknowledged, and to display these aspects of self for a girlfriend (or several if the first does not respond with sufficient love and attention). It also creates an opportunity for the girl to feel that at such times she *really knows* the boy — breaking through the normal (i.e. public) shell of toughness and hard confidence (see Eichenbaum and Orbach, 1984:56). We are suggesting, in other words, that such behaviour can be seductive.

In suggesting all this, of course, we are not denying that pharmacology and, sometimes, real dependence have their parts to play, but rather that 'coming off' remains a sexually scripted encounter. The point is that the feelings experienced by the boy (vulnerability, need) and by the girl (mothering, needed), and their probable reflections in actual behaviour, firmly place the latter in the position of nurse and social worker to which McRobbie refers. The girl thereby finds legitimate the expenditure of considerable time and emotional effort to help the boy in his hour of need, and conventional sexual divisions are strongly reaffirmed both in the encounter itself and in its subsequent retelling.

It is not difficult to see what a young man may get out of this: refreshed, fed, and wearing clean clothes, he rises and goes back on the street, having had the type of 'holiday' that sexual divisons provide a young man 'working' in the irregular economy. A whole series of episodic cycles of consumption of heroin and of girlfriend-assisted 'coming-off' may follow. All aspects of the cycle — work, consumption, and the temporary retirement from and rejuvenation of masculinity — may be enjoyable in their ways.

(b) Younger boys and their families. In the case of boys in their lower teens and occasionally younger, who try heroin or talk of it, we suggest that a similar set of motivations to that described above may be in play. In the case of younger boys, however, it is family members and, in particular, mothers, who are likely to be most concerned over the possibility or fact of heroin use. It seems to us likely that some younger males have discovered that to declare oneself or to be revealed as someone who has tried heroin provides one way in which they can gain an unusual amount of care and attention. Furthermore, because heroin experimentation is more or less equated with heroin addiction within the discourse on health and social problems to which most parents subscribe — and because local doctors, social workers and police, together with local newspapers generally underwrite that conflation of heroin and addiction — young boys who

present themselves as teetering on the edge of the abyss of involvement can find themselves in a position of considerable power. This is an aspect of the relations between younger males and their families that requires research: it was originally suggested to us by members of a community centre. And it would hardly be surprising were younger males to be using heroin to 'wind up' their families, since similar kinds of interactions occurred around solvent sniffing throughout the 1970s. We may now be seeing a reprise in which the substances involved differ but the patterns of interaction within the family remain pretty much the same. It will be very important to understand these recurrent processes if parents and practitioners are to be given realistic advice about how to respond. Saying 'don't panic' to parents and other family members who find themselves in such situations is to offer advice that they may find difficult to act upon.

We now attempt to apply the perspectives outlined above on heroin, the irregular economy, modes of administration and masculinity, applying them to the pressing issue of prevention policy.

Prevention — can a realistic control policy be found?

However jaded a ring the term prevention may have in certain crimin-ological and social policy circles, it is a term that connotes questions of pressing importance for a wide range of practitioners working with persons involved to varying degrees with heroin and other drugs.

Social workers, advice workers, youth workers, probation officers and police officers come across drug-related incidents and problems in their everyday work, and are by no means always sure how to respond to them. These problems may be divided into the immediately demanding, such as a client who presents as heavily intoxicated or overdosed, and longer-term questions about how to define the significance of, say, heroin use in a particular 'case' and how to respond most usefully over a period of time (ISDD, 1984). We shall be restricting ourselves to the longer term issues here. These issues are also of concern to management in statutory and non-statutory services and to national-level policy-making and advisory agencies. Most recently there has been an upsurge of community-level concern about heroin use and responses to it, and a range of non-professional and non-statutory groups, including parents' groups, have begun to address the problems that they see as being related to heroin, their families and communities. We have already mentioned unemployment centres as providing a potential source of information on and perspective upon drug-related problems. This paper has, first and foremost, been an attempt to synthesize some of the information and perspectives coming up from a variety of the statutory and non-statutory organizations, and we wish now to relate it to formal prevention policy as promulgated at governmental level.

The most recent government report on drug abuse is that published on *Prevention* by the Advisory Council on Misuse of Drugs (1984). This document is the outcome of many years deliberation by a working group of persons most of whom were originally brought together to consider ethical aspects of drugs misuse. The working group was subsequently renamed as having a concern with prevention, a concept that has found increasing favour in the context of both expenditure controls on the health and welfare services and enthusiasm for self-help at individual and local community levels. It was in this general context that the ACMD working group produced its recommendations about a problem the management of which ranges from health services to enforcement and is becoming almost the paradigmatic 'social problem'. The report identified two related aims on the prevention of drug-related problems:

> We decided that we should concentrate on preventive measures which satisfied two basic criteria: a) reducing the risk of an individual engaging in drug misuse; b) reducing the harm associated with drug misuse. It is clear that not all preventive measures could be equally effective in terms of both criteria (ACMD, 1984: 4).

In the paragraphs that follow, we discuss ways and means of addressing these two aims from the vantage point of the perspective upon heroin use that we have tried to develop. It may be useful, as a preliminary, to summarize the main components of our argument so far:

1. Extent. Heroin smoking and snorting is far more widespread in the mid–1980s than either smoking, snorting or injection has been hitherto. Most users currently use episodically and few consider treatment relevant.

2. Irregularity. The episodic nature of heroin use as a consumption practice is underpinned by the irregularity of work and leisure generally in that part of the expanding irregular economy within which heroin circulates as a commodity. Heroin use was always episodic for a proportion of users — those lacking wage work or clinic supply — and this proportion is now clearly in the majority.

3. Administration. The most common modes of administration of heroin — smoking and snorting, rather than injection — are compatible with a more casual approach to heroin use free of the medical and sick-role associations of the needle. Lower cost and greater purity may facilitate relatively casual and episodic patterns of use insofar as there is less concern over getting every last bit of the drug into the body by injecting it.

4. Masculinity. An exploration of the pharmacological properties of heroin and of the associated discourses on 'addiction' provides a new arena for the reproduction of traditional concepts of masculinity and femininity. Playing at 'coming-off' heroin provides an opportunity for boys to be unusually demanding, and for girls to go along with this as an 'exceptional situation' — yet one that reinforces sexual divisions in the longer term.

In short, we can say that the bringing together of these four elements — an expanding irregular economy as the primary public sphere for many young unemployed or soon-to-be unemployed males; the incorporation of supply of heroin into the relations of exchange of that economy; widespread knowledge about modes of consumption other than by injection; and, finally, continuing struggle between young men and women over the rights and duties of the sexes — has resulted in new patterns and meanings of involvement with heroin. In what ways, we now ask, can such an analysis be related to the ACMD's policy aims of reducing levels of use *or* minimizing associated problems and harm?

The aim of reducing drug use has for years been the main aim of British drug policy, and the reduction of supply has been the main strategy for achieving that aim. The ACMD report identifies 'the availability of drugs as one important influence upon both the level and nature of drug misuse. For that reason, attempts have been made for many years to minimize this influence by the use of statutory controls' (paragraph 3.5). The report goes on to mention controls on importation of drugs, prescribing by doctors, and legal penalties against cultivation and supply of drugs (as laid down by the Misuse of Drugs Act, 1971). The report does not mention taxation of businesses and individuals involved in illegal importation and supply. However, tax claims by the United States tax authorities have long been a means of acting against North American suppliers, even when the evidence against the latter was insufficient to bring criminal charges or secure convictions. There are now signs that British tax authorities, faced with evidence of income from drug trafficking that may provide sufficient grounds for purposes of taxation (although it is often insufficient to prove criminal activity 'beyond reasonable doubt' in a court of law), are beginning to think along American lines:

> Crime is no longer taxfree. In a move which has profound implications for burglars, bank-robbers and brothel-keepers, the Inland Revenue is levying tax on the proceeds of what it believes to be illegal £1.5 million marijuana operations. The tax demand is based on an estimated income over a four-year period and states unequivocally: 'Source of profits or income: drug-trafficking.' Hitherto, the taxman has been wary of attempting to raise revenue from illegal trade on the ground, as one senior official put it, 'if we are knowingly taking it, we are condoning it. We are then open to the criticism that we are tacitly accepting a situation that is illegal'. Now, however, the Inland Revenue has grasped the nettle, by levying a tax demand against Mr Howard Marks, said to be a former employee of MI6 who was acquitted in a 1981 Old Bailey trial of smuggling 15 tons of marijuana. Inland Revenue special investigators say they reject the jury's verdict in the case. ('Taxman sniffs out drug profit', *Observer*, 17 June 1984: 1)

What is being considered here is a move to bring part of the informal (and incidentally illegal) economy that is currently outside the tax net *into* that net, and hence partly into the mainstream of the regular or formal economy. This would not legalize the business, but would regularize it as regards tax, the amount of which would depend upon a process of bargaining between accountants on the two sides — as is the normal procedure in respect of calculation of taxes owed by other major businesses (such as pharmaceutical corporations). Now it is questionable whether taxation of drug businesses, legal or illegal, can be said to constitute any kind of control over their activities (e.g. by forcing them to reduce the amount of drugs supplied or to adopt different marketing and distribution strategies), and it is very doubtful whether this is the primary concern of the tax authorities anyway. We need to scrutinize any such partial regularization of the top end of the drug supply business and to evaluate any implications for changes in the patterns of drug supply and consumption that may follow. But it seems unlikely, in view of the increasing use of tax havens and other means of money laundering noted earlier in this paper, that the consequences will be dramatic.

A more immediate course of action — but one only applicable to the small minority of drug traffickers (a term generally reserved for large-scale suppliers and importers of proscribed drugs) who are prosecuted and convicted — has recently been announced by the government. As Mr David Mellor, the Home Office Minister who chaired the new Inter-departmental Committee on drug misuse, told the House of Commons on 13 July 1984: 'We shall be introducing legislation during the present Parliament to deprive major criminals, including drug traffickers, of the proceeds of their crime.'

We have said that the attempt to reduce or at least restrain supply of drugs has traditionally been the main strategy for achieving the aim of reductions of drug use. A subsidiary strategy, however, has been the attempt to reduce demand for drugs. As the ACMD *Prevention* report puts it: 'As an additional measure to trying to restrict the availability or supply or drugs, current prevention policy also includes educational measures which seek to discourage misuse' (paragraph 3.9). Throughout the report, education — 'of the community, of specific groups, and training of professionals' — is put forward as the main means of discouraging demand for drugs. Unfortunately, review of the international literature suggests that none of the available methods are capable of reducing experimentation with drugs (Dorn, 1983: chapter 3). However, belief in education as a means of solving social problems generally remains high, and drug use is no exception to this. It is possible, we suggest, that education and training *might* contribute to a reduction in drug use — either initial experimental use, or episodic and irregular continuing use, or even heavy use — if such measures addressed themselves not only to facts about the drugs involved and to the 'values' of individuals who may choose to take them, but also to the economic and social circumstances and cultures of the social groups within which individuals make their choices.[7] However, such educational materials as do exist with such an orientation do not relate specifically to the conditions of unwaged persons or those in the informal economies, nor to the possibilities for minimization of harm in such conditions. This seems one useful area of future work for practitioners in youth work, YTS and education generally.

Reduction of drug-related harm

One of the more encouraging features of current patterns of illegal drug use, including heroin use, is the relatively low 'use/harm' ratio. Of the literally millions of persons who have tried some illegal drug, few have gone on to become heavily involved or to suffer any clearly definable harm. To recognize this is not to condone drug use — whatever that may be taken to mean — but to build upon positive features of the existing situation. The ACMD report on prevention recognizes that reduction of drug-related harm is not necessarily dependent upon a reduction in drug use, and goes so far as to suggest that certain measures aiming at reduction of use may actually increase harm:

> In the first place, we need to improve our knowledge of the effectiveness of policies on supply, education and the media aimed at reducing harm. Secondly, the balance between reduction of harm and reduction of levels of misuse should be explored by studies to show whether, and in what circumstances, the relationship between levels of harm and levels of use is positively correlated, reciprocal or insignificant (ACMD, 1984: paragraph 6.15).

This is a reference to the dangers of labelling or self-labelling of drug users as 'addicts', and to the possibility that a side-effect of deterrent measures may be to deter users from seeking information, advice or treatment that might minimize harm. The reference to strategies of harm-minimization as being distinct from use-minimization opens up new perspectives, especially when considered alongside some findings of research into sequelae of education. One study of social education in the United States found that education can marginally accelerate young people's experimentation with drugs, whilst stabilizing existing moderate patterns of involvement and hence retarding heavy use and casualties, relative to control groups (Blum, 1976; Blum et al., 1978).

This raises the issue — what discourses on drugs in relation to work and sexuality can be relevant to existing patterns of heroin use in Britain? The place to look, of course — or rather the place to listen — is in the groups of the young men and women who people the social and economic relations that we have described in this paper. Until policy-makers and practitioners — and parents — regain sufficient self-composure to listen and learn about harm-minimization *as it is already practised*, then we shall not be in a position to build upon these positive features. We have suggested that a sensitivity to new patterns of use, modes of administration, relations to other irregular work and consumption practices, and sexual divisions is a prerequisite of such listening.

Conclusion

Throughout 1984 there was public debate over increasing penetration of the British market by heroin from the Far and Middle East. By the end of that year a disparate number of interest groups were united in defining the drug problem primarily in terms of importation of the product — the Conservative administration, the Society of Civil and Public Servants (representing customs officers, whose numbers had been cut), parent organizations and (keeping the pot boiling) the media. In October 1984 Health Minister Mr Kenneth Clarke, replying to a debate on drugs at the Conservative Party Conference, announced some minor amendments to and extensions of present control measures, the most newsworthy of which was life sentences for drug traffickers and dealers. This was described by Labour MP Clive Soley as 'putting on a show of toughness which has failed to prevent other criminal activites.... Deterrent sentences don't work'.[8] Soley suggested that a possible consequence of such sentencing would be to make the criminals more determined to avoid arrest and hence more prepared to use arms. Simplistic responses may be comforting — but they can backfire.

Overall, however, Conservative and Labour politicians generally share commonsense assumptions that drug supply causes drug addiction and crime, that the way to reduce drug problems is to cut supply, and that this can be done by suppression of production and distribution — i.e. by crop substitution programmes in third world countries[9] and by increasingly sharp penalties for traffickers. Among other observers, there are small sections of opinion on both the right and the left that champion legalization of supply (the commercial model) and/or decriminalization of possession (the libertarian stance, which can be allied either with free market economics,[10] or with leftist sentiments). The debate between those who favour stricter controls on supply and those who favour liberalization tends to define the issue as one of drug supply, and to exclude other frameworks of discussion.

In this paper we have consciously avoided the ever-present invitation to enter into a debate on what to do about drug supply. We want to say only that we think that liberalization of supply, either through an easing of currently tight medical prescribing policies or through commercial supply, would do no more than create a licit parallel market alongside the current irregular one. With the general economic and social conditions in society remaining unchanged, the end result of any legalization would be: *more drug use and same conditions = more harm.* On the other hand, advocates of greater restrictions on supply should in our view recognize that, even if such measures were successful (which they could be only marginally), there will continue to be a high level of heroin and other drug use in Britain for the foreseeable future. It is therefore incumbent upon all involved — whatever their views about policies bearing upon supply — to say how their analysis of the problem relates to the question of how to reduce, or at least not increase, the harm that may be associated with continuing and quite possibly increasingly widespread patterns of drug use. It is for these reasons that we have focused upon the situation in Britain, rather than giving credit to jingoistic fantasies by discussing the prospects of sorting out the conventional 'baddies' — Third World drug producers, drugs traffickers, corrupt law enforcement persons, and others involved in supplying heroin to meet British demand.

Within Britain, heroin use is becoming more widespread, in the sense that more people today have intimate knowledge of heroin than previously. This does not, however, mean that all users are on a slow boat to addiction, since the biographical consequences of intermittent use are mediated by cultures and meaning systems constructed around current economic circumstances and sexual divisions. In understanding the drug consumption practices of any social group, we might do well to ask four questions. Specifically:

1. How much of what drug do they use at one time, by what mode(s) of administration and with what expectations?

2. In what economic and cultural context do they use it, and do they do so regularly or irregularly?

3. What is the relation of the experience of intoxication, and of *not* using, to the form taken by sexual divisions in the groups concerned?

4. What opportunities do current patterns of use offer for reduction of future use and/or reduction of harm?

These questions may be useful as a simple checklist for appraising existing policy and practical proposals and for developing new ones. The questions may be summarized as relating to *drug practices*, *contexts*, *sexuality*, and prefigurative *harm-minimization* aspects, and may be useful in understanding and responding to the drug-related practices of any social group. In this paper we have focused upon the circumstances and drug use of young males in the irregular economy; the priority for future work must be to examine the circumstances and drug practices of other social groups (as distinguished by race, gender, age, circumstances and cultural concerns). Only when more is known about the ways in which a variety of social groups are involved in heroin and other drug use will it be possible to say in what ways those diverse involvements would be affected by any given policy. What stands in the way of a rational drug policy in Britain is the projection of the causes of our problems onto 'evil men' and foreigners and the failure to examine the *domestic* situation.

What signs are there of an improvement in drug-related policies? As of mid-1985, when this paper went to press, the signs were not encouraging.

The Home Office strategy paper *Tackling Drug Misuse* (1985) invoked an 'attack' on the problem 'by simultaneous action on five main fronts:
— reducing supplies from abroad
— tightening controls on drugs produced and prescribed here
— making policing more effective
— strengthening deterrence
— improving prevention, treatment, and rehabilitation.' (Home Office, 1985: 7).

The strategy also involves a high-profile public information campaign in the press and on television. It was in this context that the Parliamentary All-Party Home Affairs Committee recommended increased use of the armed forces — whilst the Committee's chairman wanted the death penalty restored for drug traffickers. 'We see [the drug problem] as the most serious peace-time threat to our national well-being', the All-Party report stated: 'Western society is faced by a warlike threat from the hard drugs industry'. But the nature of this industry — spawned by Britain in its opium wars with China, and now domesticated in these Small Islands — cannot be understood within this discourse on national mobilization. In this paper we have tried to suggest elements of a more constructive approach.

Notes

1. Over the decade 1973 to 1983, persons notified as addicts who were 'not previously known' rose from 807 to 4,189, and those 'no longer recorded' from 1,207 to 5,156. *Source*: Home Office, 1984.

2. Personal communication to second author by workers and management committee members at the Centre, June 1984.

3. For a description of social work practice in some non-statutory agencies which have tried to overcome these and other problems in helping drug users see Dorn and South, 1984.

4. For a description and analysis of how femininity is enforced through forms of language used by boys and girls, see Cowie and Lees, 1981 and new book by Lees, S, 1985.

5. This is not to say that young women are not involved in a variety of activities in other sectors of the informal economy, particularly in and between households and in exchange networks between friends and family members.

6. For a review of work on the pharmacological actions of heroin see the chapter by Stimmel and Kreek, 1976, and other parts of the same book.

7. For a teacher's manual along such lines see *Health Careers*, London: ISDD.

8. Remarks made at a meeting organized by the Society of Civil and Public Servants, 13 October, 1984, London.

9. For a recent discussion of the failure of the efforts of western countries to prevent Third World drug production, see McNicoll, 1983.

10. Writing in the *Spectator* of 13 October 1984, Geoffrey Wheatcroft said, 'If the Prime Minister tried harder she might see that economic and social liberalism are indivisible...Is it too much to hope that we might one day see England free rather than England compulsorily "drug free"?'

9

Beyond Wolfenden?
Prostitution, politics and the law

Roger Matthews

During the height of the moral panics surrounding prostitution at the end of the nineteenth century, August Bebel, one of the few socialists to address the question of prostitution, identified it as a 'Sphinx to modern society, the riddle which society cannot solve' (Bebel, 1971: 150). In one sense Bebel was correct in that the multiplicity of legislation directed at prostitution had not succeeded in eradicating it. But his indictment is also wide of the mark in that the various European states were not primarily concerned with 'solving' the problem in Bebel's terms but rather sought to maintain a more manageable form of prostitution divested of its disruptive and politically embarrassing characteristics.

For almost a century the various European states have, in pursuing this 'regulationist' strategy, achieved — albeit at a price — a considerable degree of success in containing prostitution through the sanctioning of 'public women', and also employing it as a vehicle for influencing the relation between the female labour market and the marriage market.

One of the most sophisticated formulations of regulationism is the internationally famous 'Wolfenden Report on Homosexual Offences and Prostitution' (1957) which has remained until recently the main reference point for post-war legislation on prostitution and related offences in Britain. It was the first major British report on prostitution and street offences since the McMillan Report in 1928. Although Wolfenden was seen to be a radical and path-breaking approach, it did not, unlike its predecessor, argue for a thoroughgoing revision of the antiquated body of legislation which related to prostitution; instead it attempted to bring the existing disparate body of legislation into a new synthesis.

As a number of commentators have indicated, Wolfenden's approach to prostitution involved a threefold offensive (see Hall, 1980; Greenwood and Young, 1980) which aimed firstly, to apply a more rigid distinction between law and morality, crime and sin, claiming that however 'immoral' prostitution may be it was not the law's business (see Morris and Hawkins, 1970; Schur, 1963; Kaplan, 1977). Secondly, it aimed to rationalize resources directed towards the control of prostitution while increasing the certainty of convictions; and thirdly, it encouraged a more systematic policing of the public sphere in order to remove the visible manifestations of prostitution in London and other urban centres (see Bland, McCabe and Mort, 1979; Smart, 1981).

The net effect of this offensive was to afford the law only a minimal role in confronting prostitution itself. The law should only be concerned, it was argued, with 'the manner in which the activities of prostitutes and those associated with them offend against public order and decency, expose the ordinary citizen to what is offensive and injurious, or involve the exploitation of others' (Wolfenden, 1957: 80). In the application of these proposals Wolfenden sought to streamline the process of apprehension and conviction of offenders by removing the formal need to prove annoyance and by increasing police discretion through the introduction of the cautioning system. Through this system the woman entered the court as a 'common prostitute' whose guilt was assumed in advance and who could be safely convicted on police evidence alone. In this way the offender was never in a position to challenge the (double) moral standard on which the legislation was constructed, which in turn reinforced the claim that the law was not concerned with private morality. In this way legislation in the form of the Street Offences Act 1959 proved extremely successful in removing prostitution from view and encouraging the growth of more clandestine, privatized and commercialized operations.

Through the implementation of this threefold offensive Wolfenden was able to effect a narrower but deeper level of intervention which, while excluding different elements of prostitution from direct state control through selective privatization, it also employed more punitive and repressive measures which were to be directed at a smaller, more manageable and more vulnerable population. As the policing of 'public women' became more cost-effective there was a simultaneous diminution of civil liberties and the erosion of legal rights, while the legislation on soliciting was increasingly constructed around certain categories of offenders, rather than specific acts.

But the past decade has brought changes which have increasingly unbalanced Wolfenden's triangulated strategy. Deep and long-term economic recession, changed employment practices among women, the resurgence of the women's movement, changing gender roles, the growth of community groups and organizations representing prostitutes and the growing problem of kerb-crawling have all combined to create a different political and moral climate in which the 'liberalism' associated with Wolfenden as well as much sixties legislation is gradually being undermined.

The introduction of three Private Members' Bills in the House of Lords between 1967 and 1969 indicated elements of dissatisfaction within parliamentary circles even towards the tail-end of the sixties. These Bills were concerned mainly with deleting reference to 'common prostitutes' in the law and suggestions that the law against the client, in the form of the kerb-crawler, should be initiated. None of these Bills achieved a second reading but nevertheless indicated a growing concern with women's rights and legal inequalities which were increasingly emphasized by the supporters of the Women's Movement. But even by 1974 the Working Party on Vagrancy and Street Offences remained stoically complacent and concluded in its Report that 'the Street Offences Act of 1959 is very substantially meeting the objectives of the Wolfenden Committee, and while we have considered with care the objections which have been made to it, we have no amendments to suggest to the substance of the law' (Working Paper on Vagrancy and Street Offences, 1974: 78).

Two further Private Members' Bills in 1979 and 1981 again did not receive a second reading, but the latter introduced by Clive Soley, MP on 'The Imprisonment of Prostitutes (Abolition) Bill' was influential in ultimately achieving the abolition of imprisonment for prostitutes convicted of soliciting. Campaigning behind these Private Members' Bills were the various organizations speaking on behalf of prostitutes who were them-selves publicly questioning the implicit moralism, the double standard, and the various anomalies which were contained within the legislation. Organizations like PUSSI (Prostitutes United for Social and Sexual Integration), PLAN (Prostitution Laws are Nonsense) and PROS (Pro-gramme for Reform of the Laws on Soliciting) actively drew attention to some of the inequities and inconsistencies within the legislation (see McLeod, 1982: 119–47).

As these various groups representing prostitutes have become more organized they have sought to defend the civil liberties of prostitutes, resist discretionary methods of law enforcement by the police, and expose some of the legal anomalies in court by, for example, making it incumbent upon the prosecutor to prove, rather than assume, that they *are* prostitutes, and by demanding trial by jury, they have brought pressure to bear on the criminal justice system and disturbed its relative complacency. Similar movements organized around groups like COYOTE (Call off your old Tired Ethics) in America, together with civil rights groups, have challenged prostitution laws on the basis that they infringe civil liberties and the individuals' rights of privacy, while enforcement of solicitation laws infringe on rights of free speech and are enacted through selective and discriminatory enforcement. Also vagrancy-type laws which are used to round up or harass 'disorderly persons' have been deemed unconstitutional in that they deprive those arrested of due process and arrest people on the basis of their 'type' rather than their acts. Punishing someone for what they are rather than for what they do has been ruled to constitute 'cruel and unusual' punishment. (See Rosenbleet and Pariente, 1973; Milman, 1980; Parnas, 1981; Wade, 1975.)

As the economic recession has deepened and the gains which women had made in the labour market were increasingly attacked, halted or reversed, many women who had found employment, particularly in the seasonal, unskilled, non-unionized occupations, were the first to suffer the assault on jobs and the 'rationalization' of the workforce (see Eisenstein, 1982). This, combined with the growing movement towards single parent families and the rapid increase in divorce, has forced many women to become increasingly dependent upon inadequate welfare benefits. Under these conditions it is not surprising that prostitution becomes an increasingly attractive option — or rather a decreasingly unattractive option — for many women, resulting, as a number of observers noted, in the growing incidence of street-walking. Thus the removal of the visible and public spectre of women on the streets, which many had considered Wolfenden's central achievement, was gradually being overturned as more and more women took to the streets. Not only were street-walkers becoming more numerous, but they also appeared to be getting younger (see Swingler, 1969; Cunnington, 1980).

During this period characterized by a growing 'feminization of poverty', a re-emphasis upon the monogamous family, and attacks on female promiscuity, there emerged a new contradictory movement in the punishment of female prostitutes. That is: a movement towards the decarceration of prostitutes through the removal, in 1983, of imprisonment as a punishment for soliciting on one side, and a simultaneous increase in the number of female prostitutes appearing in court on soliciting charges on the other. The number of convictions for this offence rose from just under 6,000 in 1982 to approximately 10,000 in 1983 (see Criminal Law Revision Committee 1984: 6) while the rate of incarceration rather than decreasing, substantially increased between 1982 and 1983 through the non-payment of fines such that in 1982 eighty-three women were incarcerated for the non-payment of fines, in 1983 it was 172 and in the first quarter of 1984 alone it was eighty. Paradoxically, the formal removal of incarceration in a period of growing anxiety about prostitution, has served to increase the level of fines inflicted on prostitutes which many found themselves unable to pay, and thus many have ended up in prison by a more circuitous route. This situation has created an apparent impasse in sentencing policy such that in the words of one Magistrate 'the problem of prostitution and the role of the courts in dealing with this problem is becoming acute' (Quentin-Campbell, 1984). Some Magistrates attempted to overcome this impasse by 'bending' the law and binding prostitutes over to be of good behaviour for twelve months (see Hansen, 1982).

Part of the reason for the increased prosecution of female prostitutes has been the growing pressure brought by community groups, tenants' associations and local councils onto the police to deal with the problem of prostitution. The intervention of these groups has also highlighted the effects of kerb-crawling and turned attention towards the problems created by clients. Although kerb-crawling was becoming a national problem of major proportions, with the kerb-crawler creating a greater level of nuisance than the prostitute, the Working Party on Vagrancy and Street Offences (1974), following Wolfenden, consciously avoided the problem. However, recently there has been a dramatic shift in policy and the Criminal Law Revision Committee (1984) in its report on 'Prostitution in the Street' has recommended the introduction of legislation to deal specifically with clients and kerb-crawlers and the harassment of women in the street and public places. However, when these recommendations will reach the Statute Books they involve a substantial increase in police and court time and costs, and a 'widening of the control net' which Wolfenden was at pains to avoid.

As opposed to the complacent attitudes expressed by the Working Party on Vagrancy and Street Offences (1974) the approach of the Criminal Law Revision Committee (1984) is noticeably less self-assured about the problem, and in response to the changing conditions and the growing criticisms of existing legislation they only feel 'content to draw one safe conclusion, that this is not the time to amend the law to make it less effective in dealing with street prostitution. It is rather time to consider tightening it by penalizing also the men who solicit the services of the prostitutes' (CLRC, 1984: 6). Although the Criminal Law Revision Committee maintain a formal commitment to Wolfenden's style of regulationism, there is clearly a marked shift in approach towards a more overt and more systematic 'enforcement of morals', together with a broader shift to the Right, and a gradual erosion of that brand of liberalism which once underpinned Wolfenden's approach (see Wolfe, 1981; David, 1983). Within this general shift the question of morality, although playing a more central role, remains conveniently disguised.

The recent contributions of the Criminal Law Revision Committee (1982–84) indicate a potential restructuring of regulationism, involving a broadening of the base of illegality to include for the first time in British history the criminalizing of the male heterosexual client. But this proposal to extend the parameters of control and thereby effect a more systematic policing of the public sphere is certain to undermine the delicate balance which Wolfenden achieved. Although there remains a formal commitment to Wolfenden's basic approach, and a continued emphasis on the public and visible apsects of prostitution, the emerging brand of regulationism is caught in the contradiction of both wanting to extend the range and effectiveness of legislation and simultaneously limit police and court time and expenditure. In the wake of these uncertainties alternative forms of intervention have made considerable ground as the search for solutions becomes more desperate and more urgent.

Legalization

The recurring response to the current range of problems confronted by the regulationist stance, is the legalization, or the state control of prostitution through the organization of brothels which promises to remove the trade from the streets and relocate it within a more comfortable and manageable setting. Like regulationism, it accepts that prostitution is inevitable, although it sees it as potentially performing a more positive social function providing a necessary and useful social service.

Although there has been a general historical movement in Europe and America away from state sponsored prostitution and the brothel, in periods of crisis when the tensions within the regulationist position surface, the legalization of prostitution is invariably suggested. Legalization receives support from local councils, residents' associations and others who argue that if offers a more efficient and less hypocritical response to prostitution (see Sandford, 1975: 160). Since they see prostitution as both inevitable and functional for society in that it supports the family and caters for lonely and single individuals, they suggest that we ought to formally recognize its value and try to benefit from it rather than deny its existence. State control of prostitution would also, it is claimed, provide a healthier, safer, and more congenial form of organization both for the client and the prostitute. By placing the prostitute under state control if offers her protection from the police, pimps and dangerous clients, while giving her regular hours within a more congenial setting (see Yondorf 1979).

Legalization, it is argued, will clear the streets both of prostitutes and kerb-crawlers, thus reducing the nuisance usually associated with soliciting by both prostitutes and clients. Legalization would also save the prostitute the inconvenience and stigmatization of criminalization; while allowing intervention by social work and other welfare agencies, who could provide assistance for women who might want to leave the game, and offer the prospect of rehabilitation. Finally, state control would provide a double economy in that by bringing prostitution into the regular, formal economy it would provide an opportunity for the state to benefit, through taxation, from the profits of prostitutes, while removing the costs of police and court time.

These familiar arguments for legalization clearly have a continuing attraction to a number of agencies and groups directly involved with prostitution; while the growth of a number of 'eros centres' in various European countries suggests that municipal authorities are finding such 'solutions' increasingly attractive. However, despite the immediate short-term advantages which attract some prostitutes and clients towards these state run or licensed enterprises, legalization has a number of undesirable and often unanticipated consequencies.

One of the central justifications for legalization historically, has been in terms of the control of venereal diseases. Control, at best, however, has always been one-sided, concentrating on the female prostitute, while giving no protection against the unchecked male client. At worst, it has

involved the forced examination of all 'suspected' women whether
prostitutes or not. Compulsory, and often perfunctory and brutal examina-
tions have historically been actively resisted by all women; while infected
women often learn to conceal the infection or simply move to another
district. According to Abraham Flexner's comprehensive research at the
beginning of the century there is in fact no evidence that legalization and
regular medical inspections reduced the incidence of venereal disease, but
rather only managed to conflate crime and disease, inferring that becoming
infected is in itself a crime. Flexner's study of prostitution in Europe also
convincingly showed that the decline of the brothel had not led to an
increase in venereal disease, but rather led to a decrease in its incidence
(Flexner, 1917: 260). The extent of venereal disease amongst prostitutes
has tended to be exaggerated, and recent studies in both Britain and
America indicate that prostitution accounts for less than 10 percent of
its current incidence. Also, venereal disease has, with the development
of effective medicine, lost much of its former terror, while many prostitutes tend to take stringent precautions against infection (see Jennings,
1976; Caughterty, 1974).

A second major contention emanating from this position is that the
legalization of female prostitution, by providing a readily available outlet
for sexual drives, would reduce the incidence of sexual attacks. This line
of argument, based upon a 'hydraulic' model of male sexuality, sees the
basis of prostitution in the spontaneous demand for an available 'outlet'
for sexual drives. Like the arguments concerning venereal disease, the
empirical evidence does not support the hypothesis. On the contrary it
suggests that where prostitution has been prohibited the incidence of
sexual crimes, including rape, has declined (see Schwendingers, 1983).
Thus rather than reducing rape the legitimation and commercialization
of prostitution may more readily be seen to objectify women and reduce
sexual relations to cash values, reinforcing the notion that women are
primarily sexual objects to be purchased or abused.

As for making prostitution more congenial and comfortable, the main
benefactor appears to be the male client, in that it potentially provides
a better alternative than draughty streets, uncertain advertisements,
expensive clubs and dubious agencies. For the working prostitute the
experience in brothels or the newly emerging eros centres is ultimately
less attractive for:

> it's a lousy job. You get all sorts in Eros Centres and Saunas. They're the
> pure and simple equivalent to brothels. There's no way you can actually
> refuse a client. The girls are forced to work, just to pay for the place
> they're working in. It's worse than science fiction, a society completely
> organized around the men who've got enough cash, and their pleasure (Jaget,
> 1980: 173).

The expansion of eros centres in various European countries, although it may appear at first sight to mark an elevation in the status of the prostitute, more realistically marks a new level of exploitation and deterioration in the position of women in general. Recent reports of the injection of large amounts of capital into these modern brothels exemplifies one of the main dangers of legalization — the legitimation of the further commercialization of prostitution in which the physical coercion characteristic of nineteenth century brothels is superseded by new forms of economic coercion (see Haft, 1976). The setting up of these eros centres marks not so much movement towards greater freedom, as some have suggested, but rather a reversion to neo-slavery and traditional modes of female dependence.

The ultimate limitation of the legalization argument is that it does not solve the problem of the social nuisance associated with prostitution, but merely exacerbates it. For legalization creates a dual system of control in that only a percentage of prostitutes ever register, as forced registration is invariably resisted, while a voluntary system of registration will only attract a small percentage of women. The net result is that only a limited percentage of prostitutes ever come within the state system, while the formal recognition of the state and the legitimization of prostitution serves as an encouragement for the recruitment of women outside the state system who feel that they too are more socially acceptable and can more freely operate on the streets. In fact:

> The establishment of Eros Centres (apartment buildings devoted to the exclusive use of licensed prostitutes) in Germany has not succeeded in containing prostitution either; the number of freelance prostitutes has increased in Germany while the number of registered ones has decreased. The majority of German prostitutes now work in apartment houses, bath houses, massage parlours and automobiles (Boles and Tatro, 1978: 76).

But the state cannot tolerate competition from 'outsiders' who might threaten the viability of its organization, and thus rather than being more tolerant of prostitutes who remain on the street, it tends to adopt a harsher system of penalties and sanctions against these women. The invariable result is that there is both an increase in street solicitation, and more vigorously enforced legislation. Rather than 'solve' or reduce the problem of prostitution, it only produces a contradictory system which on one hand both encourages prostitution and its exploitation, while on the other hand it attempts to suppress prostitution and the prostitute.

Decriminalization

A more attractive alternative strategy to many, and prostitutes' organizations in particular, is the decriminalization of prostitution and related offences. Although different groups and representatives suggest different levels of decriminalization, most advocates are agreed on two fundamental points. Firstly, that the existing legislation relating to prostitution does not improve the situation but often serves to make matters worse; and secondly, the need to humanize and normalize the prostitute, by reducing the social stigmatization associated with legislation, and by allowing prostitutes to operate more openly and freely.

Like the supporters of legalization the decriminalization lobby assume the inevitability of prostitution, while stressing its functional role in reinforcing the family and providing a necessary social service. But unlike the legalization position it offers a different conception of the motivation behind prostitutes' activities and rejects the assertion that prostitution is the result of individual psychologies, but rather that the motivation is, at root, determined by economic pressures. The lack of available employment opportunities, low pay, the particular problems of single parenthood and child care, make 'the life' particularly attractive to some women (see McLeod 1982: 12).

The justification for decriminalization arises from a dual response to the 'non-victim' status of prostitution. On one hand, it is claimed, following the regulationists, that prostitution is a non-victim crime and, therefore, it is not the law's business and that legal intervention is unnecessary and based upon an outmoded morality. On the other hand it is argued that the illegality of the prostitute's activities is not justified since she already suffers from economic and social disadvantage, and since she is driven by poverty and has little choice but to turn to prostitution, she cannot be held culpable for the offence. Thus she is already a victim or, rather, a 'double victim' propelled into a position of quasi-illegality. She is maintained in a subordinate relation to customers and pimps, as well as the police and other official agencies who are able to enforce discriminatory and often arbitrary methods of intervention (see Women Endorsing Decriminalization, 1973; Jennings, 1976).

The strategy of decriminalization derives its main strength from its promise to resolve three of the central tensions generated within the dominant regulationist position. Firstly, it offers a solution to the discreet but persistent moralism which informs the system of sanctions around soliciting and which punishes people not so much on the basis of their actions, but more directly on the basis of their status and sexual orientation. Secondly, it offers to overcome the subsequent legal anomalies and inconsistencies in the operation of the law by removing the legislation itself. It would also remove the costly and counter-productive effects of legislation, as well as the 'domino-effect' of intervention by which the 'problem' of prostitution is reproduced in continually new forms. Thirdly, by removing the quasi-illegality surrounding prostitution, decriminalization, it is claimed, will remove the criminal associations of the prostitute and simultaneously free her from the exploitation and domination of clients, pimps and official agencies who see her as an available and vulnerable target of control. Prostitution is in itself more properly seen as a job of work rather than a 'crime' as such.

The decriminalization lobby, both in Britain and America, have provided a detailed critique of existing legislation related to prostitution, showing that it is often inequitable, inconsistent and discriminatory in nature. In Britain, Eileen McLeod has argued that the present laws 'inflict particularly heavy penalties on street prostitutes; they seek to protect prostitutes in a paternalistic way; they blend attempts at rehabilitation and punishment and are generally discriminating against women' (McLeod, 1982: 12). There are growing critiques of the operation of soliciting laws which have maintained a one-sided preoccupation with the female prostitute whilst carefully excluding the male client. More specifically, it is argued that sanctions directed towards the female prostitute are inappropriate, ineffective and unsupported.

Soliciting related laws, it is argued, are inappropriate in that the nuisance and social disruption associated with street prostitutes does not constitute a serious enough problem to require the intervention of the criminal law. Even if there were a problem it could be adequately dealt with under other legislation (such as the Public Order Act, 1936), and there can be no justification for making any specific reference to prostitution.

The advocates of decriminalization also claim that sanctions are ineffective and even counter-productive; mainly on the grounds that despite the substantial outlay of time and money by the police and the judiciary, prostitution is alive and well. Legal intervention tends to have only a temporary and local effect in dealing with prostitution in clearing certain streets. Soliciting laws are an unnecessary burden on society as they are upon the women who are penalized. The enforcement of these laws through a combined process of stigmatization and fines, serves to reinforce women in 'the game'.

Current legal sanctions are held to be ineffective or counter-productive in that they are directed predominantly towards individual female prostitutes. As a result they reify certain ideologies constructed around 'pure' and 'fallen' women, the 'respectable' woman and the 'whore'; sustaining the judicial and social reinforcement of the female sex role (see Edwards, 1981: 55–8). Penalizing the prostitute and ignoring the client reinforces the ideology of an imperious male sexual instinct, and by implication it also supports 'the structures of male dominance, male privilege and monogamy' (McIntosh, 1978: 63). Further, the operation of current legislation also serves to undermine the rule of law, in that conviction of the prostitute is dependent upon the police having to mobilize all the evidence, while the women being introduced to the court as a 'common prostitute' is not in a position to seriously contest the issue.

The arguments for decriminalization have gained widespread support over the past few years, and must be taken seriously. Their critiques of current legislation have demonstrated its discriminatory and inequitable character and emphasized the pressing need to reconsider the laws relating to prostitution — particularly those concerned with soliciting. Increasingly influential within the decriminalization lobby are organizations representing the interests of prostitutes who understandably feel that a more open, legitimate, laissez-faire situation unhindered by the fetters of legality and police interference will make prostitution a more tolerable and less hazardous way of earning a living (see English Collective of Prostitutes, 1984). But it is far from certain that the decriminalization strategy (however far it is pursued) is in the current context likely to reduce the problems associated with prostitution. On the contrary, it might have other effects. As Symanski cryptically points out:

> The battery of arguments for decriminalization is formidable and difficult to ignore. Arguments, counter alternatives and appeal to common sense, elementary notions of justice, and the allocation of scarce resources. And not of least significance decriminalization appeals to the best interests of those who make use of prostitutes (Symanski, 1981: 228).

Although identifying some serious inconsistencies in the existing regulationist approach, decriminalization is not as radical as it might first appear, for the state, where it has sought to minimize expenditure, has readily embraced non-interventionist arguments. Decriminalization also embodies an acceptance of, and indeed the fulfilment of, the liberal conception of harm on which existing legislation is built, rather than offering a critical alternative. Moreover, many of the specific legal anomalies surrounding prostitution have been recognized and accepted by the official bodies who are in the process of effecting legislative changes including the removal of imprisonment for soliciting offences, the removal of the term 'common' prostitute, and are promising to provide a more even-handed approach by sanctioning the client and the kerb-crawler where they cause a nuisance or are offensive (see CLRC, 1982).

Decriminalization also shares with the official response an underlying theoretical commitment to nominalism which sees the problem of prostitution primarily in terms of individual motivation. Although it replaces psychological determinants by economic ones, the focus remains predominantly individualistic. Consequently legislation is evaluated primarily in terms of its effects upon individual prostitutes, rather than on social relations in general.

In the same vein, its conception of the role of the law and the state emphasizes the negative, constraining and limiting power of the state on individual freedom (see Foucault, 1978: 83–6). The law in these terms is seen as an essentially negative entity in setting unnecessary or arbitrary limits on individual freedom. There is little recognition from this perspective of the role of law as a positive and productive mechanism, or if its capacity to act as a protective instrument of social defence. The role and effects of law tend to be exclusively evaluated in terms of its impact on 'individual' prostitutes and on specific deterrence, rather than its role as a general deterrent. Although it is obviously difficult to quantify the role of law as a general deterrent, we must, in the period of advanced capitalism, ask ourselves the question posed by Kingsley Davis — not why so many women turn to prostitution, but rather why so few do (Davis, 1971). There can be little serious doubt that legal intervention over the past century, with all its anomalies and inconsistencies, has acted to reduce the level of prostitution and provide some protection for women and girls against exploitation. Decriminalization minimizes the important role of protective legislation which, however paternalistic, recognizes the real vulnerability of certain groups of women. There is nothing very radical in turning a blind eye to the wide range of asymmetrical power relations within society between classes, sexes and races, and until such differences are materially overcome, protective legislation remains necessary.

The decriminalization lobby may be correct to point out that maintaining prostitution in a state of semi-illegality may allow the intervention of various exploitative agencies. But decriminalization is unlikely to reduce the overall level of exploitation of prostitutes but rather to increase it. For as Elizabeth Wilson has pointed out 'wholesale decriminalization would simply mean a free for all for men' (Wilson, 1983: 224), and would undoubtedly encourage large financial and business interests pursuing the vast profits potentially available through the extensive commercialization of prostitution.[1] The removal of legal constraints would give a free hand to entrepreneurs to organize prostitution as a legitimate business. The criminalizing of prostitution by reducing its legitimacy also reduces the potential profit and thus the overall rate of exploitation.

Legislation against the organization of brothels is also important in this respect since significant profits can only accrue if prostitution can be organized on a large scale 'production line' system. The choice between existing regulationism and decriminalization in real terms may strategically be a choice between relatively small scale local exploitation by pimps and various parasites, and the large scale exploitation by well organized faceless business interests. Ultimately such interests are unlikely to 'allow' the kind of laissezfaire system which the decriminalization lobby envisage, but will undoubtedly attempt to control the market in sexuality, restrict competition, undermine individual competitors, in order to maximize profits. Like legalization, decriminalization would almost certainly encourage more women onto 'the game', particularly in periods of economic crises or recession.

If it is the case that decriminalization may in reality do little for the majority of prostitutes, it is certain that it will do even less for the majority of women. Indeed, the acceptance and legitimization of prostitution would act to reinforce the ideology of women as sex objects to be bought and sold indiscriminately on the market. As Mary McIntosh has argued:

> the way that the idea of male sexual needs supports institutionalized female prostitution is obvious, not so obvious perhaps in the way in which prostitution reinforces that ideology. Yet the existence of female and not male prostitution must to some extent bolster the idea that women do not need sex enough to demand it in the market and that men need it enough to be willing to pay dearly for it. Like rape, like contemporary forms of pornography, like beauty competitions, like much of our public culture, prostitution contributes to the casting of women as object and men as subject, and thus to the prevailing ideology (McIntosh 1978a: 63–4).

If the prevailing ideology is to be confronted and transcended then the material relations upon which it is constituted must also be transcended. This suggests that the erosion of such ideologies involves the control and reduction of prostitution not its legitimation or expansion.

However, it has also been constantly argued by the decriminalization lobby that the sanctioning of prostitution, and the reinforcement of ideologies between 'pure' and 'fallen' women serves to divide women into apparently oppositional groups, which acts ultimately to reinforce the notion that enduring relationships and monogamous marriage — with their various constraints — are the only legitimate option for most women. The sanctioning of prostitution, therefore, acts as a sanction against women in general who may have aspirations to retain their 'independence'. From this vantage point prostitution is identified as a progressive and liberating option, as the prostitute refuses to give up her 'independence'. But it is not the case that all anti-monogamous strategies are necessarily progressive, for as Simone de Beauvoir has pointed out, the 'greatest misfortune of the hetairae is not only that her independence is the deceptive obverse of a thousand dependencies, but also that this liberty is itself negative' (de Beauvoir, 1975: 585).

The decrminialization lobby are correct to emphasize that the erosion of the prostitute's rights acts to undermine the legal and social standing of women in general. But there are other rights at stake, in the form of the nuisance and disturbance created by prostitutes and their clients. Although the level of this nuisance is often exaggerated it is, however, a real and growing problem within many working-class districts, all of which invariably already suffer from relatively high levels of noise, crime and pollution, and have a reasonable interest in legally limiting and controlling the disruptive elements of prostitution (see Kingdom, 1981; Hirst 1980).

In one recent account of the experience of living on an estate near Kings Cross in north London, Eileen Fairweather writes that:

> Over the years, you get used to being kerb-crawled every night, every day, asked if you do fellatio when you just pop out to the shops. But with the number of brothels and pushers' flats now on the estate, the leerers and the weirdoes are literally on our doorsteps. Almost all of the women want the eviction of those flats known to 'cause or attract violence'. But the men just berate us for our lack of compassion for victims of society. We stare open-mouthed, having naïvely imagined that perhaps we were among them (Fairweather, 1982: 375).

Most tellingly she describes the horror, violence and intimidation which reigns on this estate and its devastating effect on everyday life, and the ways in which the 'law of the jungle' when left to operate freely, generates fear and hostility, rather than understanding and solidarity.

We have already noted the ambivalent response to the question of the non-victim status of prostitution by the various advocates of decriminalization. However, the majority concur with the articulation of the 'liberal' conception of harm embraced by Wolfenden, arguing that prostitution is relatively innocuous and involves no victim and therefore is not a legitimate object of legal sanctions (see Reiman, 1979). Since the client and the prostitute *freely* enter into a contract and a consensual relation, there can within existing legal relations be no justification for sanctioning either the prostitute or client, or outlawing their relation. But as Jock Young has argued:

> To represent consensus between partners as an argument for the innocuousness of an activity is to ignore that a contractual agreement in Capitalist society is very often not an agreement between equals, but one between those of unequal power; nor is such a 'free contract' beset merely by material constraints, the ideological domination of bourgeois ideas and categories scarcely makes for a rational contract between free individuals (Young, 1977: 7).

The decriminalization arguments are, in the main, governed by a pluralistic vision of society composed of free-willed atomistic individuals freely pursuing their own best interests apart from the unnecessary interference by the state. Because of the apparently consensual nature of prostitution, the problems of policing, the low reportage, the difficulties of providing objective evidence, it appears at first sight as an eminently reasonable object for decriminalization, but such a response ignores the possible structural or legislative solutions which may be available. Nor does this non-interventionist strategy provide a basis for distinguishing between the range of so-called non-victim crimes and their desirability in a just society.

In sum, decriminalization will not provide a strategy which will ultimately benefit prostitutes or women in general. Neither will it do much for the working class as a whole, particularly those who live in 'red light' districts. Those who would gain most in the long run from this strategy would be the clients and entrepreneurs. For decriminalization, like legalization, would open the flood gates for a thoroughgoing commercialization of prostitution, and encourage large-scale legitimate capital investment. Law, therefore, is not neutral in this respect; neither is existing legislation ineffective or necessarily counterproductive. Even with its serious limitations it has still managed to provide important defensive and protective elements, while acting as a general deterrent.

Towards an alternative strategy

If we are to move beyond the existing official response to prostitution with all its tensions and limitations, as well as the decriminalization strategy and its associated liberal pessimism, and the legalization approach with its dual strategy and undesirable consequences, then we need to examine the ways in which the law can be used more effectively and constructively. This necessarily involves transcending the liberal—libertarian discourse which has informed so much ostensibly radical intervention, and the notion of 'freedom' which it employs, as expressed for example, in Professor Honoré's account of prostitution; in which he claims that:

> It is viewed differently only in that, in free societies, respect for liberty generally ensures that a women can choose to be a prostitute if she wants. Where, as in Marxist states, freedom is not highly valued, especially if it takes the form of private enterprise, prostitution is repressed, though it has not so far been wiped out (Honoré, 1978: 134).

This kind of simplistic polarization obscures the complex nature of prostitution and its predominant modes of regulation in capitalist society characterized by the over-arching imperatives of impersonal class control on one hand, and the anarchistic market mechanism on the other. Paradoxically, although the capitalist state can find no justification for making prostitution itself a crime, it has historically, even at its most liberal, been unable and unwilling to allow full reign to such 'freedoms'. But Honoré is correct to indicate that most socialist states are preoccupied with the control and reduction of prostitution. Why should this be so? It is not simply because prostitution constitutes a form of unproductive labour, or that socialist states have a compelling desire to repress sexual freedom. It is rather that prostitution, more than any other activity, is seen as a critical indicator of the level of social and human emancipation. For if the level of the liberation of women is held to be a barometer of the level of emancipation as a whole, then prostitution as a form of female sexual slavery is a critical reference point of the level of social and sexual emancipation. The continuation of prostitution is, therefore, identified as a drag upon the demands for emancipation. As Christabel Pankhurst once argued: 'When women are politically and economically strong they will not be purchasable for the base use of vice' (Pankhurst, 1913: 8).

One possible radical response which might be suggested, in opposition to the liberal—libertarian tradition, is that the resolution to the contemporary situation could be found by simply making prostitution illegal. This would necessarily broaden the base of intervention in two significant directions. On one side it would logically include the client who would probably be more susceptible to sanctions than the prostitute acting under economic pressures. On the other side it would necessarily move beyond the immediately visible and vulnerable street-walker and would involve sanctioning clubs, dubious 'escort' agencies, massage parlours, and the like, hitting the middle-class trade as well as business organizations.

Punishing the client, of course, would be an obvious strategy to pursue if the aim was to reduce prostitution, not only because clients are numerically greater than prostitutes, or because, as Eileen McLeod argues, 'their sexuality and emotion are cramped and distorted by existing social conditions' (McLeod, 1983: 271), but because clients would almost certainly be more systematically deterred by the kind of sanctions currently directed towards female prostitutes. This possibility has led some socialists to argue for a more systematic sanctioning of clients (see Gannon and Gannon, 1980).

But illegality, as evidence from America all too clearly demonstrates is, within advanced capitalism, an extremely difficult course to pursue. Again, because of the formally consensual nature of the prostitute—client relation, gaining evidence and convictions is problematic and often depends upon entrapment, enticement and various decoy methods which are often embarrassing and have become the object of popular jokes and ridicule. Alternatively, the police can employ equally questionable surveillance strategies so that:

> When a police officer believes a solicitation has taken place, he follows the pair to the hotel or motel room. He may then stand outside the door to gather further evidence, open the door with a pass key obtained from a co-operative desk clerk, or break down the door. Once arrested the pair are separated for interrogation. Even when the parties' actions or state of undress indicate that sexual acts have taken place, however, statutory limitations on the use of un-corroborated accomplice testimony makes prosecution for the act itself difficult. In practice, then, the police attempt to determine who solicited whom and arrest the probable solicitor, using the testimony of the other party as evidence (Jennings, 1976: 1255).

Thus the practical difference between the American system in which prostitution itself is illegal in the majority of states, and the current British system of regulationism, is much less than one might expect. Both systems conceive of the problem of prostitution in predominantly the same terms. It is the visible public activities of female prostitutes which have been the principal object of intervention on both sides of the Atlantic. Both these systems operate in practice a mode of selective enforcement designed primarily to sanction those elements of prostitution which involve the transgression of conventional sex roles or pose a threat to public order. Clearly, some of these concerns draw upon the interests of the mass of the population — particularly those relating to problems of nuisance and disturbance — but they have historically been framed in such a way that these sanctions are used to enforce the privatization of women, reinforce monogamy, undermine rights, negate civil liberties, and shape sex roles in specific ways.

Given the practical limitations of a straightforward policy of illegality we are forced, if we want to attempt to use the law to reduce the incidence of prostitution and minimize its undersirable effects, almost in a full circle back to regulationism as the only viable response towards prostitution in advanced capitalist societies. Regulationism, itself, however, is not a break with illegality as such, but rather allows the possibility of implementing a selective illegality, and therefore making it possible to construct an alternative type of *radical regulationism* which could channel socialist objectives.

But how would such a socialist or radical regulationism differ from the traditional liberal strategies and the approach currently being outlined by the New Right? Unlike Wolfenden and its liberal predecessors it would not necessarily be preoccupied with the public and visible aspects of female prostitution, nor with the elevation of expediency over justice, nor with denying that the mobilization of legal sanctions is based on moral concerns. And in opposition to the brand of regulationism currently being developed by the New Right it is not based exclusively upon traditional religious moralities which objects to prostitution on the grounds that it is 'dirty', that it is a nuisance which interferes with the 'normal' processes of reproduction, and that it is embarrassing in that it is a constant reminder of the inherent limitations of monogamy based on private property and of the continuation of poverty and inequality in 'civilized' societies. Left regulationism would also, unlike other variations, see prostitution as a social and historical and, therefore, transformable product, rather than a 'natural' or trans-historical entity (see Olmo, 1979; James, 1951: 91–101)

Without entering into the specific details of legislation, and noting that legislative demands will always be socially and historically specific, it is possible to outline four general legislative strands through which the general aims of a radical regulationism could be formulated. These involve: a) a clear commitment to general deterrence; b) the reduction of annoyance, harassment and disturbance; c) protection from coercion and exploitation; and d) the reduction of the commercialization of prostitution.

a) General deterrence
Although it is difficult to quantify in precise terms (see Cook, 1980; Van den Haag, 1975), there can be little doubt that the semi-illegality of prostitution has served, although not always intentionally, as a general deterrent to many women who may have otherwise turned to prostitution.

Because prostitution itself does not threaten the 'morality' of political economy and remains in an ambivalent position to the capital accumulation process, traditional liberal regulationism has generally refrained from condemning the prostitute relationship itself, and from explicitly attempting to reduce the incidence of prostitution. Instead it has remained content to focus legal sanctions almost exclusively on the female prostitute. But any attempt to significantly reduce the incidence of prostitution must involve the 'demand' as well as the 'supply' and necessarily broaden the base of illegality. In this way a comprehensive general deterrent strategy is capable of explicitly condemning the prostitution relation itself and the network of social and gender relations which sustain it, and within which prostitution and its patronage remain an attractive, or at least acceptable, choice. Broadening the base of illegality to include the punishment of clients through the type of sanctions which are currently exclusively directed towards the female prostitute in Britain (i.e. fines) would probably be more effective and more appropriate. Clearly clients outnumber prostitutes and because of their different motivation may well be more generally responsive to a policy of general deterrence, but the critical role of legislation of this type is to question and potentially undermine the widely-held male expectation that women and/or young men ought to be purchasable to service their sexual desires and fantasies. (Indicatively, a continual theme in popular science fiction is the portrayal of future 'advanced' societies as narcissistic utopias in which the reward for personal success is the ability to purchase sexual services.) For this reason it is necessary to construct offences with specific reference to prostitution, although such offences should be framed in gender neutral terms. Of course not all forms of solicitation can be effectively or reasonably policed, and intervention should be limited to those forms of soliciting or importuning which involve annoyance, harassment or public disturbance.[2]

b) Disturbance, nuisance and harassment
Soliciting-type legislation was originally introduced in the nineteenth century as an outcome of a process involving the more systematic policing of working-class districts. For:

> In the Metropolis and in the larger provincial towns there came into being, in the course of this process, a body of legislation designed to prevent the occurrence in the streets of conduct, of many instances of trivial character,

which was considered to be prejudicial to the safety, health or convenience of the public, including such miscellaneous items as stone-throwing, playing games, letting off fireworks, hanging out washing, disposing of refuse, dangerous driving of vehicles and numerous other activities likely to occasion obstruction, nuisance or danger. In this body of statute law the common prostitute again appears as a named person in relation to certain offences (McMillan Report, 1928: 9).

Although some of these specific activities were in themselves fairly innocuous their combined effect often had a more profound influence upon the day-to-day quality of life in working-class communities than many other more 'serious' crimes. There has been a real and continuing problem of nuisance and annoyance associated with solicitation by female prostitutes as well as male clients. Although as we have seen, the British state has recognized the problem for some time, it has been extremely reticent to introduce or enforce legislation which might deter the client who creates annoyance or harasses women. Even in the American states where prostitution is illegal it is the female prostitute who is the main focus of intervention, while the client is often employed by the police to gain a conviction. Recently, however, the state has bowed to mounting pressure and has introduced, after some controversy, the Sexual Offences Act 1985 to deal with the problem of nuisance created by clients – particularly in the form of kerb-crawling. This Act, however, has been constructed in such a way that not only will it be difficult to enforce but also it serves to extend the existing inequitable body of legislation on soliciting (see Matthews 1985). What is urgently needed is a thorough reworking of this disparate body of legislation in a way which responds to the offence and not the offender, which treats all parties equally, and respects the rights and civil liberties of both the prostitutes and clients, as well as those who are subject to harassment and annoyance. Convictions against either party should require some proof of annoyance based upon objective evidence and should not be reliant upon police evidence alone.[3]

Although soliciting is the primary form in which prostitution is normally socially apprehended, it is itself the end point of a number of more fundamental processes through which women are recruited and maintained in prostitution. If we are to seriously confront the problem of prostitution it is to these more basic processes that we must also turn our attention.

c) Exploitation and corruption
The existing legislation which is designed to control these processes, particularly those which involve enticing or forcing women into prostitution, are grossly inadequate. Much of it is a product of the panics around white slavery and the largely exaggerated stories of the abduction

of young innocent girls by unscrupulous foreigners who invariably shipped them off to unpronounceable destinations. These inflated stories, however, served to deflect attention away from the more mundane and indigenous forces — both economic and interpersonal — which pressured women into prostitution. As a consequence, the legislation which arose was mainly directed at foreign and distant targets and the protection of 'respectable' young women and girls. One does not have to embrace a crude version of 'corruption theory' which sees women as entirely passive and a-sexual, however, to recognize the critical mediating and reinforcing role which some agents can play in encouraging or forcing poor and vulnerable women into prostitution or in preventing them from giving up 'the game' (see Gorham, 1978).

Existing legislation, rather than squarely confront these processes is only able to offer a minimal degree of protection and appears more concerned, as in the offence of 'living off immoral earnings', with role violations and inversions. The point is that the existing range of legisla-tion is unconcerned and unable to effectively differentiate between the friend and the parasite who extracts money under threat of violence or procures women into prostitution.

A central problem with such legislation, as in cases of domestic violence, is creating the conditions under which the woman is either willing to bring charges against the accused, or to stand up in court as a witness. The relative isolation and the maintenance of prostitutes as a pariah and outcast group, has served to occlude the real levels of violence and exploitation to which they are often subject. Like many married women, they often feel trapped and helpless, and even in cases of extreme and enduring violence and abuse wives are often unwilling to bring charges unless they feel safe from future attacks and reprisals (see Wilson, 1983: 80–97). Just as it was necessary to provide refuges for battered wives, so it is neces-sary to make available hostels or refuges which could also accommodate prostitutes who may wish to extricate themselves from coercive and damaging situations.

Alternatively, prostitutes could, in some cases, make use of civil law rather than criminal law in order to gain an injunction, for example against a violent pimp. The advantage of such a strategy is that it might provide some protection from the pimp without bringing criminal charges against him; while the standard of proof is lower in civil courts. Its disadvantage is that it involves a certain delay of time and requires a level of personal organization which a woman suffering from a violent attack may be in no position to consider, and whose immediate response is more likely to involve calling in the statutory agencies.

The way in which the problem has been conceived, together with the difficulties of eliciting evidence, has meant that to date the number of convictions against pimps and ponces has been extremely low. In contrast to the thousands of women who are processed through the criminal courts every year for soliciting-type offences, many of whom receive relatively severe sentences, the number of people tried at the Crown Court for procuring in 1978, for example, reached the grand total of fourteen, of whom only eleven were convicted. Of these one offender was put on probation, five were given suspended sentences and five were given prison sentences (see CLRC, 1982: 44). In that year the total number of procuration offences reported to the police was 143 (Criminal Statistics, 1978). Like all forms of sexual violence against women, there is a major problem in persuading the police to take such reports seriously and to respond constructively (see Chambers and Millar, 1983). These problems are undoubtedly exacerbated in the case of prostitutes, who will probably be seen either as 'hysterical' and exaggerating the problem, or being a 'loose' woman who 'asked for it'. As in the struggles around rape, domestic violence and other forms of violence against women, the dichotomies of 'loose' and 'respectable' women have to be contested and ultimately rejected as an acceptable criteria for protective intervention.

Current proposals in Britain to amend the existing legislation on procuring and related offences, while recognizing the limitations of the offence of 'living off immoral earnings' still remains unable to provide a clear constructive and potentially effective response to the problem. The seriousness which is attributed to these various coercive and exploitative activities is reflected in recent recommendations that there should be a general *reduction* in maximum sentences from seven years to five years for the most serious offences (see CLRC, 1982: 9–18). However, procuring and organizing prostitution in its most coercive forms can only be considered as a form of rape and should therefore be subject to a similar level of punishment (see Box-Grainger in this volume).

d) Commercialization

Equally crucial to the control of prostitution is the legislation relating to brothels. For if legislation directed at the pimp and the procurer is designed to limit personal coercion and exploitation, then legislation on brothels can be used to minimize economic exploitation. If prostitution is to be efficiently exploited, it has to be organized on a large scale basis, preferably under one roof. Only in this way can the capitalist guarantee the quality and the quantity of the service and control profits. Legislation relating to brothels has historically tried to reduce the size of an establishment which might be considered to be a brothel, partly to reduce the profitability of prostitution and partly to reduce the noise and disturbance often associated with brothels. Thus a brothel has come to be defined as 'any premises where two or more women practice prostitution'. The problem with this definition is that it has encouraged the further isolation of the prostitute and made her more vulnerable to violent and dangerous clients, as well as encouraging her to fall back onto the 'protection' of a pimp. To avoid this dilemma it is necessary to allow a minimum degree of cohabitation of prostitutes in order to allow some degree of protection and autonomy (see CLRC, 1982: 9–25).

It is the central failure of the legalization and non-interventionist approaches that they view the institutionalization and commercialization of sexuality as either a positive achievement or with indifference, particularly in the present period in which most European countries appear to be witnessing the growth of new style brothels which, although more discreet and luxurious than their predecessors, have ultimately the same undesirable effects. The growth of eros centres, massage parlours, and 'escort agencies' suggests the need for the extension of existing legislation to contain the operation of these agencies, reduce the overall rate of exploitation of prostitution, and redirect attention towards the expanding use of prostitution within the business community.

The combined effect of concentration and restructuring these four areas of legislation would be ultimately to reduce the level of exploitation and coercion directed towards women — particularly those who are most vulnerable — and ultimately reduce the incidence and profitability of prostitution. Although the problems often associated with soliciting and kerb-crawling are real and demand urgent attention, there is also a need for a radical shift in emphasis away from the most visible and public manifestations of prostitution and towards the less conspicuous but ultimately more fundamental processes of exploitation and coercion associated with procuring and pimping. The pursuit of such a strategy, combined with wider movements aimed at improving work opportunities ensuring pay and conditions for all women, might help to move us towards the kind of solution which August Bebel had in mind.

Notes

1. Although Elizabeth Wilson is sensitive to the problems of a general decriminalization policy and clearly sees the client as the main benefactor of such a strategy, she does, however, when specifically addressing the question of prostitution, surprisingly advocate a decriminalization strategy. Ian Taylor also asserts that 'a "transitional" socialist criminology must demand the abolition of laws criminalizing prostitution', seeing such laws as merely a product of 'puritanical and repressive moralities' (Taylor, 1980: 188). He, however, is less liberal when discussing rape and pornography for which 'transitional' demands involve the consolidation and extension of legislation.

2. One possible tactic which has been widely used is zoning, although this approach is often associated with legalization policies. It is necessary to distinguish between 'positive' and 'negative' zoning; that is, between licensing or promoting prostitution in certain areas (positive zoning) and banning or prohibiting prostitution from particular areas (negative zoning). The latter policy may be used selectively in places where the flourishing of prostitution is seen for whatever reasons to be particularly undesirable, and has no necessary implication concerning the tolerance or desirability of prostitution being practised elsewhere.

3. I have suggested elsewhere (Matthews, 1985) that a more appropriate formulation for such an offence designed to cover troublesome soliciting by both clients and prostitutes, male and female, whether on foot or in a car, need not have any specific reference to the sex of the person concerned and could simply read that: 'It would be an offence for any person in a street or public place to accost or importune another person or persons for the purpose of prostitution: where "importuning" would be defined as pestering a passenger by obstructing, following, addressing or molesting him or her whether from a vehicle or on foot'.

Bibliography

Adamson, C. (1984) 'Towards a Marxist Penology', *Social Problems*, 31: 435–58.

Adler, F. (1975) *Sisters in Crime*. McGraw-Hill.

Adorno, T. et al. (1950) *The Authoritarian Personality*. New York.

Advisory Commission on Civil Disorders (1968) *Report of* New York: Bantam.

Advisory Council on the Misuse of Drugs (1982) *Treatment and Rehabilitation*. London, DHSS/HMSO.

Advisory Council on the Misuse of Drugs (1984) *Prevention*. London: Home Office/HMSO.

Advisory Council on the Penal System (1978) *Sentences of Imprisonment — A Review of Maximum Penalties*. HMSO.

Ainlay, J. (1975) 'Review of the New Criminology', *Telos*, 26: 213–25.

Alderson, J. (1984) *Law and Disorder*. London: Hamish Hamilton.

Amir, M. (1970) 'Patterns of Forcible Rape' in M. Wolfgang, et al. (eds.), *The Sociology of Crime and Delinquency*. New York: Wiley.

Amir, M. (1971) *Patterns of Forcible Rape*. University of Chicago Press.

Anderson, P. (1968) 'Components of the National Culture', *New Left Review*, 50: 3–57.

APT Associates (1980) *American Prisons and Jails*. Washington DC, Government Printing Office.

Auld, J., Dorn, N. and South, N. (1984) 'Heroin Now. Bringing it all back home', *Youth and Policy*, 9 Summer: 1–7.

Babcock, B. A. (1973) 'Women and the Criminal Law', *The American Criminal Law Review*, 11 (2), Winter.

Balkan, S., Berger, R. and Schmidt, J. (1980) *Crime and Deviance in America*. Wadsworth.

Banfield, E. (1972) *The Unheavenly City*. Boston: Little, Brown.

Bankowski, Z., Mungham, G. and Young, P. (1977) 'Radical Criminology or Radical Criminologist', *Contemporary Crises*, 1 (1): 37–52.

Bard, M. and Sangrey, D. (1979) *The Crime Victim's Book*. New York: Basic Books.

Barnhorst, S. (1978) 'Female Delinquency and the Role of Women', *Canadian Journal of Family Law*, 1 (2).

Barrett, M. (1980) *Women's Oppression Today*. Verso.

Bayley, D. and Mendelsohn, H. (1968) *Minorities and The Police*. New York: Free Press.

Beauvoir, S. de (1975) *The Second Sex*. Penguin.

Bebel, A. (1971) *Women under Socialism*. Shocken Books.

Becker, H. (1963) *Outsiders: Studies in the Sociology of Deviance*. New York: Free Press.

Beechey, V. (1979) 'On Patriarchy', *Feminist Review*, 3.

Bell, D. (1962) *The End of Ideology*. New York: Collier Books.

Bernstein, I. N., Kelly, W. and Doyle, P. (1977) 'Societal Reaction to Deviants: the Case of Criminal Defendants', *American Sociological Review*, 42: 743–55.

Berridge, V. and Edwards, G. (1981) *Opium and the People. Opiate Use in Nineteenth Century England*. London: Allen Lane.

Bertrand, M. A. (1967) 'The Myth of Sexual Equality before the Law Quebec Society of Criminology Proceedings', *Fifth Research Conference on Delinquency and Criminality*.

Bertrand, M. A. (1979) *La Femme et le crime*. Editions l'Aurore.

Berzins, L. and Cooper, S. (1982) 'The Political Economy of Correctional Planning for Women', *Canadian Journal of Criminology*, 24 (4).

Biderman, A. D. and Reiss, A. J. (1967) 'On Exploring the "Dark Figure" of Crime', *Annals of the American Academy of Political and Social Science*, 374 November: 1–15.

Biles, D. (1979) 'Crime and the Use of Prisons', *Federal Probation*, 43: 39–43.

Biles, D. (1982) 'Crime and Imprisonment: An Australian Time Series Analysis', *Australian and New Zealand Journal of Criminology*, 15: 133–53.

Biles, D. (1983) 'Crime and Imprisonment', *British Journal of Criminology*, 23: 166–72.

Binney, V., Harkell, G. and Nixon, J. (1981) *Leaving Violent Men*. Women's Aid Federation, England.

Black, D. and Reiss, A. (1967) 'Patterns of Behaviour in Police and Citizen Transactions', in *Studies in Crime and Law Enforcement in Major Metropolitan Areas*, 2 (1). Washington DC: US Government Printing Office.

Bland, L., McCabe, T. and Mort, F. (1979) 'Sexuality and Reproduction: Three Official Instances', in M. Barrett, et al. (eds.) *Ideology and Cultural Production*. Croom Helm.

Blaxall, M. and Reagan, B. (eds.) (1976) *Women and the Workplace: the Implications of Occupational Segregation*. University of Chicago Press.

Blom-Cooper, L. and Drewry, G. (eds.) (1976) *Law and Morality — A Reader*. London: Duckworth.

Blum, R. (1976) *Drug Education. Results and Recommendations*. Lexington Books.

Blum, R. et al. (1978) 'Drug Education: Further Results and Recommendations', *Journal of Drug Issues*, 8, 4: 379–426.

Blumstein, A., Cohen, J. and Gooding, W. (1983) 'The Influence of Capacity on Prison Population', *Crime and Delinquency*, 29: 1–51.

Boles, J. and Tatro, C. (1978) 'Legal and Extra-Legal Methods of Controlling Female Prostitution', *International Journal of Comparative and Applied Criminal Justice*, 2 (1), Spring: 71–85.

Bonger, W. (1916) *Criminality and Economic Conditions*. Boston: Little Brown.

Bottomley, A., Gieve, K., Moon, G. and Weir, A. (1984) *The Cohabitation Handbook*. Pluto.

Bottoms, A. E. (1981) 'The Suspended Sentence in England 1967–1978', *British Journal of Criminology*, 21: 1–26.

Bowker, L. H. (1981) 'Crime and the Use of Prisons in the United States: a Time Series Analysis', *Crime and Delinquency*, 27: 206–12.

Box, S. (1980) 'Where Have All the Naughty Children Gone?', in National Deviancy Conference, *Permissiveness and Control*, London: Macmillan.

Box, S. (1981) *Deviance, Reality and Society* (2nd edition). Holt Rinehart and Winston.

Box, S. (1983) *Power, Crime and Mystification*. Tavistock.

Box, S. and Hale, C. (1982) 'Economic Crisis and the Rising Prisoner Population in England and Wales', *Crime and Social Justice*, 17: 20–35.

Box, S. and Hale, C. (1984) *Bibliography on Unemployment and Crime*. Unpublished, available from authors.

Box-Grainger, J. (1982) 'RAP — A New Strategy?', *The Abolitionist*, 12: 1114–20.

Braithwaite, J. (1980) 'The Political Economy of Punishment', in E. L. Wheelwright and K. Buckley (eds.) *Essays in the Political Economy of Australian Capitalism*, Sydney: ANZ Books.

Braithwaite, J. (1981) *Corporate Crime in the Pharmaceutical Industry*. Routledge and Kegan Paul.

Brake, M. (1980) *The Sociology of Youth Culture and Youth Subcultures*. Routledge and Kegan Paul.

Brenner, M. H. (1976) *Estimating the Social Costs of National Economic Policy*. Washington DC: Joint Economic Committee, Congress of the United States.

Bridges, L. (1983) 'Policing the Urban Wasteland', *Race and Class*, Autumn: 31–48.

Bristow, E. (1977) *Vice and Vigilance: Purity Movements in Britain since 1700*. Dublin: Gill and MacMillan.

Brody, S. and Tarling R. (1980) *Taking Offenders out of Circulation*. Home Office Research Study, 64. HMSO.

Brown, J. (1977) *Shades of Grey*. Cranfield Beds: Cranfield Institute of Technology.

Brownmiller, S. (1975) *Against Our Will: Men, Women and Rape*. Harmondsworth: Penguin (new edition 1976).

Bunyan, T. (1982) 'The Police Against the People', *Race and Class*, Winter: 153–170.

Calvin, A. D. (1981), 'Unemployment among Black Youths, Demographics and Crime', *Crime and Delinquency*, 27: 234–44.

Campbell, A. (1981) *Girl Delinquents*. Blackwell.

Campbell, A. and Schuman, H. (1968) 'Racial Attitudes in Fifteen American Cities', in *Supplementary Studies for the National Advisory Commission on Civil Disorder*. Washington DC: US Government Printing Office.

Campbell, J. Q. (1984) 'Prostitution and The Courts', *Justice of the Peace*, September: 579–80.

Cambridge Dept. of Criminal Science, (1957) *Sexual Offences*. London: Macmillan.

Carlen, P. (1983) *Women's Imprisonment: A Study in Social Control*. Routledge and Kegan Paul.

Carlen, P. and Collinson, M. (eds.) (1980) *Radical Issues in Criminology*. Martin Robertson.

Carr-Hill, R. A. and Stern, N. H. (1979) *Crime, The Police and Criminal Statistics*. London: Academic Press.

Carr-Hill, R. A. and Stern, N. H. (1983) 'Crime, Unemployment and the Police', unpublished paper.

Carrington, F. C. (1975) *The Victims*. New Rochelle: Arlington House.

Carter, T. and Clelland, D. (1979) 'A Neo-Marxian Critique, Formulation and Tests of Juvenile Dispositions as a Function of Social Class', *Social Problems*, 27: 96–108.

Casburn, M. (1979) *Girls Will Be Girls*. Women's Research and Resources Centre.

Cashmore, E. and Troyna, B. (eds.) (1982) *Black Youth in Crisis*. George Allen and Unwin.

Caughterty, M. (1974) 'The Principle of Harm and its Application to Laws Criminalising Prostitution', *Denver Law Journal*, 51: 235–62.

Cave, J. and Crowe, E. (1984) 'Ethnic Minorities and the Courts', *The Criminal Law Review*: 413–17.

Cernkovich, S. A. and Giordano, P. C. (1979) 'A Comparative Analysis of Male and Female Delinquency', *The Sociological Quarterly*, 20 Winter.

Chambers, G. and Millar, A. (1983) *Investigating Sexual Assault*. Edinburgh: Scottish Office Central Research Unit, HMSO.

Chambliss, W. (1978) 'The Political Economy of Smack: Opiates, Capitalism and Law', in R. Simon (ed.), *Research in Law and Sociology*. 1. Greenwich, Conn: JAI Press.

Chesney-Lind, M. (1973) 'Judicial Enforcement of the Female Sex Role', *Issues in Criminology*, 8 (2): 51–69.

Chesney-Lind, M. (1977) 'Judicial Paternalism and the Female Status Offender', *Crime and Delinquency*, 23.

Chester, L., Hodgson, G. and Page, G. (1969) *An American Melodrama: The Presidential Campaign of 1968*. London: Deutsch.

Chiricos, C., Jackson, P. D. and Waldo, G. P. (1972) 'Inequality in the Imposition of a Criminal Label', *Social Problems*, 19: 553–72.

Christiansen, K. O., Elers-Nielson, M., Le Maire, L. and Sturup, G. K. (1965), 'Recidivism among Sexual Offenders' in Christiansen, K. O., (ed.) *Scandinavian Studies in Criminology*. London: Tavistock.

Christian, L. (1983) *Policing by Coercion*. GLC: Police Committee Support Unit.

Christie, N. (1978) 'Conflicts as Property', *British Journal of Criminology*, 17: (1) 1–15.

Cicourel, A. V. (1976) *The Social Organisation of Juvenile Justice*. London: Hutchinson.

Clark, D. (1984) 'Police Out of Step in Kerb-Crawl Cleanup', *The Observer*, 6 February.

Clark, L. and Lewis, D. (1977) *Rape: The Price of Coercive Sexuality*. Toronto: The Women's Press.

Clark, R. (1970) *Crime in America; Observations on its Nature, Prevention and Control*. London: Cassell.

Clarke, R. (1980) 'Situational Crime Prevention: Theory and Practice', *British Journal of Criminology*, 20 (2): 136–47.

Clark, S. H. (1975) 'Getting 'Em out of Circulation', *Journal of Criminal Law and Criminology*, 65: 528–35.

Clarke, S. H. and Koch, G. C. (1976) 'The Influence of Income and Other factors on Whether Criminal Defendants go to Prison', *Law and Society Review*, 11: 57–92.

Cloward, R. and Ohlin, L. (1960) *Delinquency and Opportunity: A Theory of Delinquent Gangs*. London: Routledge and Kegan Paul.

Cohen, A. K. (1965) *Delinquent Boys*. New York: Free Press.

Cohen, L. E. and Klugel, J. R. (1979) 'The Detention Decision', *Social Forces*, 58: 146–61.

Cohen, S. (1972) *Folk Devils and Moral Panics*. MacGibbon and Kee/Paladin.

Cohen, S. (1979) 'Guilt, Justice and Tolerance', in Downes, D. and Rock P. (eds.) *Deviant Interpretations*. Oxford: Martin Robertson.

Cohen, S. (1980) *Folk Devils and Moral Panics* (2nd edition). Oxford: Martin Robertson.

Cohen, S. (1981) *Footprints in the sand*, in Fitzgerald, M. et al., op. cit.

Cohen, S. (1983) 'Social Control Talk', in Garland, D. and Young, P. (eds.) *The Power to Punish*. Heinemann.

Cohen, S., and Young, J. (1981) *The Manufacture of News* (revised edition). London: Constable; Beverly Hills: Sage.

Coleman, A. and Gordon, L. P. (1982) 'Conservatism, Authoritarianism and Dogmatism in British Police Officers', *Sociology*, 16 (1) February.

Committee on Mentally Abnormal Offenders (1975), *Report of*, HMSO.

Conklin, H. (1975) *The Impact of Crime*. New York: Collier-Macmillan.

Cook, P. (1980) 'Research in Criminal Deterrence: Laying the Groundwork for the Second Decade', in Morris, N. and Tonry, M. (eds.) *Crime and Justice: An Annual Review of Research*, 2, University of Chicago.

Coote, A. and Gill, T. (1975) *The Rape Controversy*. London: NCCL.

Corrigan, P. (1979) *Schooling the Smash Street Kids*. Macmillan.

Counter Information Service. (1976) *Racism, Who Profits?* CIS.

Cousins, M. (1980) 'Mens Rea: A Note on Sexual Difference, Criminology and the Law', Carlen, P. and Collinson, M. (eds.) op. cit.

Coussins, J. (1979) *The Shift Work Swindle*. National Council for Civil Liberties.

Cowie, C. and Lees, S. (1981) 'Slags or Drags', *Feminist Review*, 9 Autumn: 17–32.

Cowie, J., Cowie, V. and Slater, E. (1968) *Delinquency in Girls*. Heinemann.

Cressey, D. (1978) 'Criminological Theory, Social Science, and the Repression of Crime', *Criminology*, 16: 171–91.

Criminal Law Revision Committee (1980) *Working Paper on Sexual Offences*. HMSO.

Criminal Law Revision Committee (1982) *Working Paper on Offences relating to Prostitution and Allied Offences*. HMSO.

Criminal Law Revision Committee (1984) *Sixteenth Report*, 'Prostitution in the Street', Cmnd. 9329. HMSO.

Crites, L. (ed.) (1976) *The Female Offender*. Lexington.

Cross, (1981) *The English Sentencing System* (3rd edition). London: Butterworth.

Cunnington, S. (1980) 'Some Aspects of Prostitution in the West End of London', in West, D. J. (ed.) *Sex Offenders in the Criminal Justice System*, Cropwood Conference Series, 12. Cambridge.

Currie, E. (1974) 'Review of the New Criminology', *Crime and Social Justice*, Fall-Winter: 109–13.

Dadrian, V. N. (1976) 'An Attempt at Defining Victimology', in Viano, E. (ed.) *Victims and Society*, Washington DC: Visage.

David, M. (1983) 'The New Right in the USA and Britain: A New Anti-Feminist Moral Economy', *Critical Social Policy*, 2 (3): 31–45.

Davis, K. (1971) 'The Sociology of Prostitution', in Merton, R. and Nisbet, R. (eds.) *Contemporary Social Problems* (3rd edition). Harcourt Brace Jovanovich Inc.

Davis, M. (1980) 'The Barren Marriage of American Labour and the Democratic Party', *New Left Review*, Nov.-Dec.

Davis, N. (1982a) 'Yard Statistics Reveal 1981 as a Violent Year'. *The Guardian*, 15 March.

Davis, N. (1982b) 'Police Disclose Ethnic Crime Figures'. *The Guardian*, 11 March.

Dean, M. (1982a) 'Mugging Offences Higher in Capital'. *The Guardian*, 13 March.

Dean, M. (1982b) 'Making the Link Between Crime and Unemployment', *The Guardian*, 1 May.

Dean, M. (1983) 'Figures Show Misuse of Part-Suspended Sentences', *The Guardian*, 1 October.

Dean, M. (1984a) 'Brittan May Move on Fine Defaulters'. *The Guardian*, 11 February.

Dean, M. (1984b) 'Brittan Puts Forward Plan for Weekend Imprisonment'. *The Guardian*, 30 June.

Deem, R. (ed.) (1978) *Women and Schooling*. Routledge and Kegan Paul.

Dell, S. (1971) *Silent in Court*. Occasional Papers on Social Administration, 42, Bell.

Delphy, C. (1977) *The Main Enemy*. Women's Research and Resources Centre.

Delmuth, C. (1978) *'Sus' a Report on the Vagrancy Act 1824*. Runnymede Trust.

Dinitz, S. (1979) 'Nothing Fails Like Success', *Criminology: New Concerns*, Sagarin E. (ed.) Beverly Hills: Sage.

Dobash, R. E. and R. (1979) *Violence Against Wives*. New York: Free Press.

Dobbins, D. A. and Bass, B. (1958) 'Effects of Unemployment on White and Negro Prison Admissions in Louisiana', *Journal of Criminal Law and Criminology*, 48: 522–5.

Dodd, D. (1978) 'Police and Thieves on the Streets of Brixton'. *New Society*, 16 March.

Dorn, N. and South, N. (1983) *Of Males and Markets: A Critical Review of Youth Culture Theory*, Research Paper No. 1 Centre for Occupational and Community Research. Middlesex Polytechnic.

Dorn, N. (1983) *Alcohol, Youth and the State*. Beckenham, England: Croom Helm.

Dorn, N. and South, N. (1985) *Helping Drug Users*. Aldershot, England: Gower.

Downes, D. (1966) *The Delinquent Solution*. London: Routledge and Kegan Paul.

Downes, D. (1979) 'Praxis Makes Perfect: A Critique of Critical Criminology', in Downes, D. and Rock, P. (eds.) *Deviant Interpretations: Problems in Criminological Theory*. London: Martin Robertson.

Downes, D. and Rock, P. (1982) *Understanding Deviance*. Oxford: Clarendon Press.

Duberman, L. (ed.) (1975) *Gender and Sex in Society*. Praeger.

Durisch, P. (1982) *The Observer*, 24 January.

Dworkin, A. (1981) *Pornography: Men Possessing Women*. London: Women's Press.

Eastwood, M. (1971) 'The Double Standard of American Justice', *Valparaiso University Law Review*, 5 (2).

Edwards, S. (1981) *Female Sexuality and The Law*. Martin Robertson.

Eekelaar, J. (1978) *Family Law and Social Policy*. Weidenfeld and Nicolson.

Eichenbaum, L. and Orbach, S. (1984) *What do Women Want?* Britain: Fontana/Collins.

Eisenstein, Z. R. (ed.) (1979) *Capitalist Patriarchy and the Case for Socialist Feminism*. Monthly Review Press.

Eisenstein, Z. R. (1982) 'The Sexual Politics of the New Right: Understanding the "Crises of Liberalism" for the 1980s', *Signs: Journal of Women in Culture and Society*, 7 (3): 567–88.

Elshtain, J. B. (1981) *Public Man, Private Woman*. Princetown University Press.

Engels, F. (1969) *The Conditions of the English Working Class*. London: Panther.

English Collective of Prostitutes (1984) *Response to The Criminal Law Revision Committee's Working Paper on Offences Relating to Prostitution and Allied Offences*. London.

Ennis, P. (1967) *Criminal Victimisation in the United States: A Report of National Survey. President's Commission on Law Enforcement and the Administration of Justice*, Field Studies II. Washington DC: US Government Printing Office.

Erikson, K. T. (1966) *The Wayward Puritans*. Wiley.

Ermann, D. and Lundman, R. (eds.) (1978) *Corporate and Governmental Deviance*, Oxford University Press.

Ewing, B. G. (1977) 'Unemployment and Crime: Are they Bed Fellows?', *LEAA Newsletter*, 6, December.

Eysenck, H. (1964) *Crime and Personality*. London: Routledge and Kegan Paul.

Fairweather, E. (1982) 'The Law of the Jungle in Kings Cross', *New Society*, 2 December: 375–7.

Fattah, E. A. (1979) 'Recent Theoretical Developments in Victimology', *Victimology*, 4 (2): 198–213.

Ferman, L. and Ferman, P. (1973) 'The Structural Underpinnings of the Irregular Economy', *Poverty and Human Resources Abstracts*, 8, March: 3–17.

Fienberg, S. E. (1980) 'Victimisation and the National Crime Survey: Problems of Design and Analysis', in Fienberg, S. E. and Reiss, A. J. (eds.) *Indicators of Crime and Criminal Justice: Quantitive Studies*. Washington DC: US Government Printing Office.

Fine, B. et al. (1979) *Capitalism and the Rule of Law*. London: Hutchinson.

Firestone, S. (1971) *The Dialectic of Sex*. Morrow.

Fitzgerald, M., McLennan, G. and Pawson, J. (1980) *Crime and Society*. London: Routledge and Kegan Paul.

Fitzmaurice, C. and Pease, K. (1982) 'Prison Sentences and Population: A Comparison of some other European Countries', *Justice of the Peace*, 146: 575–9.

Fleisher, B. M. (1963) 'The Effect of Unemployment on Juvenile Delinquency', *Journal of Political Economy*, 71: 543–53.

Flexner, A. (1917) *Prostitution in Europe*. New York.

Floud, J. and Young, W. (1981) *Dangerousness and the Criminal Justice System*. London: Heinemann.

Foucault, M. (1978) *The History of Sexuality, Vol. 1, An Introduction*. Allen Lane.

Fox, R. G. (1971) 'The XYY Offender: A Modern Myth', *Journal of Criminal Law, Criminology and Police Science*, 62 (1).

Frank, A. G. (1966) 'Functionalism, Dialectics and Synthesis', *Science and Society*, 30 (2): 136–48.

Frankel, L. (1973) 'Sex Discrimination in the Criminal Law: The Effect of the Equal Rights Amendment', *American Criminal Law Review*, 11 (2) Winter.

Freeman, J. (1973) 'The Origins of the Women's Liberation Movement' in Huber, J. (ed.) op. cit.

Friedrichs, D. O. (1980) 'Radical Criminology in the United States: an Interpretative Understanding', in Inciardi, J. A. (ed.) *Radical Criminology: the Coming Crisis* . Beverly Hills: Sage.

Friedrichs, D. O. (1982) 'Crime, Deviance, and Criminal Justice: in Search of a Radical Humanist Perspective', *Humanity and Society*, 6 (3): 200–26.

Friedrichs, D. O. (1983) 'Victimology; a Consideration of a Radical Critique' *Crime and Delinquency*, 29, April: 283–94.

Friend, A. and Metcalf, A. (1981) *Slump City*. London: Pluto.

Frisbie, L. and Dondis, E. (1965) *Recidivism Amongst Sex Offenders*, California Mental Health Monograph, 5.

Fryer, B., Hunt, A., McBarnet, D. and Moorhouse, B. (1981) *Law, State and Society*. Croom Helm.

Galaway, B. (1983) 'The Use of Restitution as a Penal Measure in the United States', *Howard Journal*, 22 (1): 8–18.

Galaway, B. and Hudson, J. (eds.) (1978), *Offender Restitution in Theory and Action*. Lexington: D.C. Heath.

Galaway, B. and Hudson, J. (eds.) (1981) *Perspectives on Crime Victims*. St Louis: Mosby.

Gannon, I. and J. (1980) *Prostitution: The Oldest Male Crime?* September, Dublin: Jig Publications.

Gebhard, P., Gagnon, J., Pomeroy, W., Christenson, C. (1965) *Sex Offenders — An Analysis of Types*. London: Heinemann.

Gibbens, T. N. C. and Prince J. (1963) *Child Victims of Sex Offences*. London.

Giddens, A. (1976) *New Rules of Sociological Method*. London: Hutchinson.

Giddens, A. (1982) *Profiles and Critiques in Social Theory*. London: Macmillan.

Gilroy, P. (1982) 'Police and Thieves', in Centre for Contemporary Cultural Studies, *The Empire Strikes Back*. London: Hutchinson.

Giordano, P. C. and Cernkovich, S. A. (1979) 'On Complicating the Relationship between Liberation and Delinquency', *Social Problems*, 26 (4) April.

Gladstone, F. (1979) 'Crime and the Crystal Ball', *Research Bulletin*, 7, London: Home Office.

Glaser, D. and Rice, K. (1959) 'Crime, Age and Employment', *American Sociological Review*, 24: 679–86.

Goff, C. H. and Reasons, C. (1978) *Corporate Crime in Canada*. Prentice Hall.

Gordon, D. (1973) 'Capitalism, Class and Crime in America', *Crime and Delinquency*, 19, April.

Gordon, P. (1985) 'If They Came in the Morning...The Police, The Miners and Black People', in Fine, B. and Millar, R. (eds.) *Policing the Miners' Strike*, London: Lawrence and Wishart.

Gordon, R. A. (1982) 'Preventive Sentencing and the Dangerous Offender', *British Journal of Criminology*, 22 (3) July.

Gorham, D. (1978) 'The Maiden Tribute of Modern Babylon Revisited', *Victorian Studies*, 21 (3) Spring: 353–69.

Graham, H. (1983) 'Do Her Answers Fit His Questions? Women and the Survey Method', in Gamarnitow et al. (eds.) *The Public and The Private*. London: Heinemann.

Greenberg, D. (1975) 'The Incapacitative Effect of Imprisonment: Some Estimates', *Law and Society Review*, 9: 541–80.

Greenberg, D. F. (1977) 'The Dynamics of Oscillatory Punishment Processes', *Journal of Criminal Law and Criminology*, 68: 643–51.

Greenberg, D. F. (1979) *Mathematical Criminology*. New Brunswick: Rutgers University Press.

Greenberg, D. F. (1980) 'Penal Sanctions in Poland: A Test of Alternative Models, *Social Problems*, 28: 194–204.

Greenberg, D. F. (1983) 'Reflections on the Justice Model Debate', *Contemporary Crisis*.

Greenberg, D. F. (1984) 'Age and Crime: In Search of Sociology'. Mimeo.

Greenwood, V. (1981) 'The Myths of Female Crime', in Morris, A. (ed.) *Women and Crime*, Cropwood Conference Series No. 13. University of Cambridge.

Greenwood, V. (1983) 'The Role and Future of Female Imprisonment', Middlesex Polytechnic. Mimeo.

Greenwood, V. and Young, J. (1979) *Notes on the theory of Rape and its Policy Implications*. Middlesex Polytechnic. Mimeo.

Greenwood, V. and Young, J. (1980) 'Ghettos of Freedom' in National Deviancy Conference (ed.) *Permissiveness and Control: The Fate of the Sixties Legislation*. Macmillan.

Gregory, J. (1981) 'The Future of Protective Legislation', Occasional Paper No. 3. Middlesex Polytechnic.

Griffin, S. (1979) *Rape: The Power of Consciousness*. New York: Harper and Row.

Griffin, S. (1981) *Pornography and Silence*. Women's Press.

Griffiths, J. A. (1977) *The Politics of the Judiciary*. London: Fontana.

Gross, B. (1982) 'Some Anticrime Proposals for Progressives', *Crime and Social Justice*, Summer: 51–4.

Guttentag, M. (1968) 'The Relationship of Unemployment to Crime and Delinquency', *Journal of Social Issues*, 1: 105–44.

Gutzmore, C. (1983) 'Capital, Black Youth and Crime', *Race and Class*, Autumn: 13–30.

Hacker, H. M. (1975) 'Class and Race Differences in Gender Roles', in Duberman, L. (ed.) op. cit.

Haft, M. (1976) 'Hustling For Rights', in Crites, L. (ed.) *The Female Offender*. Lexington: D. C. Heath.

Hall, R., James, S. and Kertex, J. (1981) *The Rapist who Pays the Rent*. Falling Wall Press/Women Against Rape.

Hall, R. E. (1985) *Ask Any Woman — A London Enquiry into Rape and Sexual Assault*. Falling Wall Press.

Hall, S. and Jefferson, T. (1976) *Resistance through Rituals*. Hutchinson.

Hall, S., Critcher, C., Jefferson, T., Clarke, J. and Roberts, B. (1978) *Policing the Crisis: Mugging, the State and Law and Order*. London: Macmillan.

Hall, S. (1980) 'Reformism and the Legislation of Consent', in NDC (ed.) *Permissiveness and Control: The Fate of the Sixties Legislation*. Macmillan.

Halper, S. (1975) *The Heroin Trade*. Washington: Drug Abuse Council.

Hanmer, J. and Saunders, S. (1984) *Well-Founded Fears: A Community Study of Violence to Women*. London: Hutchinson.

Hanson, O. (1982) 'Magistrates Bend Law to Ban Prostitutes', *LAG Bulletin*, September: 3.

Harding, J. (1982) *Victims and Offenders: Needs and Responsibilities*. London: Bedford Square Press.

Harrington, M. (1972) *Socialism*. New York: Saturday Review Press.

Harrington, M. (1977) *The Twilight of Capitalism*. London: Macmillan.

Harrison, P. (1983) *Inside the Inner City: Life Under the Cutting Edge*. Harmondsworth: Penguin.

Hart, H. L. (1963) *Law, Liberty and Morality*. Oxford.

Hartnoll, R., Lewis, R. and Bryer, S. (1984) 'Recent Trends in Drug Use in Britain', *Druglink*, 19, Spring: 22–4.

Haskell, M. R. and Yablonsky, L. (1973) *Crime and Delinquency*, Rand McNally.

Hawkins, K. (1984) *Unemployment*. London: Penguin.

Hay, D. (1975) 'Property, Authority and Criminal Law', in D. Hay, et al. (eds.) *Albion's Fatal Tree*. London: Allen Lane.

Hebdige, D. (1979) *Subculture: The Meaning of Style*. Methuen.

Heidensohn, F. (1968) 'The Deviance of Women: A Critique and an Inquiry', *British Journal of Sociology*, 19, June.

Heidensohn, F. (1981) 'Women and the Penal System' in Morris, A. (ed.) op. cit.

Helmer, J. (1975) *Drugs and Minority Oppression*. New York: Seabury Press.

Henry, S. (1982) 'The Working Unemployed. Perspectives on the Informal Economy and

Unemployment', *Sociological Review*, 30: 460–77.

Hentig, H. von. (1948) *The Criminal and His Victim: Studies in the Sociobiology of Crime*. New Haven: Yale University Press.

Hewitt, P. (1982) *Abuse of Power*. London: Martin Robertson.

Hindelang, M. (1971) 'Age, Sex and the Versatility of Delinquent Involvements', *Social Problems*, 18.

Hindelang, M. et al. (1978) *Victims of Personal Crime: An Empirical Foundation For a Theory of Personal Victimisation*. Cambridge: Ballinger.

Hirst, P. (1975) 'Marx and Engels on Law, Crime and Morality', in Taylor, I. et al. (eds.) *Critical Criminology*. London: Routledge and Kegan Paul.

Hirst, P. (1980) 'Law, Socialism and Rights', in Carlen, P. and Collison, M. (eds.) *Radical Issues in Criminology*. London: Martin Robertson.

Holdaway, S. (1982) *Inside the British Police*. Oxford: Blackwell.

Home Office (1984) *Statistics of the Misuse of Drugs in the United Kingdom, 1983*, London: Home Office Statistical Dept.

Home Office (1985) *Tackling Drug Abuse: A Summary of the Government's Strategy*. London: HMSO.

Honoré, T. (1978) *Sex Law*. London: Duckworth.

Horan, P. M., Myers, M. A. and Farnworth, M. (1983) 'Prior Record and Court Processes; The Role of Latent Theory in Criminology Research', *Sociology and Social Research*, 67: 40–58.

Hough, M. and Mayhew, P. (1983) *The British Crime Survey: First Report*. London: Home Office Research and Planning Unit.

House of Lords, (1982) *Report of the Select Committee on Unemployment*. London: HMSO.

Huber, J. (ed.) (1973) *Changing Women in a Changing Society*. University of Chicago Press.

Hutter, B. and Williams, G. (1981) *Controlling Women: The Normal and the Deviant*. Croom Helm.

ISDD Research and Development Unit, (1984) *Drugs Demystified Training Pack*. London: Institute for the Study of Drug Dependence.

ISDD, (1983) *Health Careers Teacher's Manual*. (Contains thirteen units of health and social education covering health-related aspects of work, environment, cultures and leisure.)

Jackson, G. (1971) *Soledad Brother*. Penguin Books.

Jacobs, D. and Britt, D. (1977) 'Inequality and Police Use of Deadly Force', *Social Problems*, 26: 403–12.

Jaget, C. (ed.) (1980) *Prostitution: Our Life*. Falling Wall Press.

James, T. E. (1951) *Prostitution and The Law*. Heinemann.

Jankovic, I. (1977) 'Labour Market and Imprisonment', *Crime and Social Justice*, 9: 17–31.

Jardine, J. (1982) 'Capital Punishment: A Message From the Police Federation', *The Guardian*, 10 March.

Jay, P. and Rose, B. (1977) *Children and Young Persons in Custody*, Report of a Working Party. NACRO.

Jennings, A. M. (1976) 'The Victim as Criminal', *Californian Law Review*, 64, September: 1235–84.

Johnson, H. G. (1971) 'The Keynesian Revolution and Monetarist Counterrevolution', *American Economic Review*, 16 (2): 1–14.

Joubet, P. E., Picou, J. S. and McIntosh, W. A. (1981) 'US Social Structure, Crime and Imprisonment', *Criminology*, 19: 344–59.

Judson, H. (1973) *Heroin Addiction in Britain*. New York: Harcourt Brace Jovanovich: 116–18.

Kaplan, J. (1977) 'Non-Victim Crime and the Regulation of Prostitution', *West Virginia Law Review*, 79: 593–606.

Katznelson, S. (1975) 'The Female Offender in Washington DC'. Paper Presented at The American Society of Criminology, Toronto.

Kellner, P. (1982) 'For Richer, For Poorer', *New Statesman*. 22 October.

Kellough, D. G., Brickley, S. L. and Greenaway, W. K. (1980) 'The Politics of Incarceration: Manitoba, 1918–1939', *Canadian Journal Sociology*, 5: 253–71.

Kerridge, R. (1983) 'How Many Lies to Babylon?', *Police Magazine*, April: 44–51.

Kettle, M. (1984) 'The Police and the Left', *New Society*, 70 (1146): 366–7.

Kilroy-Silk, R. (1983) 'Scandal Missing Millions', *Sunday Times*, 1 May.

King, M. (1978) 'Mad Dances and Magistrates', *New Society*, 14 September.

Kingdom, E. (1981) 'Sexist Bias and the Law', *Politics and Power*, 3: 97–113.

Kinsey, R. (1985) *First Report on the Merseyside Crime Survey*. Liverpool: Merseyside County Council.

Kinsey, R. (1985) 'Working Class Victims'. Paper given at the Centre for Criminology, Edinburgh.

Kinsey, R. and Baldwin, R. (1985) 'Rules, Realism and The Police Act', *Critical Social Policy*, 12 Spring: 89–102.

Kinsey, R., Lea, J. and Young, J. (1986) *Losing the Fight Against Crime*. Oxford: Blackwell.

Kinsey, R. and Young, J. (1982) 'Police Autonomy and the Politics of Discretion', in Cowell, D., Jones, T. and Young, J. (eds.) *Policing the Riots*. London: Junction Books.

Kinsey, R. and Young, J. (1983) 'Life and Crime', *New Statesman*, 7 October: 12–13.

Kitsuse, J. I. and Cicourel, A. V. (1963) 'A Note on the Use of Office Statistics', *Social Problems*, 11 Autumn: 131–9.

Klein, D. (1973) 'The Etiology of Female Crime: A Review of the Literature', *Issues in Criminology*, 8 (2): 3–30.

Klein, D. and Kress, J. (1976) 'Any Woman's Blues: A Critical Overview of Women, Crime and the Criminal Justice System', *Crime and Social Justice*, 5 Spring/Summer: 34–47.

Klockars, C. (1980) 'The Contemporary Crisis of Marxist Criminology', in Inciardi, J. (ed.) *Radical Criminology: The Coming Crisis*. Beverly Hills: Sage.

Kraus, J. (1979) 'Juvenile Unemployment and Delinquency', *Australian and New Zealand Journal of Criminology*, 12: 37–42.

Krause, K. (1974) 'Denial of Work Release Programs to Women: A Violation of Equal Protection', *Southern Californian Law Review*, 47 (4).

Krisberg, B. (1975) *Crime and Privilege: Toward a New Criminology*. Prentice Hall.

Kruttschnitt, C. (1980) 'Social Status and Sentences of Female Offenders', *Law and Society Review*, 15: 247–65.

Kruttschnitt, C. (1982) 'Respectable Women and the Law', *Sociological Quarterly*, 23: 235–51.

Kuhn, A. and Wolpe, A. M. (eds.) (1978) *Feminism and Materialism*. Routledge and Kegan Paul.

Laite, J. (ed.) (1982) *Bibliographical Reviews on Local Labour Markets and the Informal Economies*. London: Social Science Research Council. (Now ESRC.)

Lambert, J. (1970) *Crime, Police and Race Relations*. Oxford University Press.

Landau, H. (1981) 'Juveniles and the Police', *British Journal of Criminology*, 21: 143–72.

Lea, J. (1980) 'The Contradictions of the Sixties' Race Relations Legislation', in National Deviancy Conference, *Permissiveness and Control*. London: Macmillan.

Lea, J. and Young, J. (1982) 'The Riots in Britain 1981', in Cowell, D., Jones, T., Young, J., (eds.) *Policing the Riots*. London: Junction.

Lea, J. and Young, J. (1984) *What is to be Done About Law and Order?* Harmondsworth: Penguin.

Lemert, E. M. (1967) *Human Deviance, Social Problems and Social Control*. Prentice Hall.

Leng, R. and Sanders, A. (1983) 'The CLRC Working Paper on Prostitution', *Criminal Law Review*: 645–55.

Leonard, E. B. (1982) *Women, Crime and Society*. Longman.

Lombroso C. and Ferrero, W. (1895) *The Female Offender*. Fisher Unwin.

London Rape Crisis Centre (1984) *Sexual Violence — The Reality for Women*. Women's Press.

Lotz, R. and Hewitt, J. D. (1976) 'The Influence of Legally Irrelevant Factors on Felony Sentencing', *Sociological Inquiry*, 47: 39–48.

MacNamara, J. (1967) 'Uncertainties of Police Work' in Bordua D. (ed.) *The Police: Six Sociological Essays*. New York.

McBarnet, D. (1983) *Conviction*. London: Macmillan.

McDonald, L. (1976) *The Sociology of Law and Order*. London: Faber and Faber.

McDonald, W. (ed.) (1976) *Criminal Justice and the Victim*. Beverly Hills: Sage.

McGuire, W. J. and Sheehan, R. G. (1983) 'Relationships Between Crime Rates and Incarceration Rates', *Journal of Research and Delinquency*, 20: 73–85.

McIntosh, M. (1978a) 'Who Needs Prostitutes? The Ideology of Male Sexual Needs' in Smart, C. and Smart, B. (eds.) *Women, Sexuality and Social Control*. Routledge and Kegan Paul.

McIntosh, M. (1978b) 'The State and The Oppression of Women', in Kuhn, A. and Wolpe, A. M. (eds.) op. cit.

McLeod, E. (1982) *Women Working: Prostitution Now*. Croom Helm.

McLeod, E. (1983) 'A Fresh Approach? A Critique of the Criminal Law Revision Committee's Working Paper on Offences Relating to Prostitution and Allied Offences', *Journal of Law and Society*, 10 (2) Winter: 271–7.

McMillan Report (1928) *Report of the Street Offences Committee*, HMSO.

McNicoll, A. (1983) *Drug Trafficking. A North-South Perspective*. Ottawa: North-South Institute: 94.

McRobbie, A. (1980) 'Settling Accounts with Subcultures: A Feminist Critique', *Screen Education*, 34 Spring: 37–50.

Maguire, M. (1982) *Burglary in a Dwelling: The Offence, The Offender*. London: Heinemann.

Maltz, M. (1977) 'Crime Statistics: An Historical Perspective', *Crime and Delinquency*, 23, January: 32–40.

Mannheim, H. (1965) *Comparative Criminology: A Textbook — Vol. 2*. London: Routledge and Kegan Paul.

Mannheim, K. (1949) 'Crime and Unemployment', *Social Aspects of Crime and England Between the Wars*, 5. London: Allen and Unwin.

Marenin, O., Pisciotta, A. W. and Juliani, T. J. (1983) 'Economic Conditions and Social Control', *Criminal Justice Review*, 8: 43–53.

Marx, E. (1976) *The Social Context of Violent Behaviour*. London: Routledge and Kegan Paul.

Marx, K. (1977/1867), Transl. Ben Fowkes, *Capital*, 1. New York.

Mathiesen, T. (1974) *The Politics of Abolition*. London: Martin Robertson.

Matthews, J. (1981) *Women in the Penal System*, NACRO (National Association for the Care and Resettlement of Offenders).

Matthews, R. (1985) 'Streetwise? A Critical Review of the Criminal Law Revision Committee's Report on "Prostitution in the Street"', *Critical Social Policy*, Spring 103–11.

Matza, D. (1964) *Delinquency and Drift*. Wiley.

Matza, D. (1969) *Becoming Deviant*. Prentice Hall.

Maxfield, M. (1984) *Fear of Crime in England and Wales*. Home Office Research Study: HMSO.

Melossi, D. (1983) 'Is "Critical Criminology" in Crisis?'. Paper prepared for the Ninth International Congress in Criminology, Vienna: Mimeo.

Melossi, D. (1985) 'Punishment and Social Action', in McNall (ed.) *Current Perspectives in Social Theory*. Greenwich, Conn: JAI Press.

Millet, K. (1971) *Sexual Politics*. Hart-Davis.

Millet, K. (1975) *The Prostitution Papers*. Paladin Books.

Milman, B. (1980) 'New Rules for the Oldest Profession; Should We Change Our Prostitution Laws?', *Harvard Women's Law Journal*, 3.

Morris, A. (ed.) (1981) *Women and Crime*. Cropwood Conference Series No. 13. University of Cambridge.

Morris, A. and Giller, A. (1980) *Justice for Children*. Macmillan.

Morris, N. and Hawkins, G. (1970) *The Honest Politicians' Guide to Crime Control*. Chicago University Press.

Morris, T. (1957) *The Criminal Area*. London: Routledge and Kegan Paul.

Moxon, D. (1983) 'Fine Default: Unemployment and the Use of Imprisonment', *Research Bulletin*, 16. London: Home Office.

Mukherjee, S. A. and Fitzgerald, R. W. (1982) 'The Myth of Rising Female Crime', Mukherjee and Scutt (eds.) op. cit.

Mukherjee, S. A. and Scutt, J. A. (eds.) (1982) *Women and Crime*. Australian Institute of Criminology in Association with George Allen and Unwin.

Mungham, G. (1980) 'A Career of Confusion: Radical Criminology in Britain', in Inciardi, J. A. (ed.) *Radical Criminology: The Coming Crisis*. Beverly Hills: Sage.

Mungham, G. and Pearson, G. (1976) *Working Class Youth Culture*. Routledge and Kegan Paul.

Myers, M. A. (1979) 'Personal and Situational Contingencies in the Processing of Convicted Felons', *Sociological Inquiry*, 50: 65–74.

Nagel, I. (1981) 'Sex Differences in the Processing of Criminal Defendants', Morris, A. (ed.) op. cit.

Nagel, S. and Weitzman, L. J. (1972) 'Double Standards of American Justice', *Society*, 9 (5) March.

Nagel, W. (1977) 'On Behalf of a Moratorium on Prison Construction', *Crime and Delinquency*, 23: 154–72.

National Association of Probation Officers (1974) *Comments on the Working Party on Vagrancy and Street Offences*. London: NAPO.

National Association of Probation Officers (1984) *Fine Default and Debtors Prison*. London: NAPO.

National Association of Victims' Support Schemes (1983) *Third Annual Report 1982–83*. London: NAVSS.

National Deviancy Conference/Conference of Socialist Economists (1979) *Capitalism and the Rule of Law*. Hutchinson.

National Institute of Justice (1981) *Victims of Crime: A Review of Research Issues and Methods*. Washington DC: US Government Printing Office.

Nelson and Amir (1975) 'The Hitch-Hike Victim of Rape: A Research Report', Drapkin, I. and Viano, E. (eds.) *Victimology: A New Focus*, 5. Lexington: D.C. Heath.

Oakley, A. (1972) *Sex, Gender and Society*. Temple Smith.

O'Connor, J. (1973), *The Fiscal Crisis of the State*. New York: St Martin's Press.

O'Connor, J. (1984) *Accumulation Crisis*. Oxford: Blackwell.

Olmo, R. del (1984) 'The Cuban Revolution and the Struggle Against Prostitution', *Crime and Social Justice*. Winter: 34–40.

Orsagh, T. (1980) 'Unemployment and Crime: An Objection to Professor Brenner's View', *Journal of Criminal Law and Criminology*, 71: 181–3.

Pankhurst, C. (1913) *The Great Scourge and How to End It*. London.

Parnas, R. (1981) 'Legislative Reform of Prostitution Laws; Keeping Commercial Sex Out of Sight and Out of Mind', *Santa Clara Law Review*, 21 Summer: 669–96.

Parsons, T. (1951) *The Social System*. London: Routledge and Kegan Paul.

Pearce, F. (1976) *Crimes of the Powerful*. Pluto.

Pearson, G. (1976) '"Paki-bashing" in a North-East Lancashire Cotton Town: Case Study and its History', in Mungham, G. and Pearson, G. (eds.) *Working Class Youth Culture*. London: Routledge and Kegan Paul.

Pease, K. and Wolfson, J. (1979) 'Incapacitation Studies: Review and Commentary', *Howard Journal*, 18: 160–7.

Petchesky, R. (1979) 'Dissolving the Hyphen', in Eisenstein, Z. R. (ed.) op. cit.

Pfohl, S. J. (1979) 'Deciding on Dangerousness: Predictions of Violence as Social Control', *Crime and Social Justice*, 11 Spring/Summer.

Phillips, A. and Taylor, B. (1980) 'Sex and Skill', *Feminist Review*, 6.

Phillips, L., Votey, H. L. and Maxwell, D. (1972) 'Crime, Youth and the Labour Market', *Journal of Political Economy*, 80: 491–504.

Phipps, A. J. (1981) 'What about the Victim?', *The Abolitionist*, 9: 21–3.

Pierce, G. (1982) 'Unleashing an Uncritical Press', *The Guardian*, 15 March.

Piliavin, I. and Briar, S. (1968) 'Police Encounters With Juveniles', in Rubington, E. and Weinberg, M. (eds.) *Deviance*. New York.

Pitts, J. and Robinson, T. (1981) *Young Offenders in Lambeth*. LITA.

Piven, F. and Cloward, R. (1972) *Regulating the Poor*. Tavistock.

Piven, F. and Cloward, R. (1982) *The New Class War*. New York: Pantheon.

Pizzey, E. (1974) *Scream Quietly or the Neighbours Will Hear*. Harmondsworth: Penguin.

Platt, T. (1975) 'Prospects for a Radical Criminology in the US', Taylor, I., Walton, P. and Young, J. (eds.) op. cit.

Platt, T. (1978) 'Street Crime: A View from the Left', *Crime and Social Justice*, 9.

Platt, T. (1982) 'Crime and Punishment in the United States', *Crime and Social Justice*, Winter: 38–45.

Platt, T. and Takagi, P. (1981) 'Intellectuals for Law and Order: A Critique of the New Realists', in Platt, T. and Takagi, P. (eds.) *Crime and Social Justice*. London: Macmillan.

Plaza, M. de (1980) 'Our Costs and their Benefits', *M/F*, 4: 28–39.

Plummer, K. (1975) *Sexual Stigma*. London: Routledge and Kegan Paul.

Police Review (Editorial) (1984) 'The Drugs Debate', *Police Review*, 15 June: 1166–8.

Political and Economic Planning (PEP) (1977) *Evidence to the House of Commons Select Committee on Race Relations and Immigration*, Session 1976–7, The West Indian Community, HC-180-1: xxxii.

Pollack, O. (1961) *The Criminality of Women*. A. S. Barnes.

Pratt, M. (1980) *Mugging as a Social Problem*. London: Routledge and Kegan Paul.

Preble, E. and Casey, J. (1969) 'Taking Care of Business: The Heroin Users Life on the Streets', *International Journal of Addiction*, 4 (1): 1-24.

President's Commission on Law Enforcement and the Administration of Justice (1967) *The Challenge of Crime in a Free Society*. Washington DC: US Government Printing Office.

Pryce, K. (1979) *Endless Pressure*. Penguin.

Quinney, R. (1972) 'Who is the Victim?', *Criminology*, 10 (3) November: 314–23.

Quinney, R. (1980) *Class, State and Crime* (2nd edition). New York: Longman.

Radzinowicz, L. and King, J. (1977) *The Growth of Crime*. New York: Basic Books.

Reasons, C. E. and Kaplan, R. L. (1975) 'Tear down the Walls? Some Functions of Prison', *Crime and Delinquency*, 21: 360–72.

Reckless, W. C. and Kay, B. A. (1967) *The Female Offender*. US Government Printing Office.

Reich, W. (1970) *The Mass Psychology of Fascism*. New York: Giroux.

Reiman, J. H. (1979) *The Rich Get Richer and the Poor Get Prison*. Wiley.

Reiman, R. (1979) 'Prostitution, Addiction and the Ideology of Liberalism', *Contemporary Crisis*, 3: 53–65.

Reiter, R. R. (ed.) (1975) *Toward an Anthropology of Women*. Monthly Review Press.

Reynolds, J. R. (1974) 'Rape as Social Control', *Catalyst*, 8 Winter.

Rider, B. (1982) 'A Prostitute Without Company', *The Company Lawyer*, 2 (2): 69–70.

Rock, P. (1977) 'Review Symposium on C. Smart, Women, Crime and Criminology', *British Journal of Criminology*, 17 (4).

Rock, P. (1979) 'The Sociology of Crime', in Downes, D. and Rock, P. *Deviant Interpretations*. Martin Robertson.

Rosenbleet, C. and Pariente, B. (1973) 'The Prostitution of the Criminal Law', *American Criminal Law Review*, 11 (2) Winter: 373–427.

Rowbotham, S., Segal, L. and Wainwright, H. (1979) *Beyond the Fragments: Feminism and the Making of Socialism*. Merlin.

Royal Canadian Mounted Police (1983) *National Drug Intelligence Estimate 1982*. Ottawa: RCMP Public Relations Branch.

Rubin, G. (1975) 'The Traffic in Women: Notes on the "Political Economy" of Sex', Reiter, R. R. (ed.), op. cit.

Rusche, G. and Kirchheimer, O. (1968/1939) *Punishment and Social Structure*. New York: Russell and Russell.

Russell, D. (1982) *Rape in Marriage*. New York: Macmillan.

Rutter, M. and Giller, H. (1983) *Juvenile Delinquency*. Harmondsworth: Penguin Books.

Sandford, J. (1975) *Prostitutes*. Secker and Warburg.

Sanko, B. (1983) 'Hidden Fears', *The Guardian*, 5 September.

Sargent, L. (ed.) (1981) *Women and Revolution: The Unhappy Marriage of Marxism and Feminism*. Pluto.

Sayers, J. (1982) *Biological Politics*. Tavistock.

Scarman, P. (1982) *The Scarman Report*. London: Penguin.

Schafer, S. (1968) *The Victim and his Criminal: A Study in Functional Responsibility*. Reston: Reston Publishing Co.

Schafer, S. (1977) *Victimology: The Victim and his Criminal*. Reston: Reston Publishing Co.

Schumann, K. F. (1976) 'Theoretical Presuppositions for Criminology as a Critical Enterprise', *International Journal of Criminology and Penology*, 4, August.

Schur, E. M. (1963) *Crimes Without Victims, Deviant Behaviour and Public Policy*. Prentice Hall.

Schur, E. M. (1971) *Labelling Deviant Behaviour*, Random House.

Schwendinger, H. and J. (1975) 'Defenders of Order or Guardians of Human Rights?', in Taylor, I., Walton, P. and Young, J. (eds.) *'Critical Criminology'*. London: Routledge and Kegan Paul.

Schwendinger, J. R. and H. (1983) *Rape and Inequality*. Sage.

Scott, R. A. and Scull, A. (1978) 'Penal Reform and the Surplus Army of Labour', Greenaway, W. K. and Brickley, S. L. (eds.) *Law and Social Control in Canada*. Ontario: Prentice Hall.

Scroggs, J. (1976) 'Penalties for Rape as a Function of Victim Provocativeness, Damage and Resistance', *Journal of Applied Social Psychology*, 6 (4) October.

Scull, A. (1977) *Decarceration*. New Jersey: Spectrum.

Seabrook, J. (1982) 'The Greatest Consumer Swindle', *The Guardian*, 21 August.

Seabrook, J. (1983) 'The Crime of Poverty', *New Society*, 14 April.

Sellin, T. (1937) *Research Memorandum on Crime in the Depression*. New York: Social Science Research Council.

Sellin, T. and Wolfgang, M. (1964) *The Measurement of Delinquency*. New York: Wiley.

Sharpe, S. (1976) *Just Like a Girl*. Penguin.

Shaw, C. (1930) *The Jackroller*. Chicago: University of Chicago Press.

Shaw, S. (1982) *The People's Justice*. London: Prison Reform Trust.

Shinnar, S. and Shinnar, R. (1975) 'The Effect of the Criminal Justice System on the Control of Crime: a Quantitative Approach', *Law and Society*, 9: 581–612.

Sinfield, A. (1981) *What Unemployment Means*. London: Martin Robertson.

Singer, L. R. (1973) 'Women and the Correctional Process', *American Criminal Law Review* Vol. 11 (2) Winter.

Singnell, L. D. (1967) 'Examination of the Empirical Relationships Between Unemployment and Juvenile Delinquency', *American Journal of Economics and Sociology*, 26: 377–86.

Sion, A. (1977) *Prostitution and the Law*. London: Faber.

Sivanandan, A. (1982) *A Different Hunger*. Pluto Press.

Skogan, W. (1981) *Issues in the Measurement of Victimisation*. Washington DC: US Government Printing Office.

Small, A. (1983) *Police and People in London*, II. Policy Studies Institute.

Smart, C. (1976) *Women, Crime and Criminology*. Routledge and Kegan Paul.

Smart, C. (1979) 'The New Female Criminal: Reality or Myth?', *British Journal of Criminology*, 19 (1): 50–9.

Smart, C. (1981) 'Law and the Control of Women: Sexuality, the Case of the 1950s', in Hutter, B. and Williams, B. (eds.) *Controlling Women, the Normal and the Deviant*. London: Croom Helm.

Smith, D. (1980) 'Reducing the Custodial Population', *Research Bulletin*, 9: 18–20. London: Home Office.

Smith, D. (1983) *Police and People in London Volume I*. Policy Studies Institute.

Smith, D. and Gray, J. (1983) *Police and People in London Volume IV*. Policy Studies Institute.

Smith, D. A. and Visher, A. C. (1980) 'Sex and Involvement in Deviance and Crime', *American Sociological Review*, 45.

Soothill, K. and Gibbens, T. (1978) 'Recidivism of Sexual Offenders: A Re-appraisal', *British Journal of Criminology*, 18 (3) July.

South, N. (1982) 'The Informal Economy and Local Labour Markets' in Laite (ed.) op. cit.

Southgate, P. and Field, S. (1982) *Public Disorder*. London: Home Office.

Sparks, R. (1971) 'The Use of Suspended Sentences', *Criminal Law Review*: 384–401.

Sparks, R. (1981) 'Surveys of Victimisation: An Optimistic Assessment', in Tonry, M. and Morris, N. (eds.) *Crime and Justice: An Annual Review of Research*, 3. Chicago: University of Chicago Press.

Sparks, R. (1982) *Research on Victims of Crime: Accomplishments, Issues, and New Directions*. Rockville: US Department of Health and Human Services.

Sparks, R., Genn, H. and Dodd, D. (1977) *Surveying Victims: A Study of the Measurement of Criminal Victimisation*. Chichester: Wiley.

Spender, D. and Sarah, E. (eds.) (1980) *Learning to Lose: Sexism and Education*. Women's Free Press.

Spitzer, S. (1975) 'Towards a Marxian Theory of Crime', *Social Problems*, 22.

Steffensmeier, R. H. and D. J. (1980) 'Trends in Female Delinquency', *Criminology*, 18.

Stern, L. T. (1940) 'The Effects of the Depression on Prison Commitments and Sentences', *Journal of Criminal Law, Criminology and Police Science*, 31: 696–711.

Stevens, P. (1979) 'Predicting Black Crime', *Research Bulletin*, 8: 16–19, London: Home Office.

Stevens, P. and Willis, C. (1979) *Race, Crime and Arrests*. London: Home Office.

Stimmel, B. and Kreek, M. (1976) 'Pharmacological Actions of Heroin', in Stimmel, B. (ed.) *Heroin Dependency. Medical, Economic and Social Aspects*, New York: Stratton International Medical Book Corp: 71–87.

Sutherland, E. (1949) *White Collar Crime*. New York: Dryden.

Swigert, V. L. and Farrell, R. A. (1976) *Murder, Inequality and the Law*. Lexington: Heath.

Swingler, N. (1969) 'The Streetwalker's Return', *New Society*, 16 January.

Sykes, G. and Matza, D. (1957) 'Techniques of Neutralisation', *American Sociological Review*, 22, December: 664–70.

Symanski, R. (1981) *The Immoral Landscape: Female Prostitution in Western Societies*. New York.

Taylor, I. (1980) *Law and Order: Arguments for Socialism*. Macmillan.

Taylor, I., Walton, P. and Young, J. (1973) *The New Criminology*. Routledge and Kegan Paul.

Taylor, I., Walton, P. and Young, J. (eds.) (1975) *Critical Criminology*. Routledge and Kegan Paul.

Taylor, L. (1972) 'The Significance and Interpretation of Replies to Motivational Questions: The Case of Sex Offenders', *Sociology*, 6 (1).

Taylor, L. et al. (1980) *In Whose Best Interests?* The Cobden Trust/MIND.

Taylor, W. (1981) *Probation and After Care in a Multi-Racial Society*. CRE and West Midlands County Probation and Aftercare Service.

Taylor, W. (1982) 'Black Youth. White Man's Justice', *Youth and Society*, November.

Teevan, J. (1979) 'Criminal Victimisation as a Neglected Social Problem', *Sociological Symposium*, 25: 6–22.

Temin, C. E. (1973) 'Discriminatory Sentencing of Women Offenders: The Argument for ERA in a Nutshell', *American Criminal Law Review*, 11 (2) Winter.

Thomas, D. A. (1970) *Principles of Sentencing*. London: Heinemann.

Thorpe, D. H., Smith, D., Green, C. J. and Paley, J. H. (1980) *Out of Care*. Allen and Unwin.

Timmer, D. (1982) 'The Productivity of Crime in the United States. Drugs and Capital Accumulation', *Journal of Drug Issues*, Autumn: 383–96.

Toner, B. (1982) *The Facts of Rape*. Arrow Books.

Trasler, G. (1984) *Crime and Criminal Justice Research in the United States*, Home Office Research Bulletin, 18, HMSO.

Triesman, D. (1973) *A Survey to Estimate the Number of Cannabis Users in the UK*, Commissioned by BBC Mid Week, London: Social Research Design Consultancy.

Unnever, J. D., Frazier, C. E. and Henrietta, J. C. (1980) 'Race Differences in Criminal Sentencing', *Sociological Quarterly*, 21: 197–205.

US Department of Justice, (1981) *Measuring Crime*, Bureau of Justice Statistics Bulletin (February), Washington DC: US Government Printing Office.

US Department of Justice (1983) *Criminal Victimisation in the United States 1981*, Bureau of Justice Statistics Bulletin, Washington DC: US Government Printing Office.

Vagrancy and Street Offences Working Party (1974) *Report of*, HMSO.

Vagrancy and Street Offences Working Party (1976) *Report of*, HMSO.

Valentine, C. (1968) *Culture and Poverty*. Chicago: University of Chicago Press.

Van den Haag, E. (1975) *Punishing Criminals*. New York: Basic Books.

Vinson, T. and Hommell, R. 'Crime and Disadvantage', *British Journal of Criminology*, 15: 21–31.

Votey, H. L. and Phillips, L. (1974) *Economic Crimes*. Springfield: US Clearinghouse Federal Scientific Technical Information.

Wade, D. (1975) 'Prostitution and the Law: Emerging Attacks on the Women's Crime', *UMKC. Law Review*, 43 (3): 413–28.

Walker, N. (1971) *Sentencing in a Rational Society*. New York: Basic Books.

Walker, N. and Marsh, C. (1984) 'Do Sentences Affect Public Disapproval?', *British Journal of Criminology*, 24: 27–48.

Walmsley, R. and White, K. (1979) *Sexual Offences, Consent and Sentencing*, 54. Home Office Research Study, HMSO.

Ward, D. and Kassebaum, G. (1966) *Women's Prison*. London: Weidenfeld and Nicolson.

Weeks, J. (1981) *Sex, Politics and Society: The Regulation of Sexuality since 1880* , Longman.

Weis, J. G. (1976) 'Liberation and Crime: The Invention of the New Female Criminal', *Crime and Social Justice*, 6 Autumn/Winter: 17–21.

Weis, K. (1978) 'On the Theory and Politics of Victimology and General Aspects of the Progress of Victimisation', in Flynn, E. and Conrad, J. P. (eds.) *The New and The Old Criminology*. New York: Praeger.

Werkentin, F., Hofferbert, M. and Baurmann, M. (1974) 'Criminology as Police Science or "How Old is the New Criminology?"' , *Crime and Social Justice*, Autumn-Winter: 24–41.

West, D. J. (1969) *Present Conduct and Future Delinquency*. London: Heinemann.

West, G. (1984) 'Phenomenon and Form', in Barton, L. and Walker, S. (eds.) *Educational Research and Social Crisis*. London: Croom Helm.

West, J. (ed.) 1982 *Work, Women and the Labour Market*. Routledge and Kegan Paul.

Wheeler, S. (1967) 'Criminal Statistics: A Reformulation of the Problem', *Journal of Criminal Law Criminology and Police Science*, 58 (3): 317–24.

Wilkerson, A. E. (ed.) (1973) *The Rights of Children*. Temple University Press.

Wilkins, L. (1964) *Social Deviance: Social Policy, Action and Research*. London: Tavistock.

Wilkins, L. (1965) 'New Thinking in Criminal Statistics', *Journal of Criminal Law, Criminology and Police Science*, 56 (3) September.

Williams, K. (1983) *Community Resources for Victims of Crime*. Home Office Research Study 14: HMSO.

Willis, P. (1977) *Learning to Labour*. Farnborough: Saxon House.

Willis, P. (1978) *Profane Culture*. London: Routledge and Kegan Paul.

Wilson, E. (1983) *What is to be Done About Violence Against Women?* Penguin.

Wilson, J. Q. (1972) 'The Police in the Ghetto', in Steadman, R. F. (ed.), *The Police and the Community*. Baltimore: John Hopkins University Press.

Wilson, J. Q. (1975) *Thinking About Crime*. New York: Vintage.

Wilson, J. Q. (1982) *Report and Recommendations of the Ad Hoc Committee on the Future of Criminal Justice Research*. Washington DC: National Institute of Justice.

Wilson, J. Q. and Kelling, G. (1982) 'Broken Windows', *The Atlantic Monthly*, March: 29–38.

Wilson, P. R. (1978) *The Other Side of Rape*. University of Queensland Press.

WLIHE. First Year CQSW Project (1982) *Black Young People in Trouble and Intermediate Treatment*. West London Institute of Higher Education. (Unpublished.)

Wolfe, A. (1981) 'Sociology, Liberalism and The New Right', *New Left Review*, 128.

Wolfenden Report (1957) *Report of the Committee on Homosexual Offences and Prostitution*. HMSO.

Wolfgang, M. (1958) *Patterns in Criminal Homicide*. Philadelphia: University of Philadelphia Press.

Wolfgang, M. (1975) 'Review of Thinking About Crime', *New York Times Review and Books*, 20 July.

Wolpe, A. M. (1976) *Some Processes in Sexist Education*. Women's Research and Resources Centre.

Women Endorsing Decriminalisation (1973) 'Prostitution: A Non-Victim Crime', *Issues in Criminology* 8 (2) Autumn: 138–61.

Women's Studies Group, Centre for Contemporary Cultural Studies (1978) *Women Take Issue*. Hutchinson.

Wootton, B. (1959) *Social Science and Social Pathology*. London: Allen and Unwin.

Wright, M. (1982) *Making Good: Prisons, Punishment and Beyond*. London: Burnett.

Yeager, M. G. (1979) 'Unemployment and Imprisonment', *Journal of Criminal Law and Criminology*, 70: 586–8.

Yondorf, B. (1979) 'Prostitution as a Legal Activity: The West German Experience', *Policy Analysis*, Autumn: 417–53.

Young, J. (1971) *The Drugtakers*. MacGibbon and Kee.

Young, J. (1976) 'Working Class Criminology', in Taylor, I., Walton, P. and Young J. (eds.) *Critical Criminology*. London: Routledge and Kegan Paul.

Young, J. (1977) 'The Politics of Indiscrimination', Middlesex Polytechnic. Mimeo.

Young, J. (1979) 'Left Idealism, Reformism and Beyond: From New Criminology to Marxism', in Fine, B. et al. (eds.) *Capitalism and the Rule of Law: From Deviancy Theory to Marxism*. London: Hutchinson.

Young, J. (1980) 'Thinking Seriously About Crime', in Fitzgerald, M., McLennan, G. and Pawson, J. (eds.) *Crime and Society: Readings in History and Theory*. London: Routledge and Kegan Paul.

Young, J. (1981) *'A Critique of Left Functionalism in Media Theory'*, in Cohen, S. and Young, J., op. cit.

Young, V. D. (1980) 'Women, Race and Crime', *Criminology*, 18 (1) May.

Yurick, S. (1970) 'The Political Economy of Junk', *Monthly Review*, 22 (7): 22–37.

Zander, M. (1982) *The Guardian*, 7 January.

Ziegenhagen, E. (1976) 'Towards a Theory of Victim-Criminal Justice System Interactions', in McDonald, W. (ed.) *Criminal Justice and the Victim*. Beverly Hills: Sage.

Ziegenhagen, E. (1977) *Victims, Crime and Social Control*. New York: Praeger.

Zimring, F. and Hawkins, G. (1973) *Deterrence — The Legal Threat in Crime Control*. University of Chicago Press.

Index

Adler, Freda, 57–8
Administrative criminology, 9, 26–7
Advisory Council on Civil Disorders, 100–2
Advisory Council on the Misuse of Drugs, 181–4
Aetiological crisis, 4–6, 20
Ainley, John, 15
Alderson, John, 160
Alternatives to prison, 91, 133, 143, 189

Bail Act (1976), 88
Bard, M. and Sangrey, D., 108
Bebel, August, 188
Box, Steven, 58
Brenner, M., 77
Brittan, Leon, 90
British Crime Survey, 22, 107, 116
Brody, S. and Tarling, R., 43, 46–7
Brothels, 194–5
Butler Report, 89

Carr-Hill, R. and Stern, N., 77
Cashmore, E. and Troyna, B., 138
Centre For Contemporary Cultural Studies, 110, 125, 158
Chicago School, 7
Clark, L. and Lewis, D., 31, 35, 55, 105
Clarke, Ron, 10, 11
Cloward, R. and Ohlin, L., 7, 14, 121
Cohen, Albert, 7, 13, 15
Cohen, Stanley, 4, 8, 15, 62, 113, 119
Coleman, A. and Gordon, L., 155
Conservative criminology, 9, 11, 90, 103, 116
Cowie, J., Cowie, V. and Slater, E., 60
Cressey, Donald, 9
Crime: aetiology of, 6, 19–20, 98, 118–23; class and, 23, 38, 75, 83, 111; and criminalization, 17–18, 157–9; dark figure of, 6, 99; fear of, 22–5; female, 38–40, 53 et seq.; imprisonment and, 73, 81; mass media and, 22, 57; poverty and, 11, 59, 135; prevention of, 10, 77; race and, 84–5, 118 et seq., 121, 161; reporting of, 74–5; unemployment and, 72, 74

et seq., 107, 121, 130, 132, 135; victimization and, 20–1, 109–116
Criminal statistics, 28, 54, 74, 125

Dadrian, V., 104–5
Dean, Malcolm, 74
de Beauvoir, Simone, 200
Decarceration, 69, 78
Deterrence, 36, 205–6
Dinitz, Simon, 6
Dodd, D., 137
Dorn, N., 183
Downes, David, 5, 11, 113, 138
Drug abuse, 166 et seq.; extent of, 168–71; and the family, 179–80; and masculinity, 176; and opium, 168; prevention of, 180–5; profits from, 169, 182; unemployment and, 171
Drug Dependency Units, 170, 178

Equal Rights Amendment, 65
Empiricism, 24
Eysenck, Hans, 5

Fairweather, Eileen, 201
Female crime, 53 et seq.; biology and, 60–1, 67; chivalry and, 55–6; liberation and, 57–8; unemployment and, 84
Feminist criminology, 38–40, 53 et seq.; Marxism and, 64–8; varieties of 63–7
Fines, 89, 205
Floud, J. and Young, W., 45
Freeman, Jo, 64
Friend, A. and Metcalf, A., 16
Functionalism, 14, 18

Giddens, Anthony, 112
Gilroy, Paul, 136, 138, 156–9
Gordon, Paul, 158–9
Greenberg, David, 28, 46, 113
Greenwood, Victoria, 53, 56, 62, 69
Gross, Bertram, 29

Hall, Stuart, 125
Handsworth Project, 131–3, 135
Hebdige, Dick, 136

229